THE
EVERYTHING®
GREEN WEDDING BOOK

Plan an elegant, affordable, earth-friendly wedding

Wenona Napolitano

Adamsmedia
Avon, Massachusetts

This book is dedicated to my mother, ClaraBelle Casey, who has always loved me and been there for me no matter what, and to my ever patient and understanding husband, Robert, and my beautiful children, Timothy, Arianna, and Robby Napolitano, for believing in me and putting up with me even though I drove you guys crazy while I was writing this book. I love you all.

An Everything® Series Book.
Everything® and everything.com® are registered trademarks of F+W Media, Inc.

Published by Adams Media, an F+W Media Company
57 Littlefield Street, Avon, MA 02322 U.S.A.
www.adamsmedia.com

ISBN 10: 1-59869-811-7
ISBN 13: 978-1-59869-811-4

Printed in the United States of America.

J   I   H   G   F   E   D   C   B   A

Library of Congress Cataloging-in-Publication Data
is available from the publisher.

This publication is designed to provide accurate and authoritative information with regard to the subject matter covered. It is sold with the understanding that the publisher is not engaged in rendering legal, accounting, or other professional advice. If legal advice or other expert assistance is required, the services of a competent professional person should be sought.

—From a *Declaration of Principles* jointly adopted by a Committee of the American Bar Association and a Committee of Publishers and Associations

Many of the designations used by manufacturers and sellers to distinguish their products are claimed as trademarks. Where those designations appear in this book and Adams Media was aware of a trademark claim, the designations have been printed with initial capital letters.

The pages of this book are printed on 100% post-consumer recycled paper.

This book is available at quantity discounts for bulk purchases.
For information, please call 1-800-289-0963.

Contents

Acknowledgments

First of all I want to thank my agent, Barb Doyen, for bringing this opportunity my way, and I'd like to thank everyone who provided information and ideas for this book: all the ladies who shared suggestions in the groups at Cafemom.com, all the websites that offered great ideas and inspired green thinking, and everyone else who helped make this book a reality. Thank you.

I'd also like to thank my family for putting up with me while I wrote this book and my friends for being there when I was done, since I didn't get to see or talk to them much during the process.

Top Ten Reasons to Choose a Green Wedding

1. Your big day can have a big impact on the environment; an eco-friendly green wedding can reduce that damaging footprint.

2. For those of you who are already living a green lifestyle, it is natural to plan a wedding that expresses your personal beliefs.

3. You want to share your eco-friendly beliefs with your family and friends.

4. You can make a statement and raise awareness about environmental issues by having a fabulously green celebration.

5. You want everyone to know that you love the planet and you are willing to do your part to protect it. Plus, you've been dying to check out that organic gourmet caterer you've heard so much about.

6. Having a green wedding is a great way to support charitable causes.

7. Enviro-conscious weddings support retailers and providers of organic, sustainable, and recycled products and services.

8. You love shopping at thrift stores, yard sales, and consignment shops, and a green wedding gives you the perfect opportunity to go treasure hunting.

9. You want to showcase your creative side by having a green theme wedding. Naturally green, recycled retro, or vintage glamour—take your pick; you are only as limited as your imagination.

10. From simply green to eco-extravagant, you can show everyone that you can have the wedding of your dreams while being green.

Introduction

▶ CONGRATULATIONS ON YOUR engagement! You are about to embark on a whirlwind of wedding planning that can be exciting, frustrating, and simply amazing. You are ready to plan one of the biggest events of your life.

But be warned: That big event could leave a big environmentally negative footprint. The fact that you have picked up this book means you are aware of the fragility of the earth and the changes that need to be made to save it. Living in harmony with the earth would be much simpler without the consumer mentality that is programmed into us. We have lost the ability to live simple lives. We have been brainwashed into thinking that money buys happiness and that the more stuff we have, the happier we'll be. We've forgotten how to listen to and follow our hearts. Instead, we listen to the constant buzz of what the media tells us to think, do, or buy. Greed drives our economy and pulls the strings of politicians. We buy, buy, buy, always wanting and thinking we need more— the latest fashions, the newest technology. Our lives are filled with things we don't need, and landfills quickly pile up with items we quickly cast off and replace with equally unnecessary objects.

This excessive spending has overflowed into the wedding industry. In 2006, the average American wedding cost $27,825. Every year, more than $125 billion is spent on weddings in the United States alone, and the costs keep going up. According to the Fairchild Bridal Group, the amount spent on photography and videography leapt 103 percent in the six years from 1999 to 2005. In the same time period, music for the ceremony and reception jumped 68 percent, and the cost of the rehearsal dinner increased 51 percent.

Increasingly, brides and grooms like you want to spend their wedding dollars on environmentally friendly products and services. In the past five years, more and more couples are including green concepts in their special day, from hemp wedding gowns to eco-responsible honeymoons. They want a day to remember, not one that remembers them.

Perhaps you are already living a green lifestyle but you're not sure how to incorporate that into your wedding. Maybe preparing for a new life together has inspired you to think about the future. You may wonder how that future is going to look. You want to do your part to save the environment, and what better way to start than by including eco-friendly choices in your big day? Your celebration of love for each other can also celebrate your love of the earth. Diving into this book is the first step. Enjoy the journey!

CHAPTER 1

The Environmentally Conscious Couple

Your wedding is the perfect opportunity to show off your unique style and your values. From the location to the theme you choose, this day is all about you. While some couples may choose to do something wild like jumping out of a plane to profess their love for each other, having a green wedding means you want to make a difference when you say "I do."

Choosing to Go Green

The damage humans have done to the planet becomes more apparent every day. Clean land, air, and water are quickly disappearing, while natural resources dwindle or become so polluted they are unusable. Landfills are piling up with items that could have been reused or recycled. While the United States consists of only 5 to 7 percent of the earth's total population, it uses more than one-third of the world's resources. Our consumer mentality has us living in excess, and nowhere is that more apparent than in the wedding industry.

Weddings were once small, intimate affairs that focused on the joining of two hearts and two families. Today the wedding industry has grown to a multibillion-dollar business of excess and ecological damage. One wedding can leave behind one large, environmentally damaging footprint.

By choosing to have a green wedding you are saying loud and clear that you love the planet and want to leave behind as small an ecological footprint as possible. By choosing to incorporate green elements into your special day you are not giving up your dreams and ideas of a fairy-tale wedding. You are just being more conscious of the products and services that will be involved.

If you choose to fly under the radar with your green wedding, that is perfectly acceptable. No one has to know you're wearing a used gown or a dress made of hemp unless you want them to. Some people like to keep their choices private, but even if you keep quiet you'll have the satisfaction of knowing that your choices made a difference.

There are approximately 2.5 million weddings in the United States every year, and the average nuptial celebration costs around $25,000. There's a lot of potential for weddings to be more environmentally friendly, and increasing numbers of couples are trying to reduce the amount of waste their weddings generate.

Many people like to shout it from the rooftops and make a big statement with their green choices, and that is okay as well. If you want everyone to know about your green choices in an eco-friendly way, post it on your wedding website, announce it in your e-mails, or even create an elegant poster that can be displayed at your eco-event. However you choose to share the news, you can include a map with local organic farms, orchards, and wineries along with other green retailers.

Your Wedding, Your Beliefs

Your wedding is a unique expression of your love for each other and the ideals and beliefs you will take into your new life together. A green wedding is a wonderful way to show your friends and family how much you love each other and the earth. It expresses how much you want your guests to be a part of making the world a better place.

Your carbon footprint is an estimate of how much carbon is produced to support your lifestyle and activities. You can plant trees to help offset your footprint, and you can also donate to programs that will plant the trees for you. Calculate your footprint by visiting websites like *www.carbonfootprint.com*.

From donating to carbon offsetting organizations to purchasing a gently used gown from a charitable organization, it is worth it to start your life together in a way that meshes with your values and beliefs. Don't let anyone talk you out of doing what you feel is right. Don't let people tell you that you are crazy or that it doesn't make a difference. Every little thing can make a difference somewhere, to someone. It will be worth the extra effort to make your big day extra special.

One person can make a difference. Two people who care can do more than double what just one could. You are considering planning an event with many people. By having an eco-conscious wedding, you are making environmental and socially responsible choices for all of your guests. That is a big deal, especially when you think of the positive impact it can have.

By having a green wedding you can:

- Save trees.
- Reduce pollution.
- Cut down on landfill waste.
- Cut down or offset carbon emissions.
- Promote the growth and consumption of organic crops.
- Support green businesses.
- Increase the demand for green products.
- Support your local economy.
- Buy from companies that support and practice fair trade.
- Say no to products made in sweatshops.
- Give to charitable organizations.
- Inspire others to have green weddings or live greener lifestyles.

The possibilities of what one green wedding can accomplish are endless. You never know how much of an impact you may have on someone or how much one person can do. However, be careful not to force your guests to do anything they don't want to do. Suggest they donate to charities or ask them to help out with whatever cause you choose to support, but make sure everyone knows it is only a suggestion. You want to inspire change in a positive way, not gain a reputation as an eco-tyrant.

Your Green Wedding

You can have a traditional wedding in a green way or you can be a trendsetting eco-couple and celebrate your special day in an unconventional way. Your wedding should be as unique as you are while showcasing your beliefs and values. From the smallest eco-detail to the largest wedding expense, there are no rules to how green you have to be to qualify as having a green wedding. It may depend on what you are comfortable with or what is readily available in your area. How green your wedding is can also depend on your planning timeline or your budget. Perhaps you are planning a quick wedding and don't have time to shop around, or maybe there are not enough eco-conscious vendors in your area.

Being green is not an all-or-nothing endeavor. You can do as little or as much as you are comfortable with. What matters is that you do something; every little bit counts. Now that the wedding industry has embraced the concept of the green wedding, it is easier than ever to find green products. Every day, more products, services, and companies are showing up with eco-friendly solutions for all your planning needs.

Choosing to celebrate your big day in a green way can manifest in many ways, from hiring an organic caterer to buying a hemp wedding gown to using recycled products. It is your wedding and your choice in what to use and how green to go.

FACT

According to a Condé Nast wedding survey, there were approximately 44,230 weddings in the United States every weekend in 2006. That's 2.3 million weddings for the entire year. The average wedding had 178 guests, who collectively spent $19 billion on items from couples' gift registries.

It is easy to incorporate earth-friendly ideas into your wedding planning. Some people may say it is an inconvenience or will take too much time and effort, but that simply is not true. Consider that a traditional bride will search high and low for the perfect dress, the most fabulous shoes, or the fanciest accessories with the biggest wow factor. You'll be doing the same thing—with one slight difference. Instead of making the choices all about you, your choices will reflect what's best for the environment.

Every aspect of your wedding can be earth friendly; the attire, decorations, food, flowers, gifts, favors, travel, and even the honeymoon can be green. Earth-friendly options are all around you, from simple and sustainable to eco-extravagant. You just have to open your eyes and look.

Don't get discouraged if you can't find what you are looking for in an earth-friendly material. It matters that you tried and every little bit counts. You can incorporate just one or two green concepts or you can go all the way and try to make sure that every possible part of your special day is done in the most eco-friendly way.

You will have many things to consider, from the availability of products and services in your area to budget and time constraints. You have a multitude of options when it comes to how green to make your wedding. Let your creativity come out; by thinking outside the box, you will have your fairy-tale day in a new and sparkling green way.

Reduce, Reuse, Recycle

While you plan your big green day there are three words to remember: reduce, reuse, and recycle. Incorporate these three words into your wedding planning to help make it fabulously green.

The Environmental Protection Agency estimates that Americans discard 220 million tons of garbage every year. Each person produces 4.4 pounds of rubbish per day. That's down from a high of 4.5 pounds in the early 1990s, but it's significantly higher than the 2.7 pounds of trash each person generated each day in 1960.

Reduce

You want to reduce the impact your wedding will have on the environment as much as possible. By reducing the amount of waste you produce, from the garbage left behind to the carbon emissions you create, you cause less damage. Understand that there is no way to have zero impact; the key is to making your impact as small as possible. You can do this in many ways.

You could have a smaller wedding, which means fewer resources are used and less waste is created. You could make sure your ceremony and reception are close to home so you travel less. Another possibility is to keep traveling guests to a minimum to keep carbon emissions as low as possible. Little details count; consider using fewer decorations and forgoing favors. It all depends on what you are comfortable with and what can easily be accommodated.

Reuse

By reusing objects, you keep trash out of overflowing landfills and save energy because you are sending fewer items through the recycling process. You are also lessening the need for new products to be made. Reusing what is available is the greenest solution possible. Reusing is often confused with or used interchangeably with recycling. Reuse lengthens the life of an item; recycling reprocesses the material into a new form to create a completely new product, such as tires that are recycled into belts or shoes.

There are many reasons why reusing is the best choice, including the following:

- Reuse keeps items out of landfills.
- Reuse preserves energy by reducing the need for new items to be produced.
- Reuse reduces the need for resources such as fuel, energy, water, and wood.
- Reuse causes less pollution.
- Reuse can conserve financial resources.

The concept of reusing is fun and creative, and you can incorporate it into your wedding in many ways. You can buy a gently used wedding gown, reuse decorations and centerpieces found at yard sales and thrift stores, and wear heirloom jewelry. Purchase items that you can reuse in your home after the wedding: Baskets found at a thrift store can be reused as storage containers in your home, tablecloths made from organic fibers can always be reused, toasting goblets made from recycled glass will do double duty as wineglasses, and unique centerpieces can be recreated as art or trendy storage solutions.

One great way to use the reuse concept is to have an era-theme wedding: the roaring '20s, the fabulous '30s, the glamorous '50s, the psychedelic '70s, or the awesome '80s. Pick a theme and search for treasures from that era that can be reused in your wedding; from clothing to jewelry to crafty decorations, you'll create a memorable wedding while being green as can be.

Recycle

The third concept—recycling—is easy to include in your green wedding. Make an effort to purchase recycled products or products made from recycled materials. You could use invitations made from recycled paper, rings and jewelry made from reclaimed and recycled gold, or glassware made from recycled glass.

In the past fifteen years the amount of recycling in the United States has almost doubled. Today Americans recycle about 32.5 percent of their waste. However, landfills are still rapidly filling with goods that can be reused or recycled. More and more companies are embracing the recycling concept by purchasing recycled goods or by recycling the manufacturing waste materials that once would have been discarded. Currently the materials that are recycled the most are aluminum, plastic bottles, newspaper, corrugated cardboard, steel cans, glass containers, magazines, and mixed paper.

To learn more about what and where to recycle check out *www.recyclingmarkets.net*. There you can look up information according to product or material.

ALERT!

Some eco-experts argue the value of recycling, saying that it takes more energy and resources to recycle than it would to make something new. The problem is that resources are dwindling and landfills are overfull. Recycling is a necessity.

You might be surprised at the wide variety of items that can be made from recycled materials. There's a lot more than paper, glass, and plastic items. Shoes can be made from recycled tires and other fibers, belts made from recycled bicycle tires, bowls and art made from old records, and photo frames made from recycled bike chains. Any of these items can be creatively used on your special day. The Green Glass Company (*www .greenglass.com*) and Fire & Light (*www.fireandlight.com*) have beautiful recycled glassware, and Eco-Artware.com (*www.eco-artware.com*) turns reused and recycled items into useful objects of art.

Savvy Solutions

While planning your earth-conscious affair, other green keywords you should look for and consider are organic, sustainable, renewable, and fair-trade.

Organic

Organic products are those that are grown without use of pesticides and other unnatural products, and they are processed without use of harmful chemicals. When you shop for organic products, don't just think food. Flowers are grown organically and many products are made from organically grown crops, including wine, beer, cotton, and hemp fabrics, and even bath and beauty items. Not only can your menu be organic, but so can your flowers, your cosmetics, and your dress.

Bamboo is the fastest growing plant on earth. Ecologists claim bamboo is the best renewable resource because it can be used for everything from building materials to food. In the right environmental conditions, bamboo can grow as much as four feet per day.

Sustainable Resources

Sustainable resources are those that can be used without fear that they will run out. A material is also considered to be sustainable if it can be created or harvested and used without harming the environment. Hemp and bamboo are sustainable resources because even though the plants are destroyed for manufacturing, new ones quickly grow in their place, and the supply can be maintained. Petroleum is not a sustainable resource; once petroleum resources are depleted, we cannot make more.

Hemp fabric combines warmth and softness with extreme durability. It is very versatile and is used to make numerous products including clothing, shoes, accessories, linens, and furniture. You can use many hemp products in your wedding, from paper made from hemp to hemp fabric used in the bridal attire.

Bamboo may show up in many products you use for your green wedding. Bambu (*www.bambuhome.com*) has biodegradable single-use plates and utensils, called Veneerware, made from bamboo. Several bridal designers offer gowns made from bamboo and bamboo fabric blends.

Renewable Resources

Renewable resources are those not completely depleted by human consumption and the afterlife of which does not contribute to the waste system. Solar energy, wind energy, geothermal energy, and bio-fuels are all renewable resources. Look for green businesses that utilize renewable resources.

Fair Trade

Fair trade products are those that have been produced by businesses that promote fair wages, environmentally sustainable practices, and healthy work conditions. Many big businesses have factories in other countries where workers are exploited. Clothing is made in sweatshops by workers who are treated poorly. Research the companies you purchase from at sources such as Co-op America (*www.coopamerica.org*), SweatFree (*www.sweatfree.org*), and the Fair Trade Federation (*www.fairtradefederation.org*).

Some people may view you as a little eccentric for going the green route, but to most people you'll be the height of style, an eco-trendsetter. The hottest thing right now is being green. Remember that change occurs when people decide to discard the old way of doing things. You'll be moving in the right direction, changing the way people view weddings and the world.

By purchasing products that are organic, sustainable, fair trade, and recycled you are supporting the conservation of the planet's natural resources and practicing responsible consumerism. That makes you and your wedding even more meaningful.

CHAPTER 2

Planning Green

Planning a green wedding is the same as planning a traditional one. It will be exciting, stressful, fun, tiring, time consuming, and completely worth it. Planning a wedding is a big deal even if you are having a small, simple wedding. Don't worry too much or take all the stress to heart. All that planning will culminate in a beautiful day filled with love and hope for the future—your future together as a married couple and the future of the planet.

Wedding Planning Basics

Whether you are planning an extravagant eco-affair or a simple ceremony followed by a small green gathering, you have to decide on a lot of basics. It's best to start planning early and plan together. It is also good to let your family be involved, but remember that you are the ones in control. Sit down, start brainstorming, and make a list or two or several.

Here are some basic things you'll want to consider:

- When do you want to get married? This should be one of the first things you decide. Also consider what time of day you want to have your ceremony.
- Do you need a wedding planner? One who specializes in green weddings may be helpful, but is it necessary or in your budget?
- Who will officiate your wedding? Do you have a minister? Will you consider a justice of the peace or another nondenominational officiant?
- What is your budget? This may be the single most important aspect of your planning because it will decide every other area of your wedding.
- How many people do you want to have, and whom will you invite?
- Who will be in your wedding party? Bridesmaids, groomsmen, ushers, flower girl, ring bearer—remember, they aren't necessary, but many people have at least a maid of honor and a best man.
- What kind of ceremony do you wish to have? Traditional? Custom? Religious? Would you like to write your own vows? Would you like to have special readings of romantic passages from literature or scripture during the ceremony?
- Would you like to have an indoor or outdoor ceremony? What about the reception?
- Do you wish to incorporate a separate theme into your green wedding? Recycled retro, nature's beauty, autumn splendor—any idea and theme can be combined and used creatively with a green slant.
- Will you have pre- or postwedding parties such as a bridal shower, bachelor or bachelorette party, rehearsal dinner, or after-wedding brunch?

These are just some of the basics you'll want to consider in the early planning stages. Especially consider how you can do it all in a way that is the most beneficial and least harmful to the environment.

If you are planning an outdoor wedding, think about using solar lights, candles, or LED lights to conserve energy and save money. Just be sure to have plenty of proper fire extinguishers available if you use candles.

Give yourself plenty of time to plan your wedding the way you want it. It is not uncommon to devote as much as a year to planning your big event. The earlier you start planning, the better, especially if you have your heart set on a specific date. Some ceremony and reception sites can be booked more than a year in advance. If you are flexible about the date, you will have a better chance of finding the perfect location. For a more complete checklist and timeline, see Appendix A.

Where to Start

How can you keep track of all the things you have to do and be green at the same time? Organization is key. Get a spiral bound notebook with folders, a three ring binder, or a custom wedding planner book to keep all of your lists and receipts together.

Do your research. Search for locations that would be suitable for your green ceremony and reception. Check your area for caterers that offer organic, vegetarian, or vegan menus. Research what produce and flowers are grown locally and organically in your area. Also search for retailers and vendors that offer green products and services. If you cannot find anything in your local yellow pages, check online in Co-Op America's National Green Pages (*www.coopamerica.org/pubs/greenpages*), which lists green businesses and their products and services.

Other things to remember as you plan your green wedding:

- Make responsible choices when choosing outdoor locations. Parks and organic gardens are set up to be natural yet still accessible to people. A true wilderness location is not equipped to handle human parties. You may do more harm than good by having your wedding in a truly wild setting.
- Be sensitive in the materials you choose. Skip the balloons, crepe paper, and tulle decorations. None are natural and they all just get thrown away. Say no to Styrofoam and plastic utensils. Choose items that can be reused or recycled. Also forgo the disposable cameras. Ask everyone to bring their digital cameras, and guests can e-mail you the photos, put the photos on a disk for you, or share the photos at online sites such as Shutterfly.com or Snapfish.com.
- Think outside the wedding mindset and purchase items you can reuse, such as a great pair of shoes. Buy something you'll use again, not just something you'll use exclusively for your wedding day.
- Rent or borrow whatever possible. This reduces the need for new items to be made and purchased and greatly slashes your expenses. Items that can be rented or borrowed include large items such as altars, trellises, gazeboes, tables, and chairs, and other things such as tuxedos, table linens, dinnerware and table settings, glass bowls or vases for centerpieces, and even jewelry and other accessories.
- When it comes to clothing and linens, consider how they will be cleaned. Find a green dry cleaner for your wedding dress, and research tuxedo and table linen rental companies that use green dry cleaning processes.
- Ask yourselves, "Do we really need this?" Cut out all the unnecessary stuff and you'll save money while you help save the environment.

Look to Nature for Inspiration

The greenest options are all around you. From ideas on where to have your wedding to unique elements to include in your decorating, let nature inspire you. Natural items and materials such as leaves, twigs, grasses, fruits, and berries can be incorporated into your green wedding in stylish and creative ways. Leaves, twigs, and grasses can be used in floral bouquets and arrangements in addition to the flowers. Rocks can be used in centerpieces or as place cards. Fruits and berries can make beautiful accent pieces or fabulous focal points.

Where to Look

Let Mother Nature lend her hand and provide you with beautiful solutions for your green wedding. Take a walk through local parks, gardens, or even your own backyard. Visit with friends and family and walk through their yards. Many people, especially those who live in the country or in a semisuburban area, have an abundance of trees, plants, wildflowers, and other things that they never take advantage of.

Using What You See

Maybe you have wild grape vines growing everywhere. Those can be used as decorative vines to drape around tables or wrap around poles and columns at your reception, or they could be dried and made into wreaths.

Do you or any family or friends have fruit or nut trees? Fruit and nuts could be placed in bowls or baskets and used for centerpieces. Arrange them naturally or add some ribbon or candles for a stylish display. The fruit could also be used as favors or donated to a local homeless shelter or food bank afterward. Another creative solution would be to use the fruit instead of place cards; names could be written on them with nontoxic ink.

Small stones or river rocks are another option instead of throwaway place cards. You can write names on them with permanent markers or paint pens. After the wedding the rocks can be placed in your garden to remember everyone who shared your special day with you.

Leaves can be gathered and used in a multitude of ways, from bouquets to artful arrangements. They can be used as place cards or adornments for invitations and note cards. Leaves can also be used to stamp leaf print designs on handmade invitations, paper, and thank-you cards. Other ways to look to nature for inspiration include purchasing all-natural products made from organic hemp, cotton, and bamboo along with other natural materials.

Green Budget

Being eco-conscious doesn't mean you can't be financially responsible too. There is no reason to start your new life together in debt by going overboard on the spending for your big day. Save money instead of borrowing or charging up your credit cards. Put money aside for the wedding and budget accordingly. Going green doesn't have to break your budget.

FACT

According to Condé Nast, the average American wedding costs around $27,825. Every wedding expense has increased 20 percent since 2002, and the amount of money spent on the average wedding has increased 100 percent since 1992.

Creating a Budget

To stay within your budget, you need to first sit down and create a budget. Figure out exactly how much money you have to spend. Putting it all down on paper makes it more real. If you keep track of all your spending, you are more likely to spend less. This is where a wedding planner book comes in handy, although a spreadsheet you design yourself can also work. Charts and lists help you keep track of everything, and pocket folders help you organize all your receipts and paperwork.

If you don't use a custom planner book, create your own and use a more detailed breakdown of expenses to give you a budget average. For instance, instead of grouping bride's attire into one category, break it down into dress, veil, shoes, and accessories. Write down how much you have in your budget for each item, and then record how much you actually spend as you make purchases. If you go over budget on one thing, you can see where you can cut or recoup costs somewhere else. Say you budgeted $500 for your dress but ended up spending $750. However, you budgeted $400 for the cake but your mom offered to buy it for you for free. By keeping track, you'll know you are still within your budget with $150 to spare. There are computer programs such as Microsoft Excel that can help you keep track of your budget and your spending.

Seventy-nine percent of couples pay for part of their own weddings. The bride's family traditionally paid for the wedding, but this is becoming less common as couples marry later in life and are more financially independent when they decide to tie the knot.

Small, Simple, Sustainable

Keep your spending under control by remembering these three words: small, simple, and sustainable.

Keep your wedding small by not inviting every single person you've ever come in contact with or whom you might be related to. Keep things simple by purchasing and using only what you need. Whenever you make a purchase, try to make sure it is made from a sustainable resource.

The most eco-friendly wedding would be one that consisted of the couple, the officiant, and the legally required witnesses. This could take place at city hall, in a chapel in Las Vegas, or on a beach on a tropical island. However, no matter how appealing that may sound, the simplest solution may not be for you. For some couples, small and simple just may not work. Perhaps you have a huge family or you've always dreamed of a big wedding. That's okay; as long as you plan responsibly, you can have your big affair and still do it in a green way without going into debt.

Buying the Right Products

Some people think that buying green products and using green services costs more than using regular products and services. It doesn't. While sometimes the initial expense may be more, you will save money in the long run. For instance, the durability of hemp and bamboo fabrics means that they will last longer than their synthetic counterparts. Products made from these fabrics may cost more, but they last much longer and will not wear out and need to be replaced as quickly.

When it comes to planning your green wedding, there are many eco-options that will not hurt your pocketbook. The average cost of a wedding dress is around $1,300, and it is not uncommon for a bride to pay upward of $2,000 for a designer gown. Bridal gowns made from sustainable and organic fabrics can be as much as $1,000 but most cost much, much less. You'll pay a fraction of the original price for a used gown, and an heirloom or borrowed gown will be free, except for cleaning costs and possible alteration fees. Hemp suits cost about the same as renting a designer-brand tuxedo, but you'll have the added advantage of being able to wear it over and over again.

FACT

Some parks and local nonprofits such as museums request a donation or small fee to use their park or building for special events such as weddings. Search around in your area to see how much it costs to hold your wedding in different eco-friendly areas.

If you embrace the concept of reusing, you'll buy things that will serve double duty; they can be used at your wedding, then reused in your home. Glassware, dinnerware, table linens, baskets, potted plants, and trees are all items you can incorporate into your postwedding life.

Where to Shop

Another way to keep costs at a minimum is by shopping at local antique shops, thrift stores, and yard sales instead of bridal boutiques and wedding supercenters. You'll spend much less, find quality items that can be reused, and enjoy the treasure hunt.

There are other ways to keep costs down:

- Borrowing or renting items instead of buying them will definitely keep you within your budget.

- Keep it simple. If you don't need it, forget it. Don't let the caterer talk you into ten kinds of hors d'oeuvres or four kinds of dessert. Keep it to a minimum; four hors d'oeuvres are plenty and you only need the cake as dessert.
- There is no rule that you have to provide alcohol, which can be a big expense. If you do, keep it to a white bar to minimize the cost. A white bar consists of mostly white beverages like white rum, vodka, and white wine. These are the alcoholic beverages available for straight or mixed drinks. There is also the option of having a cash bar. Let guests get toasted on their own dime.
- Consider getting married on a weekday. Venues and vendors often charge less during the week.
- Always do plenty of research and compare prices.
- Get married in the off-season—November through April—when venues are often cheaper.
- Have your ceremony and reception earlier in the day so you don't have to provide dinner.
- Check your area for schools and/or students who would be willing to work for lower fees or maybe even just at the cost of materials. Culinary schools, floral design programs, and photography programs are all great places to find up-and-coming talent who might jump at the chance of having a project to put on their resume and in their portfolio.
- Consider a meatless menu. Meat raises food costs dramatically. Stick to veggies, breads, and pasta dishes to cut expenses.
- Use talented friends and family instead of hiring vendors. Is Cousin Billy an aspiring DJ? Is Aunt Maude an amazing baker? See who is willing to donate time and talent for a good cause—your wedding.
- Last but not least, stick to your budget by shopping local and in season. It cuts out costly shipping expenses, and you'll be supporting your local economy.

Search the Internet for more creative money-saving advice, tips, and resources.

Shop the Web for Eco-Friendly Solutions

Anything and everything can be found on the Internet these days. The Internet has become a vast resource for communication, entertainment, education, and shopping. If you can't find what you need at local stores, you can find it online. You can search for the perfect location for your ceremony and reception or scout out a site for your great green honeymoon.

ALERT!

When you purchase from online retailers, select ground delivery instead of air whenever possible. Airplanes have a much greater effect on global warming than vehicles. When you compare products, if all things are equal—product, price, and quality—always choose the retailer that is closest to you. It saves on shipping costs and it cuts down on carbon emissions.

For many people, the Internet has become a regular part of everyday life. E-commerce sites can disappear, which can make it challenging to find what you are looking for. Search engines can produce a bewildering number of results, some unrelated to what you were trying to find, and you may get frustrated and give up. Throughout this book, various websites are mentioned to help direct you to the products you are looking for or need.

Don't forget about eBay; you can find almost anything you could ever want on eBay. Be sure to search the stores, not just the auctions. The web is full of loads of information that can help you plan your green wedding; from informational sites to online retailers and vendors, you are sure to find what you are looking for. Searching the Internet can save you a lot of time, and you have the advantage of being able to plan your wedding without changing out of your pajamas.

CHAPTER 3

Location, Location, Location

The location of your wedding may be one of the most important aspects of your entire wedding. You want it to be someplace special, beautiful, and meaningful to you. The options are endless, from traditional choices such as your place of worship to unique ideas that range from mild to wild—on a boat in the middle of the sea, on the side of a mountain, or deep underwater on a sea-diving expedition. New trends include saying "I do" at vineyards, ski lodges, and far-away destinations.

3

Stay Close to Home

You don't have to sacrifice your beliefs to have an earth-friendly wedding. You can still have a traditional or religious ceremony at a place of worship and then have your eco-elegant reception at a great green location. Just be sure to choose a location that both of you agree on, whether it is a place with personal meaning or a place that you both feel comfortable in. Find a place that speaks to you. You want a location worthy of the occasion. It is here that you will exchange your vows and express your love for one another, so the setting should reflect the event. Staying close to home is a wonderful option. It's easier to plan and easier to decorate and keep in touch with all your vendors. It saves the time and expense of traveling and cuts down on transportation-related pollution.

QUESTION?

Where is the number-one location to get married in the United States?
Las Vegas, Nevada, tops the charts with an average of 114,000 weddings per year. Gatlinburg, Tennessee, is in second place with around 42,000 weddings a year.

Green Options

Having your wedding and reception in the same place is a very green option; it combines everything in one nice, neat, eco-responsible package. No traveling back and forth between venues and no need for special transportation to get you from one place to another. Open your mind to what is in your area. You don't have to get married in a traditional wedding location. Historical landmarks, museums, parks, gardens, art galleries, aquariums, old saloons, greenhouses—there are many exciting possibilities out there; you just have to look for them. Check with your local area chamber of commerce, your city's official website, your county parks, or your yellow pages to see what amazing possibilities lie in your own backyard.

Genesee County, Michigan, has the usual wedding chapels, churches, and other cookie-cutter wedding venues and plain rental halls. But if you look a little more closely, the Genesee County Parks have a wide range of exciting options that can be utilized for weddings, including the historical nineteenth-century Crossroads Village and Huckleberry Railroad. It features a quaint little church, several beautiful historic homes, a modern dining hall, and the Genesee Belle, an authentic style paddle-wheel boat. There are also many beautiful parks with river and lakefront views, pavilions, and possibly a gazebo or two. Genesee County is home to the city of Flint, which has a thriving cultural area that includes the Flint Institute of Arts, Sloan Museum, the Sarvis Center, Whiting Auditorium, the Applewood Estate, and the Whaley Historical House, a restored Victorian mansion. Many of these cultural centers have rooms and areas available to rent for special events and weddings.

Destination weddings have increased by 400 percent in the past fifteen years. All that travel releases tons of pollution into the air. Stay close to home to avoid having to worry about offsetting all those carbon emissions.

Finding Local Green Options

Other close-to-home options include restaurants, hotels, or country clubs that offer organic menus or follow green practices such as recycling and buying fair-trade or locally grown products. If you want a green location or at least an eco-conscious and socially responsible one, you can search for green restaurants at *www.dinegreen.com* and green hotels at *www.greenhotels.com/members.htm.* You can look for other green businesses in Co-Op America's National Green Pages listings at *www .coopamerica.org/pubs/greenpages.*

If you can't find a green location, find one that supports a good cause. Maybe your local museum has an event center or your public library has a meeting room that can be utilized for a wedding. Look for historic landmarks, buildings that have been renovated and opened to the public, or nonprofits and cultural centers that support the arts or other local charities.

There might be a school or college campus with a fabulous area that is suitable for weddings. Look at local locations in a new light, and you may find the perfect place.

The Great Outdoors

Nothing says green like an outdoor wedding in the middle of nature's glory. Beautiful flowers, sunny skies, big trees full of green leaves, a lake with a waterfall in the background—how enchanting.

Locales and Challenges

You have so many choices—parks, botanical and organic gardens, nature preserves, and other welcoming sites. Just make sure to choose an area that won't be harmed by humans tromping and stomping all over the place. A pristine wilderness will be damaged by a wedding party trampling through the area, whereas a park, nature preserve, or garden is made for both natural preservation and human enjoyment.

Some other interesting outdoor options include:

- A clearing in the woods by your house, along a local trail, or in a park
- A beach
- The desert
- An orange grove
- A rooftop garden
- An outdoor ice skating rink in the middle of winter
- A pumpkin patch

However, any of these outdoor locations may pose their own challenges. Weather unpredictability being the biggest issue, you'll want to find a location that has options if the weather is bad—a pavilion, a large building, or a location where a large event tent can be set up to shelter everyone in case of rain.

Another big problem in the great outdoors can be pests, specifically mosquitoes. A truly green location will not use pesticides to control the bugs, so you may have a problem. Be sure to ask about natural pest control solutions and see what can be done to lessen the possibility of getting eaten alive on your wedding day. Citronella candles, lamps, and torches may be one possibility. Others may include using all-natural sprays and foggers before the event to shoo away the mosquito population, at least for the evening. The venue may take care of it for you, or it may be an expense you'll have to cover.

No matter where you get married, you'll want to know all the location's rules and regulations. The following are just some of the questions you'll want to ask:

- How many people will the location accommodate?
- Is there electricity available?
- Does the area have its own caterer? Can you bring in your own caterer? Can you have food at the location? Some natural settings may not allow food because of the resident animals.
- Are chairs, tables, and tents available? Is there an extra charge to use them?
- Does the location offer to set up and clean up, or do you have to do everything?
- Are candles allowed?
- What kind of noise and distractions may occur?

A big problem concerning outdoor weddings is electricity; you may not have access to any. If your event will be continuing into the late evening you'll want some kind of light source. Candles, oil lamps, and solar lights are some of your options. Strands of battery-powered LED lights or battery-powered flameless candles might also be possibilities. A big bonfire may be another fun option, depending on your location and what is allowed.

A Wedding in the Park

The first place to consider for an outdoor wedding may be a park, whether local or some place you've always dreamed of.

Many people do not realize the opportunities that are available through local park and recreation resources. Does your city have a park downtown?

A riverside park? Maybe somewhere with a gorgeous gazebo or amazing amphitheater? Do you ever see signs for music or movies in the park? Those places are usually well equipped for weddings.

Drive around or surf the web for local attractions. There are probably many places you've missed, maybe even places you drive by every day on your way to work. Go exploring with your fiancé. Take a walk in the park. Have a picnic. It'll be a great way to spend quality time together while alleviating some of that wedding-planning stress.

National parks such as Yosemite have several locations suitable for wedding ceremonies. To search for information about the National Park Service and all of its beautiful locations, go to *www.nps.gov*. The park service usually charges a fee for a wedding permit, and guests are required to pay the usual entrance fees.

Garden View

If you don't find your perfect outdoor location in a park, maybe a garden is more your style. Imagine walking toward the love of your life surrounded by blooming beauties, the sweet scent of fresh flowers everywhere— romance at its best. Are there any botanical gardens near you? Perhaps an organic flower garden? There might be locations that are not listed in the phone book, and you might even consider private homes. Search for area garden clubs and garden societies; a local extension office can point you in the right direction for a garden location.

Organic Orchards, Farms, and Vineyards

Do you want to celebrate while promoting organically grown food? Consider having your wedding at an organic orchard, farm, or vineyard. You'll be supporting local farming, promoting the importance of growing organic, and helping the local economy.

Organic Orchards and Farms

Orchards and farms often have rustic charm combined with natural beauty. Maybe they have a big barn you could rent for your reception after having your ceremony in a grove of apple trees. An orchard wedding in the autumn would be perfect. Your guests could enjoy hayrides while sipping fresh apple cider after a ceremony surrounded by trees filled with ripe apples ready to be picked. The fall colors swirl in the breeze, offering a fantastic backdrop. Centerpieces could be baskets filled with apples and pears, favors could be jars of apple butter and organic jams and jellies made at the very location you are having your special event. To search for organic farms and orchards visit *www.localharvest.org*.

Organic Vineyards

Vineyards are becoming very popular places to hold wedding ceremonies and receptions. The natural beauty and gorgeous scenery combined with rustic elegance and charm make them a perfect choice. Add to that the love of fine wine and you've got the perfect location. Check out vineyard websites or visit a winery in person and you will be awestruck by their picturesque quality. They offer romance and elegance amid the beautiful and bountiful settings of nature.

Many vineyards now offer wedding packages. The Summerhill Pyramid Winery in Canada and a multitude of vineyards in California, including Deer Ridge and Rock Basin Vineyards, have wedding packages that include catering and even sleeping accommodations.

Other western U.S. vineyards that offer bridal packages include Zenith Vineyard in Salem, Oregon, and BoaVentura De Caires in Livermore, California. The eastern side of the country offers a fine selection of vineyards that have wedding packages, too. Their fees vary widely from the very reasonable (under $1,000) Alba Vineyard in Milford, New Jersey, to the extremely pricey and much sought after Wolffer Estate Vineyards and Stables in Sagaponack, New York.

While any vineyard can be a good eco-choice, an organic vineyard is the greenest choice because they grow their grapes without the use of harmful pesticides. Organic growers are often green in other ways, so investigate growing practices before booking—though you might be so amazed by the beauty of the location that it may not matter if they grow organically. If the vineyard is local, it has the benefit of allowing you to cut back on the amount of manufactured goods, paper products, and other waste. Nonorganic vineyards are still greener than many other reception areas, and they provide you with a beautiful and natural setting.

In the past five years, the popularity of vineyard weddings has grown tremendously. If a winery is your location of choice, book early. Some are so popular they are booked years in advance. Vineyards offer a unique atmosphere that lets you enjoy a momentous occasion with only your friends, family, and nature.

Webcast Your Wedding

Broadcasting your wedding live over the Internet with a wedding webcast is a new trend. This is a great green option. Though it was not originally intended to be an eco-choice, it fits very well into the green scheme of things.

The Basics

If you want to have a small wedding, you can still share it with friends or family without asking them to travel. The wedding webcast is a great tech tool that keeps loved ones from missing out on your special moment and saves on costly and pollution-creating travel.

If you are planning to have a videographer, this can be a great upgrade. Alternately, maybe a techie friend can help set it up. Prices for a live webcast usually range between $250 and $750. The service usually includes reservation of your web space, time of broadcast, and an archive of your webcast to allow easy viewing for anyone who missed the live version. You also get the option of downloading it later to save for yourself and burn copies onto DVD.

Companies that offer this service are Webcast My Wedding (*webcast mywedding.net*) out of Dallas, Texas; Vowcast (*vowcast.com*), located in Smyrna, Georgia; and the newcomer *www.liveweddingbroadcast.tv.*

Other Points to Consider

The downside is that you have to provide all the equipment. You need to have a digital video camera hooked up to a computer that has high-speed Internet access, which means your wedding site has to have broadband access, preferably wireless broadband access. This may be a problem in many locations, especially if you are holding your wedding outside or in a remote location. Your guests will also need high-speed access to view the webcast properly.

A digital recording is another option. It can be e-mailed to friends and family, saved to disk and mailed the old-fashioned way, or even uploaded to *www.youtube.com* or *www.myspace.com* for everyone to enjoy.

CHAPTER 4

Elegantly Green Wedding Attire

The wedding gown is likely one of the first and most important items the bride chooses for her special day. The most widely available bridal gowns are often made of synthetic fabrics or produced in sweatshops. Fortunately, there are many earth-friendly alternatives that will coordinate nicely with your green wedding. With the growing popularity of green weddings, even high-end designers are incorporating green and fair trade pieces into their bridal collections. As the wedding industry continues to adjust to the eco-responsible desires of brides-to-be, expect to see more popular designers using sustainable fabrics.

You Don't Have to Sacrifice Your Style

Gone are the days that equated being green with hippie clothes and Birkenstocks—though you are still welcome to those if that's your style. Today's green brides can walk down the aisle in eco-couture fashions. They can be glamorously green or revel in simple eco-elegance.

Your style is all yours and you don't have to sacrifice it to have a green wedding. You could wear something you or a stylish friend already have hiding away in the back of your closet or you can splurge on a fabulous gown you know you could wear again to an elegant New Year's Eve party or other event. You don't even have to wear white. New bridal trends feature gowns in soft colors other than white and ivory or have bold color accents on a white gown. The more color you have in your dress, the more likely you are to wear it again. Give yourself time and you will find the perfect dress—a beautiful gown that will fit your style, your green values, and your budget.

Before Victorian times, wedding dresses were not always white. Blue was the earliest color that symbolized purity, and it's probably where the "something blue" line in the old rhyme came from. In other cultures, white has never been a common wedding dress color. Norwegian brides traditionally wore green, while Icelandic brides wore black. Red is commonly worn by Asian brides.

Rich and sumptuous natural fabrics can be turned into fabulous gowns. There are many eco-conscious bridal designers and retailers that offer ready-made bridal gowns or custom made-to-order gowns. Conscious Clothing (*www.getconscious.com*) offers high-fashion wedding attire made from hemp and hemp blends. René Geneva Design (*www.mycorset.com*) offers high-fashion gowns and corsets made from hemp and hemp/silk blends at designer label pricing. Rawganique (*www.rawganique.com*) offers hemp and linen fabrics. Rawganique also has hemp gowns that can be used for bridesmaids' dresses.

The bridal gowns that are available in natural, sustainable, and organic fabrics range from simple to stunning and can rival the beauty and elegance of any synthetic gown. Many synthetic fabrics may cost less than natural and organically grown sustainable fabrics, but they are often made from petroleum-based products such as polyester that are terrible for the environment. Several retailers offer gorgeously green earth-friendly gowns at approximately the same cost—or less—as designer gowns. Threadhead Creations (*www.threadheadcreations.com*) offers many midrange gown prices. Its average gowns retail between $400 and $800, and it offers off-the-rack designs and unique custom dresses.

Natural Materials

Natural materials are good for you and for the earth. Choosing natural, organic, and sustainable fabrics for your wedding gown and other bridal attire is a great choice for the eco-conscious bride. Whether you buy the fabric and have a gown made for you or buy from an eco-friendly retailer, you won't be sacrificing style, beauty, or comfort. In fact, natural fabrics such as organic cotton, hemp, and bamboo are softer and less itchy than synthetics and won't irritate your skin.

Green designers and retailers offer gowns made from several types of natural fabrics. The most popular is hemp, followed by organic cotton and hemp combo blends such as hemp/silk. Bamboo, the newest sustainable fabric, is also making an impact in the wedding industry. Other sustainable fabrics include abaca, cashmere, ingeo, linen, canvas, twill, muslin, jersey knits, and fleece. Some may show up in wedding dresses, especially in a fabric blend, but many are not suitable for wedding finery.

Hemp

Hemp is a superior fiber known for being strong and durable. Hemp products will outlast competitive products made with other fabrics. Not only is hemp strong and durable, it is very comfortable. It wears in, not out. Hemp provides warmth and softness in a breathable material that is resistant to mold and ultraviolet light. It is nontoxic and great for those with sensitive skin.

Hemp fibers can be grown with no chemicals, making it entirely eco-friendly. It is also a sustainable product because it grows so quickly. Hemp can produce 250 percent more fiber than cotton and 600 percent more fiber than flax using the same amount of land.

What makes hemp perfect for wedding gowns is that it combines the soft elasticity of cotton with the smooth texture of silk. When hemp is blended with other fabrics it incorporates the qualities of both. A hemp/silk blend is a truly luxurious fabric perfect for the bride who wants to have a green wedding and still feel like a princess.

FACT

U.S. laws prohibit the industrial farming of hemp because of its relationship to marijuana. Industrial hemp is only 0.3 percent to 1.5 percent tetrahydrocannabinol (THC), which is the substance that causes intoxication. A cannabis plant used for intoxication purposes contains an average of 3 percent THC.

Organic and Recycled Cotton

Cotton is the most comfortable and most popular fabric in the world. However, it is very hard on the environment. Organic cotton is growing in popularity because it is raised without toxins or synthetic fertilizers. Organic cotton is more expensive to produce, so it may be more expensive to purchase.

ALERT!

Regularly grown cotton is the most pesticide-dependent crop in the world. It accounts for 25 percent of all pesticide use. According to the USDA, more than 50 million pounds of pesticides are used on U.S. cotton fields in one year.

Organic cotton clothing is available in many stores and online shops, and it is becoming popular to make green wedding dresses and other bridal attire from organically grown cotton. The dresses range from beautifully simple to naturally elegant and are often something that can be comfortably worn again.

Recycled cotton is another earth-friendly choice you can incorporate into your green wedding. Recycled cotton is made from fiber that is normally cast off during the spinning, weaving, and cutting processes. No harsh chemicals are used to process recycled cotton.

Lyocell

Lyocell, also known by the brand name Tencel, is a natural fiber made from wood pulp cellulose. It is the first new fiber in more than thirty years and the first new natural fiber in much longer. While lyocell is a manufactured fiber, it is not synthetic. The cellulose is processed with a nontoxic, recyclable agent and is naturally biodegradable.

Lyocell is popular with formalwear because it drapes luxuriously and feels like silk. It absorbs dye very well and can be made into jewel-toned fabrics. Lyocell often appears as a hemp/lyocell blend in bridalwear. Like other natural fibers, it is comfortable, breathable, and resilient. Because of its sensuous texture and appearance, lyocell has become very popular with some of the top mainstream designer fashion labels such as DKNY, Calvin Klein, Ann Taylor, and even L. L. Bean.

Silk

Silk is a natural fabric that has been used for centuries in fine and casual clothing. Silk is a very eco-friendly renewable resource. It is called peace silk when the silk is harvested without killing the worms, which is what happens when the silk is processed using conventional methods. Silk is the most luxurious natural fabric around, but it does have its limitations and can often be very expensive. Silk has to be carefully laundered and can be easily damaged by sunlight, bleach, perspiration, heat, and harsh detergents. To make silk more durable while retaining its natural beauty, hemp/silk, silk/bamboo, and other fabric blends are appearing in clothing.

Bamboo

Bamboo is an up-and-coming sustainable product that is being used for everything from flooring to sheets and now is making its appearance in the wedding dress. Bamboo fabric is spun and knit from the fibers of the bamboo plant. Bamboo can look and feel like silk—with a few key bonuses. It is machine-washable and much more durable. Bamboo and bamboo blend fabrics are appearing in bridal dresses at online retailers.

FACT

A sixty-foot tree cut for commercial use takes around sixty years to replace. A sixty-foot bamboo tree cut for consumer use takes less than sixty days to replace. Bamboo is a versatile plant that can be used for food, building materials, and decoration.

Bamboo fabric has many wonderful qualities. It is antimicrobial, antifungal, and antibacterial. Even after many washes, the fabric retains these amazing qualities. Bamboo is also suitable for anyone who is sensitive to allergens. The Bamboo Fabric Store (*www.bamboofabricstore.com*) offers a variety of fabrics to choose from if you would like to make your own wedding dress out of bamboo.

Reuse, Recycle

If you can't find what you're looking for in natural fabrics, consider another green option—gently worn, used dresses. You have many options when choosing a gently worn dress, and you can find them in many places. Raid your own closet, ask to borrow a dress from a friend or family member, or go on an expedition to the thrift store down the street. Don't forget about the endless online options such as eBay and Craigslist.

Thrift Store Chic

Chances are that if you're an earth-conscious bride you've visited some thrift stores. Not only may you find a gorgeous wedding dress for a ridiculously cheap price, but you may even find other items that can be used for decorations for your reception—glass bowls for the centerpieces, wicker baskets for the flower girl, or jewelry to wear on your wedding day.

The key to thrift store shopping is taking along your imagination to see ordinary objects in a new light. Also be prepared to dig; some stores just pile things up, although others have everything laid out nice and neat. If you don't find something on the first try, ask how often and when the store puts out new items and get there bright and early the day items are restocked. Secondhand treasures can be amazing one-of-a-kind finds, and searching for them can be quite an adventure. Take your mom, your maid of honor, or all your bridesmaids along for the hunt and make it a day of treasure hunting. You never know what you may find during your treasure-hunting adventures.

Classifieds and Consignment Stores

Local thrift stores are not the only place to find beautiful, gently used wedding gowns. Your local newspaper classifieds and online classifieds are full of ads. Make sure you also check your yellow pages for resale shops and consignment stores, and check your bridal and wedding listings for boutiques that offer used wedding gowns. Most cities have at least one store that sells used formalwear and wedding gowns.

Whether you buy your dress brand new or gently used, consider donating it to a good cause once you are done with it. Whether it is a local charity in your area or a nationwide effort such as Making Memories, your donation matters and can make a difference to someone.

Gowns for a Good Cause

For the eco-conscious bride, buying a dress from an organization that supports a charitable cause is the perfect choice. Several charities sell and even rent wedding gowns and other formalwear. Making Memories (*www.makingmemories.org*) takes in used bridal gowns and then resells them. The proceeds help make wishes come true for breast cancer patients. The organization accepts donations of any formal attire: bridal gowns, veils, mother of the bride dresses, bridesmaids' dresses, and flower girl dresses.

If you can't find a charitable cause selling gowns in your area, look for a retailer such as Blue Sky Bridal (*www.blueskybridal.com*) that donate proceeds to charities. It offers recycled wedding gowns and organic wedding dresses and donates 10 percent of each sale to environmental protection.

Vintage Wedding Gowns

You could have a green wedding and still wear high fashion—from another era. Vintage bridal gowns are becoming very popular, from the elegance of the 1920s and 1930s to the glamour of the 1950s to the psychedelic fun of the 1960s and 1970s. Perhaps you may want to go even further back in time and wear a romantic Victorian gown. You can scour thrift stores, resale shops, consignment stores, and antique stores. You never know what will turn up.

To add more meaning to your wedding and honor your family, you might consider wearing an heirloom. Even if it's not your style or doesn't fit just right, a great seamstress can update and alter the gown for you. As with other areas of your wedding, look at your dress with an open mind so you can see the possibilities.

Explore Your Options

To research vintage fashions and styles of wedding gowns, check out Daniela Turudich's *Vintage Wedding: Simple Ideas for Creating a Romantic Vintage Wedding* and Norma Shephard's *Accessorizing the Bride: Vintage Wedding Finery Through the Decades*. In *Vintage Wedding*, Daniela Turudich gives you highly detailed drawings and descriptions of wedding finery starting in the 1910s. She also gives details of attire for the bride, the groom, and the attendants and popular color schemes, drinks, food, and even favor ideas for the different decades. In *Accessorizing the Bride*, you'll find beautiful photos of bridal gowns and accessories along with historical details of the dresses and accessories from the Victorian era all the way to the 1990s. For a very in-depth look at the history of the bridal fashion industry along with fabulous photos from vintage weddings, check out *I Do: 100 Years of Wedding Fashion* by Caroline Cox.

If you are looking for a specific style or era, try shopping online. There are several trustworthy dealers that offer vintage gowns and vintage accessories such as Vintage Wedding (*www.vintagewedding.com*) and VintageVixen.com (*www.vintagevixen.com*). EBay is a good place to look, but buyer beware. What you end up with may not be authentic or it may be damaged. No matter who you are dealing with, ask for full disclosure. Ask what condition the gown is in, how fragile the material is, and whether the dress is wearable (some people just collect vintage gowns they don't plan to wear). Above all, do not rely on sizes. Get measurements. Sizes mean nothing in vintage gowns because they don't even come close to modern size charts. Even a dress made as recently as the 1970s can be very different from the sizes you're used to today. Over time, people have gotten taller and thicker and sizes have been adjusted accordingly. Vintage styles are often very small and are made for shorter women. Make sure you have accurate measurements of yourself.

When shopping for a vintage gown, avoid dresses that have stains or need other repairs because it can be very costly to have them restored. Ask about refund policies and get insurance on anything you have shipped to you. The last thing to consider with vintage dresses is undergarments. You'll want to know what kinds of undergarments were worn with a specific style of dress. Some styles may require a corset or a hoop skirt.

Turn Your Vintage Style into a Theme

One great thing about choosing a vintage gown is planning your wedding around it. You can create a vintage theme for your wedding, and it can all be done in an eco-conscious way.

If you choose a vintage gown from, say, the 1950s, you can incorporate that into your wedding. Set the tables with vintage '50s glassware or other kitchenware, such as plates and bowls made from Melmac. Dig through thrift stores for anything that can be used as decorations or even as favors.

Since nothing is new and everything is being reused, it goes along with your primary green theme.

Currently the '50s is one of the easiest eras to find items from, but you can let any era inspire you. However, just know that you'll be searching harder and will have to widen your net to include antique stores and online retailers if you want to pay tribute to an earlier era. You may also end up paying much higher prices. If you do pick an older era, allow plenty of time for the hunt.

Eco-Sexy Undergarments

Something you may not have thought about is what you will wear under your eco-elegant gown. If you are going green all the way and wearing an earth-friendly gown, shouldn't your undergarments be green, too? Of course, that is completely up to you. There are several options. Many eco-stores such as Gaiam (*www.gaiam.com*) carry undergarments made from organic cotton, hemp, and bamboo. However, many of them might not be what you envisioned for wedding attire—or more specifically, your wedding night attire. A lot of organic panties and thongs are plain. They're good for everyday comfort, but not for the woman who wants to feel like a green goddess on her wedding day. Greenloop (*www.thegreenloop.com*) has a small selection of organic intimates that are cute but not too racy or supersexy.

FACT

The United Kingdom and France have several stores that offer amazingly sexy eco-undies, but only a small selection is available in the United States. Faernyn's Grove's corsets are extremely hot, but not so cheap. U.K.-based Enamore has some very sexy organic silk lingerie, and G=9.8 in France has lingerie made from pine branches and pine needles—tres green and tres sexy.

If you're budget-conscious as well as eco-conscious, green undergarments may be a stretch. You do still have the option of gently worn or vintage undergarments. Nothing says old-school sexy like a garter belt and traditional silk stockings. Many resale shops and vintage clothing stores carry undergarments. You'll want to follow the same rules as you would if you were shopping for vintage gowns, but be aware of one specific thing— elastic. Elastic wears out over time. Many vintage items may look fabulous but can't be worn unless they are completely restored with new elastic. It takes a highly skilled seamstress to pull that off, which can be pricey. If you are in the market for retro, pull and stretch the fabric or have the shopkeeper demonstrate for you, especially anywhere there is elastic. If it doesn't bounce back or feels stiff, it is no good. If you shop online, ask if the item is wearable and inquire about refund policies.

Beautiful Attire for the Whole Wedding Party

While you shop for your own green gown, check out what retailers of natural, organic, and sustainable clothing have for the rest of your bridal party. If the bride is the only one wearing eco-conscious attire, everyone else will be green with envy.

Rawganique's commitment to making the world a better place and treading lightly on the planet extends to its online presence. The Rawganique website (*www.rawganique.com*) was created and maintained entirely off the grid. It's powered by solar and wind energy.

Eco-Retailers

Rawganique carries clothing for everyone from the bride to the flower girl. It offers casual and formal clothing options. It even carries a very nice suit for the groom and hemp shoes. Most hemp suits can be purchased for approximately the same price as renting a designer tuxedo, but you can keep the hemp suit to wear again.

Conscious Clothing has apparel for the rest of the bridal party, including beautiful bridesmaid gowns and cute flower girl dresses. Other retailers have just some of what you might need. Boll Organic (*www .bollorganic.com*) carries organic cotton men's dress shirts. For a more complete selection of organic and eco-friendly retailers, check the web resource section at the back of this book.

Borrowed or Gently Used

Everyone in the bridal party also has the same options as the bride: borrowing clothing, buying used attire, or wearing something they already have. No one says the guys have to rent tuxes or wear identical suits. They can wear suits they already own; just specify a color palette and purchase matching ties to unify the look.

> If you do want your groomsmen to rent identical tuxes, check with your rental place to see what kinds of dry cleaning practices they follow. Traditional methods of dry cleaning release large amounts of toxic pollutants, but there are many green dry cleaning options.

The bridesmaids could see what they already own in the same color scheme or hit the local thrift stores to see what they can find. The dresses don't have to be identical. If each woman bought something similar but in a style that flatters her body, she'd be that much happier and be more likely to wear the dress again instead of stuffing in it the closet and forgetting about it.

Flower girls can wear pretty dresses they already have. Ribbons, bows, or lace can be added to fancy a dress up or fit it into your color scheme. Other accessories such as hair pieces, gloves, or even just the flower girl's basket can dress up the ensemble to coordinate with your theme.

CHAPTER 5

Eco-Friendly Wedding Jewelry

Mining for gemstones and precious metals is a very dirty and hazardous business, both for the environment and for the workers. Mining for metals and gemstones destroys thousands of acres of habitat every year and causes vast amounts of pollutants to be released into the air, soil, and water. Making just one gold ring generates around twenty tons of mining waste. Toxic amounts of mercury, cyanide, and arsenic can be released into the environment through mining processes.

Jewelry Through the Ages

Enchanted by shiny metals and pretty sparkling stones, humans have been adorning themselves with jewelry since the beginning of civilization. The materials they used have varied depending on the time and culture. Primitive tribes adorned themselves with dried berries, shells, bone, leather, or whatever was available in their area. Egyptians were known for their elaborate use of gold, but it is said they favored colored glass over precious gemstones. The ancient Greeks and Romans loved jewelry, and men and women alike adorned themselves in elaborate pieces.

FACT

Roman betrothal rings were once made of iron. They were called *annulus pronubus*. They symbolized strength and permanence. The use of iron betrothal rings in Rome has been traced back to the second century B.C.

Metals

Some cultures believed copper to be the most precious of metals, although many preferred gold or silver. Researchers have ascertained through historical accounts and findings that gold and silver were the two most used metals for betrothal and wedding rings.

Ancients and alchemists described gold as the metal of the sun and silver as the metal of the moon. When platinum was discovered, it was thought to be the metal of heaven because of its purity and durability.

Renaissance Italians gave their loved ones highly ornate silver betrothal rings engraved and filled with black enamel. When gold became the metal of choice in Europe, the silver ring was still given at the betrothal, then an identical gold ring was given during the marriage ceremony. This may be where the concept of dual rings originated.

Gemstones

Diamonds have not always been the gemstone of choice for engagement rings. The popularity of the diamond is mostly a twentieth-century trend, thanks to very clever marketing. Throughout history, colored gemstones have varied in their popularity, while diamonds were something only the very, very rich could afford. In the eighteenth and nineteenth centuries, sapphires and emeralds were the most popular choices for engagement rings. Sapphires were in demand because their blue color symbolized the heavens from which love came. Rings containing aquamarine represented harmony. In medieval Europe, rubies were the stone of choice for engagement rings. Their red color associated them with the heart and love.

ALERT!

If you forgo the diamond for a colored gemstone you'll be in good company. Princess Diana had a sapphire engagement ring, and John F. Kennedy gave Jacqueline Bouvier an engagement ring with a huge—almost 3 carat—emerald surrounded by diamonds.

History of Diamond Marketing

Diamonds became extremely popular in the late nineteenth century when large quantities were discovered in South Africa. Before this, diamonds were rare and expensive. Suddenly they flooded the market and everyone could have them. This popularity is evident in the Victorian era, when diamond engagement rings became common. However, the fascination soon wore off and diamond sales plummeted.

In 1888 De Beers Consolidated Mines, Ltd. was created to control diamond supply and demand. It slowed the flow of diamonds to make them once again seem rare and priceless, but sales didn't immediately take off. It was a few more decades before De Beers launched what has to be the single most effective marketing campaign ever. "A diamond is forever" the slogan insisted, indelibly linking diamonds with everlasting love.

The materialistic ideal that equated diamonds and love was further supported by Hollywood movies such as *Gentlemen Prefer Blondes*, *High Society*, *Breakfast at Tiffany's*, and *Diamonds Are Forever*. Today, De Beers still controls the majority of the world's diamonds, especially those in the United States. It controls the diamond supply and pricing in the United States.

FACT

In 1477, the first recorded diamond engagement ring was given to Mary of Burgundy by the Archduke Maximilian of Hamburg. This was a rare event because at the time a diamond was a very rare find and something only the wealthy would have access to.

The Conflict Surrounding Diamonds

The popularity of diamonds surged in the twentieth century, propelled by one industry giant. In recent years, however, increased awareness about some diamonds' troubled origins has fueled a movement away from them.

Ecological Concerns

By its very nature, mining produces pollution and disrupts the local environment. Pipe mining is the most common method for mining diamonds. Large amounts of rock are shifted to search for diamonds. The mine itself displaces local animal populations, and pollution from diamond mining contaminates nearby waterways and can lead to devastating effects for aquatic plant and animal species. In addition, a large amount of waste is generated to unearth comparatively few gems. When the miners are done, the waste is left behind.

Responsible miners can take steps to mitigate the damage. Rock can be placed back in the mine when operations are finished, and topsoil can be saved and used as a valuable resource to encourage natural plant life to take hold. Different countries place different environmental regulations on their mining industries, so you might ask your jeweler where she gets her diamonds.

Faux diamonds have come a long way. The virtually perfect lab-created diamond is Moissanite. Indistinguishable from the real thing to the naked eye, the only difference you'll see is the price. Don't tell anyone it's not real and they'll never know.

Ethical Concerns

In the 1990s, illegal smuggling and sales of diamonds were used to fund wars in Sierra Leone, Angola, Cote d'Ivoire, and the Democratic Republic of Congo. These conflicts cost an estimated 3.7 million lives and left millions more homeless.

The Kimberley Process was enacted by the United Nations in 2003 to stop the flow of conflict diamonds and promote peace and security in these war-torn countries. Each exporting government certifies that its diamonds are conflict free, and each importer agrees not to accept shipments without proper certification or from countries that do not participate in the process. The Kimberley Process has helped make sure that the profits from legal diamond exports go back into the countries where the diamonds were mined. Thanks to the Kimberley Process, more than $125 million worth of diamonds were legally exported from Sierra Leone in 2006. In the 1990s, almost all of the diamonds coming from that area were illegal.

The Kimberley Process is credited with reducing the flow of conflict diamonds in international trade. The Kimberley Process website states that 99.8 percent of diamonds are now conflict free; in the 1990s, they made up as much as 15 percent of the trade. However, critics charge that the Kimberley Process is flawed and corruption has allowed more conflict diamonds to leak into the trade than the organization admits. You should still ask jewelers where their stones come from; make sure they can provide you with authenticity.

Buying a Diamond

Here are some tips to help you make sure your diamond is legitimate:

- Do your research. Go online and ask questions.
- Request a certificate of origin. While it is not required, your retailer should be able to provide you with some background on the stone.
- Shop for stones from conflict-free areas such as Canada, Russia, and Australia. Mining is still a very dirty process, but these areas are conflict-free and trying to mine in more eco-friendly and socially responsible ways.
- Buy vintage stones and rings.
- Shop from responsible, reliable jewelers.

FACT

Conflict diamonds have gained a lot of attention, but there are other ethical concerns associated with the diamond industry. Some suppliers take advantage of the workers—including children—who mine the diamonds, paying them scant wages and forcing them to work in unsafe conditions. Ask your jeweler if his suppliers adhere to your ethical standards.

Eco-Responsible Jewelers

Mining of any kind can have very serious consequences for the people that work in the mines and for the land that is destroyed during the mining process. Two-thirds of the world's gold production is from developing countries, where labor and fair treatment are rarely regulated and health care isn't an option. Irresponsible gold mining has been polluting land and water for decades and causes serious illness in workers and nearby populations who are exposed to toxic waste from the mining process. However, gold mining can bring considerable economic advantage to struggling countries.

Jewelers both big and small are beginning to pledge to make changes to be more socially and ecologically responsible. The Council for Responsible

Jewelry Practices was created in 2005 by members of the industry to implement change. A few very well known companies are members, including Zales, Cartier, and Piaget. Another organization is the American Gem Trade Association (AGTA), which has developed best practices guidelines for gem sourcing.

Many jewelers are making a commitment to sell only conflict-free diamonds and nondirty gold. Tiffany & Co. supports the Green Gold Program. It has pledged to sell only green gold and certified conflict-free diamonds. Tiffany deals exclusively with suppliers of conflict-free mining. Leber Jewelers sells only nonconflict, free trade, and nondirty gold items. It has the Earthwise Line, a whole line of jewelry devoted to this. The Signet Group (Kay and Sterling Jewelers) pledges to sell only nondirty gold.

Other companies are also moving in the right direction by pledging themselves to sustainable, eco-responsible, and fair-trade practices. Brilliant Earth sells high-quality jewelry made from conflict-free Canadian diamonds and renewed gold and platinum, and Cred Jewellery offers impressive jewelry and adheres to responsible social, ecological, and economic practices.

Jewelry Made from Recycled Materials

Many eco-friendly companies are opting to use recycled old gold and other precious metals and making the material into new, beautiful jewelry pieces. You may want only precious metal and real gemstones for your engagement ring and wedding band, but consider the other jewelry you may wear for your green event—and what about the bridesmaids and even the flower girl? You certainly don't need to go with expensive precious metals for all of that. The amazing one-of-a-kind finds made from recycled materials are stunning. The following companies all use recycled materials for their creations:

- GreenKarat (*www.greenkarat.com*) uses recycled and reclaimed gold for all of its jewelry. It gets the metals from used and broken pieces of jewelry and electronics.
- Seraglia Couture Gems and Jewellery (*www.seraglia.com*) uses antique, old, and reclaimed materials to make unique pieces.

- Kathleen Plate (*www.smartglassjewelry.com*) makes beautiful jewelry from recycled glass. Plate uses sterling silver and recycled glass to create earrings, necklaces, bracelets, and more. She even has a line commissioned by Coca-Cola.
- Junk to Jewels (*www.junktojewels.net*) has some very interesting ecological jewelry that turns junk into eco-fashion.
- Global Handcrafters (*www.globalhandcrafters.com*) has jewelry from all over the world made by artisans that have been provided with fair wages and good working conditions.
- Repurposed 4 You (*www.repurposed4you.com*) has creative rings and bracelets made out of soda can tabs. It is a nonprofit organization that donates all of its proceeds to charities.

You can get jewelry made from recycled materials to wear on your wedding day and purchase stunning sets for all your bridesmaids and your flower girl to wear. How green is that?

Recycle Your Old Jewelry

You probably have some broken or tarnished pieces lying around in your jewelry box or hiding in the bottom of a drawer somewhere. You could collect your old gold and take it to a jeweler and have it made into a custom wedding band. If you have gemstones from old rings, pendants, or earrings, they can be fashioned into new settings on a new ring. Get your mom, your future in-laws, or even your friends involved and sort through old jewelry to see what you can come up with.

Check out thrift stores, pawn shops, and online ads for used jewelry. If you can get something for a steal, it's worth it to have the materials that can be made into something new. eBay and Craigslist are great places to find things other people are getting rid of. Many rings were never even worn; a jilted lover may like to recoup some money from the ring and you'll get a great deal. You could even place your own ad looking for rings to buy. Make sure what you are getting is legitimate; have it appraised if necessary.

Old wives' tales consider pearl engagement rings to be bad luck because the pearl represents tears. Another old superstition states that wearing pearls on your wedding day foretells of the tears you will cry throughout your marriage.

It might be a little pricey to have a ring custom designed, but if you are providing all of the materials all the jeweler has to charge is labor, which should cut a huge chunk off your bill. Shop around to see who gives you the best deal and request to see samples of their work. If you cannot find a good jeweler, check out local artists and visit arts and crafts shows and local art galleries, even a rock and gem show. You might be able to commission a ring that is a true piece of art.

The princess ring—three to five diamonds in a row across the top—was fashionable during the early twentieth century in the United States. Sometimes you can date a ring just by the settings and the style, or even the number of stones. Today the three-stone styles are very popular, although you don't see much of the five-stone princesses anymore.

Update Heirloom Pieces

Perhaps you have your grandma's old engagement ring or maybe your mom inherited Great Aunt Helen's wedding set. The antique setting is just what you were looking for, something unique you won't see anyone else wearing.

Are you a history buff or an antique enthusiast? Maybe you love the romance of the past. Have you listened to Grandma and Grandpa's love story over and over? Wouldn't it be wonderful to have a love like that? Take a piece of that love and good karma into your marriage by wearing a family heirloom ring. Heirloom pieces can be a great green way to have a meaningful and beautiful wedding ring. If the ring is in bad shape, a jeweler can clean it and fix it up for you.

By choosing an heirloom ring you are honoring your family and your heritage. You are also saving resources and energy that would have been used to create a new ring—not to mention that you'll probably be saving a ton of money by not having to buy a brand new ring.

Even if you don't settle on an heirloom ring, maybe some heirloom jewelry will work well for your wedding day. It fits in perfectly with the old saying "something old, something new, something borrowed, something blue."

FACT

The smallest diamond engagement ring ever recorded was given to two-year-old Princess Mary, the daughter of King Henry VIII, when she was betrothed to the infant Dauphin of France, son of King Francis I, in 1518. Francis broke the betrothal off two years later.

Fashionably Vintage

Do you marvel at the beauty and elegance of items from bygone eras? An antique ring may be just for you. Vintage jewelry, just like vintage clothing, is very hot and trendy, not to mention fashionable, easy to come by, and—best of all—green.

ALERT!

There are five basic styles and time periods of antique and vintage rings that are readily available: Victorian, art nouveau, Edwardian, art deco, and retro. Anything older than the Victorian era is rare and pricey. Anything newer is considered to be modern or contemporary.

Whether you are wearing a vintage gown and want jewelry to match the era or period pieces just appeal to you, you have a lot to choose from. Get swept up in the passion of the past while searching for beautiful vintage jewelry. There is something magical and timeless about old jewelry, like a testament that love is truly timeless. You can find vintage rings in many places—in thrift stores, antique shops, estate sales, pawn shops, and even at yard sales and online.

Victorian Jewelry

The Victorian era spanned the period from about 1836 to 1901 and coincided with the reign of Queen Victoria in Great Britain. Queen Victoria was a romantic, and the clothing styles and jewelry of the era reflected that with flowers, hearts, birds, bows, and intricate lacy designs. The serpent motif often appeared as well, and Queen Victoria is said to have worn a snake ring.

FACT

The Tiffany, or solitaire, setting was introduced toward the end of the nineteenth century. The six-prong diamond solitaire was introduced in 1886. A six-prong setting protects the side of the stone and lessens the chances that the stone will fall out and be lost.

Victorian engagement rings were often set in yellow or rose gold with very intricate and elegant designs. Opals were popular during the Victorian era because the queen adored them. Garnets, amethysts, turquoise, and seed pearls were also frequently used. Diamonds gained popularity in the later part of the Victorian period after the mines were discovered in South Africa. The discovery flooded the market with diamonds, making the stones readily available. Some Victorian settings featured rows of diamonds cut with an extra facet on the bottom called a mine cut.

Art Nouveau Jewelry

The art nouveau period overlapped with the Victorian era a bit, beginning around 1890 and ending around 1905. The art nouveau period represented the turning of the century and the coming of a new age. Materials were not as important as craftsmanship, so semiprecious and nonprecious stones were often used. Amber, opals, moonstones, citrines, peridots, copper, tortoise shell, ivory, carved glass, shells, pearls, and cabochon-cut gemstones were used. The feminine form was celebrated, and jewelry reflected this with sinuous flowing lines and soft curves. Nature appeared in the jewelry in the form of butterflies, dragonflies, poppies, orchids, irises, and lilies. Designs were very dramatic.

Consider eco-friendly rings made of nonprecious materials such as shells, recycled glass, or even custom carved wooden bands. Local craftsmen or artisans can create a beautiful one-of-a-kind ring for you, so check out what you have near you and support your local economy.

Edwardian Jewelry

The Edwardian period lasted from around 1900 to 1920. Platinum was the most popular metal after the invention of the oxyacetylene torch. Jewelers used the torch to craft lacy, intricate, and scrolling detail on engagement rings. Rose-cut diamonds and brilliant sapphires were the stones of choice during this era.

Art Deco Jewelry

The age of jazz, machinery, and new thinking—the roaring '20s gave rise to the art deco period from 1920 to 1930. The name was adopted from the Exposition of Decorative Arts and Modern Manufactures, held in Paris in 1925, where a new architectural and decorative style was unveiled. The style used geometric shapes and symmetry and bold, contrasting colors, specifically black and white.

The age of exploration and symmetry was reflected in the jewelry of the time with bold geometric shapes and bright colors. Hints of Egyptian, Asian, and Native American cultures were featured, especially in engagement rings. Bold colored stones were used. Diamonds were sometimes combined with platinum, and rubies, emeralds, sapphires, turquoise, and coral were used extensively throughout the 1920s.

FACT

Platinum was very popular in the early twentieth century for engagement rings and wedding bands until World War II restricted the use of platinum to war-related projects. This gave rise again to the popularity of yellow and white gold rings. Platinum has been making a comeback recently.

Retro Jewelry

The final vintage period is the retro period, which spans the years 1935 to approximately 1950. During World War II, women had to take over masculine roles, joining the work force and doing what they could while all the men were gone. Women's fashion became more severe and masculine, but the jewelry became softer and more whimsical. Gold once again became popular since platinum was restricted. Colored gold was used in interesting combinations of yellow, rose, white, and even green. Everything was big and bold, including the gemstones. Hollywood glitz and glamour ruled the scene. Aquamarines and citrines were fashioned into large rectangular settings. Colored gemstones were boldly used, as were synthetic rubies and sapphires. Cocktail rings were trendy, along with other oversized jewelry such as bracelets and watches.

Shopping Guidelines for Vintage Rings

When you buy anything expensive it is best to shop from a reputable dealer, but you never know where a great bargain may appear. Vintage rings can show up in estate sales, pawn shops, and antique stores. They can appear in classified ads and online auctions. However, be careful, especially when shopping online or from a private person. Get the ring appraised by a reputable outside source before you make your purchase. You want to know that what you are getting is authentic, not a reproduction, and that the stones are real gemstones and not colored glass. You may be surprised at how beautiful some older costume jewelry can be. Sometimes even the experts can be fooled at first glance.

During the reign of George I of Great Britain, which lasted from 1714 to 1727, it was popular to wear big, chunky wedding rings on the thumb, even though they were originally placed on the ring finger during the wedding ceremony.

When you shop online, make sure to get a complete description of the piece, including its size, condition, color, cut, carat, and clarity of the stones. You also want to know what metals were used, what size the ring is, and whether the ring can be sized. A dealer should be able to provide a certified gemologist report for you. Reputable online dealers of antique rings include the following:

- Topazery (*www.topazery.com*) offers a tremendous selection of heirloom, antique, vintage, and estate jewelry from the 1800s to the present.
- The Marlene Harris Collection (*www.marleneharriscol.com*) carries one-of-a-kind antique and estate jewelry.
- Fay Cullen (*www.faycullen.com*) offers a very large assortment of styles, from Victorian to modern.
- Sylvia's Antique Jewelry (*www.sylviasantiques.com*) carries a wide variety of antiques, including beautiful engagement rings spanning the eras from Victorian to contemporary.

Read all descriptions carefully. Several sites carry reproduction rings in addition to authentic period pieces, and they are all mixed in together. While the actual materials are no less real, the ring itself is made to look like a vintage ring but was really made within the last few months or years. Also make sure you know the refund policy before you type in your credit card number. You don't want to get stuck with a ring that isn't what it appeared to be on screen.

When you are shopping in person, inspect the ring carefully. Make sure the stones are sturdy in their settings and the prongs are not loose or sticking out. Check out the craftsmanship to avoid ending up with a poorly made replica. Remember that methods of cutting were different in the past and the standards that apply to today's stones are not the same. Also be careful of softer stones such as emeralds, pearls, and opals. These stones are easily damaged and may have internal cracks, so be sure to get them checked out thoroughly.

Above all else, when searching for the perfect ring, the most important thing is that you fall in love with it and that it means something to you. It is, after all, a symbol of your love.

CHAPTER 6

Natural Health and Beauty

Every bride wants to be beautiful on her wedding day. Many start exercising and dieting to look and feel their best when they walk down the aisle. Many brides also experiment with new beauty routines and new cosmetics, and many treat themselves to facials, manicures, and pedicures. There are many all-natural, organic products now available from companies that are focused on being eco-conscious. Look for green companies and eco-ways to help you get ready for your big day.

Natural and Organic Beauty Products

There are already many cosmetic companies that create all-natural, safe, organic alternatives. Drugstore.com and Beauty.com sell several brands of organic and all-natural personal care products.

FACT

One of the first things you may want to do is check the labels on your cosmetics or go online to Skin Deep (*www.cosmeticdatabase.com*). According to a Skin Deep report by the Environmental Working Group, more than one-third of personal care products contain at least one chemical linked to cancer.

Other companies that offer all-natural and organic personal care products and cosmetics include the following:

- Alima Cosmetics (*www.alimacosmetics.com*) offers 100 percent natural mineral cosmetics.
- Saffron Rouge (*www.saffronrouge.com*) sells organic face and skin care products.
- Terressentials (*www.terressentials.com*) makes handcrafted certified organic skin, hair, and baby care products; it uses USDA-certified organic food-grade ingredients.
- Avalon Natural Products (*www.avalonnaturalproducts.com*) sells organic body care products and cosmetics by Avalon Organics and Un-Petroleum products by Alba.
- Tom's of Maine (*www.tomsofmaine.com*) is one of the original all-natural personal care product lines.
- Origins (*www.origins.com*) is an organic beauty brand that is a division of Estée Lauder; it sells cosmetics and bath and body products.
- Trillium Organics (*www.trilliumorganics.com*) has a nice selection of natural, organic products.
- JASON (*www.jason-natural.com*) offers organic skin care products.
- Garden of Eve (*www.garden-of-eve.com*) sells natural and organic products.

- Purely Shea (*www.purelyshea.com*) offers organic shea butter skin care.
- Mother Nature (*www.mothernature.com*) carries a wide variety of personal care products from all the big companies—Avalon, Tom's of Maine, and more—in addition to many other items.

Many mainstream companies are adding green cosmetic products to their existing lineups. Physicians Formula introduced a line called Organic Wear. It is supposed to be 100 percent natural origin makeup made with certified organic ingredients, completely free of harsh chemicals, parabens, and synthetic preservatives. It comes packaged in recyclable paper containers. Organic Wear is also the first ECOCERT certified line of organic makeup in the United States.

ECOCERT is an independent organization accredited by the French committee for accreditation, which conducts inspections and certifications to insure organic quality and integrity. It is much stricter than, and far superior to, conventional standards that govern organic cosmetics.

QUESTION?

Why are petroleum-based ingredients in beauty products unsafe?
Mineral oil, paraffin, and petrolatum are all petroleum-based products. These petroleum-based products coat the skin, clog the pores, and create a buildup of toxins. They can disrupt hormone activity, can cause early signs of aging, and are a suspected carcinogen. However, they are a major ingredient in most beauty products.

Look for other companies that support eco-issues. Check to see if companies have signed the Compact for Safe Cosmetics, pledging that their products are free of any potentially harmful chemicals that are known to cause or are suspected of causing cancer or birth defects. You can find these companies through *www.safecosmetics.org*.

You can even make your own natural beauty products with many ingredients you may already have in your kitchen: sea salt, cornstarch, cornmeal, honey, oatmeal, sugar, and many fresh fruits, vegetables, and herbs.

Food oils that are used as bases for many natural beauty products include almond, apricot kernel, avocado, castor, coconut, jojoba bean, macadamia nut, olive, sesame, soybean, sunflower seed, and wheat germ oils. These natural oils are safe alternatives to chemical-laden body lotions, creams, and oils. A good rule of thumb is "If you wouldn't put it in your body, you shouldn't put it on your body."

FACT

According to an industry researcher, Package Facts, the natural care market's sales increased from $2 million in 2002 to $6.1 million in 2006 with sales continuing to grow at a rate of nine percent annually. Natural and organic personal care products are already filtering into the mainstream in Europe, which is a leader in the market.

If you are interested in recipes and more information on how to make your own cosmetics at home, check out the books *Organic Body Care Recipes* by Stephanie Tourles and *Natural Beauty at Home* by Janice Cox. *Natural Beauty at Home* does have a few recipes that include petroleum jelly and/or mineral oil, but you can skip them or use nonpetroleum products instead. There are also many websites full of recipes and useful do-it-yourself advice. Check out *www.modernwife.com* and *www.the-cats-meow.com/naturalcosmeticindex.shtml.* Cranberry Lane (*www.cranberrylane.com*) sells DIY bath and body care supplies and, its website is full of recipes and ideas.

Naturally Beautiful

Are you interested in other ways to get naturally healthy and beautiful? Curious about alternative medicines and natural remedies to keep you healthy? Aromatherapy, herbs and vitamins, holistic living, homeopathy, yoga—what is all this stuff and how can it be beneficial? Here are some of the basics on these topics and how they can be implemented into your life.

Aromatherapy

You may use aromatherapy and not even know it: lighting a scented candle, putting on scented body lotion or perfume, sinking into a warm scented bath, simmering potpourri, or enjoying a walk through a scented garden. These are all essentially forms of aromatherapy. The actual practice of aromatherapy uses pure and natural essential oils that are scientifically proven to elicit certain physical and emotional responses.

The sense of smell occurs in the limbic portion of the brain, the most primitive part of our brain that stores and processes memories and emotions. A scent can take us back in time and make us recall memory. Learned odor responses are our brain's reaction to odors that have memories attached to them. They can be triggered by any scent, whether it's synthetic or natural. However, the scientific research of aromatherapy focuses on natural scents.

Synthetic oils, or oils reproduced chemically in labs, do not have the same properties or effects as natural essential oils and experts believe they are not effective in aromatherapy. Synthetic oils are also blamed for causing unpleasant effects, allergic reactions and headaches among them.

Essential oils can cause physiological changes in the mind and body of a person. "Smells act directly on the brain, like a drug," says Alan Hirsch, M.D., a neurologist and psychiatrist. Essential oils are highly concentrated essences of aromatic plants. Aromatherapy is the art of using the oils of the plant to promote the healing of the mind and body. Essential oils can be used alone or in combinations.

Essential oils are effective not only through inhalation but also when used topically. When used in massage, the oils are both inhaled and absorbed through the skin. They penetrate tissue, find their way into the bloodstream, and are transported to the organs and systems of the body.

There are many ways to use and enjoy the benefits of aromatherapy. Essential oils can be added to humidifiers, vaporizers, candle wax, diffusers, spray bottles of water, baths, and light bulb rings. They can be inhaled directly from the bottle or added to massage oils, bath oils, bath salts, powders, or body lotions. The proper use of essential oils can be very beneficial. Most natural body care products use essential oils. If you are interested in essential oils or herbs, check out *www .mountainroseherbs.com*. It carries a great selection of essential oils, bulk herbs, and tea and supplies for do-it-yourself bath and body products.

FACT

With rising health care costs and the dangerous side effects of some prescription medications and medical treatments, many people are looking for natural ways to stay healthy. Herbal therapy has become extremely popular because herbs are often cheaper than prescription medicines and have fewer to no side effects compared to prescription drugs.

Herbal Therapy

No one knows when humans started using plants as medicine, but some prehistoric sites suggest that Neanderthals used healing herbs more than 60,000 years ago. Many pharmaceuticals are derived from herbs. Aspirin was derived from the bark of a willow tree. Oral decongestants containing pseudoephedrine are made from the ephedra plant. At least one-fourth of all drugs that doctors prescribe contain active ingredients derived from or synthesized from plants. Scientists have learned how to isolate the active ingredients in herbs and produce more potent, faster-acting medicine. Unfortunately, with more potent medicine comes more powerful problems and side effects. With all the added chemicals and preservatives, and the synthetic formulations, the safety of the original herb is gone.

Most herbal remedies are safe and have no known side effects, but some can be dangerous. Combining the remedies with prescription or over-the-counter drugs or using them if you have a pre-existing health condition can be particularly dangerous. Always exercise caution. Consult a trained physician or herbalist before taking herbal remedies. Herbal remedies can commonly be found in pill and capsule forms, in teas, extracts, tinctures, ointments and creams, and in raw, dried forms.

Holistic Practices

Holistic medicine is a healing approach that considers a person's body, mind, and spirit when evaluating health or treating a disease. Holistic medicine promotes an individual's overall health and well-being to ensure the proper functioning of the body as a whole. The term *holistic* (sometimes *wholistic*) comes from the unification of the mind and body.

Holistic practitioners treat the whole person, not just the organs or areas where the symptoms occur. Holistic medicine emphasizes the need to look at the whole person and all areas of her life, including physical, nutritional, environmental, emotional, social, spiritual, and lifestyle values.

The beauty and cosmetic industries are recognizing the growing popularity of natural medicine and therapies and are incorporating holistic approaches and formulas into their products. Holistic skin care is a regimen that recognizes your skin as a reflection of your body's internal state. Outward appearance is a reflection of what is going on inside the body. Rather than just treating the surface symptoms that destroy beauty, holistic skin care targets the roots of your problems and treats them. Holistic approaches take into consideration all aspects of your life and all your symptoms so your entire body will be revitalized and rejuvenated.

There are many therapies and remedies that fall into the categories of holistic, alternative, and natural medicine. The practices may be used alone, together, or as a complementary therapy alongside conventional medicine.

Homeopathy

Homeopathy relies on minute amounts of herbs, minerals, and other substances to stimulate a person's natural defenses and help the body heal itself. It is thought to be able to heal illnesses with just a single dose of medicine with few to no side effects.

Homeopathy is based on the law of similars, which has been verified in experiments and in clinical studies throughout the past 200 years. The law of similars basically boils down to the statement "like is cured by like." The same principle is behind the creation of modern vaccinations and some allergy medications. In vaccines, a small amount of the disease is used to create a substance that will encourage immunity to the disease.

Today more than 1,200 substances are recognized as homeopathic remedies. In the United States, homeopathic medicines are drug products made by homeopathic pharmacies in accordance with processes described in the *Homeopathic Pharmacopoeia of the United States* and are regulated by the U.S. Food and Drug Administration, unlike most herbs and herbal remedies that you will find in a store. Many homeopathic remedies can be purchased in health food stores or drug stores, through catalogs, or online.

A homeopathic remedy is prescribed based on an assessment of all your symptoms and should be done by a trained homeopath. Homeopathic medicines are not something you should prescribe for yourself or ever try to make yourself. They are not quick and easy home remedies. Use caution before deciding if homeopathic medicines are right for you.

ALERT!

If you choose to walk or bicycle to places you would normally drive, you are simultaneously getting yourself in shape and reducing the amount of transportation pollution being released into the air. It's also a money-saver; you can conserve your financial resources by using your vehicle less and spending less money on gas.

Yoga

Yoga is the most basic of natural remedies and exercise. All you need to practice yoga is a quiet place with a level floor, comfortable clothing, and a few minutes each day to practice breathing, stretching, and meditation.

Yoga is extremely effective in increasing flexibility and massaging all organs of the body. It is excellent for toning the muscles, and there are many other benefits, both physical and psychological. Yoga can act as both a preventive and curative therapy for many illnesses and conditions.

The whole system of yoga is built on three main structures: postures, breathing, and meditation. To receive the maximum benefits of yoga you should practice all three. Yoga brings the mind, body, and spirit together.

Green Exercise

Research studies and programs are being implemented to explore the benefits of green exercise. Green exercise is any physical activity that takes place within the natural environment: gardening, walking, bicycling, running, jogging, playing outdoor sports, skiing, hiking, swimming, or anything else you want to do outside.

Get in shape while enjoying the great outdoors. Great ways to implement green activity into your life include:

- Walk or bicycle to work and other locations instead of driving.
- Go outside and walk around on your lunch break instead of surfing the Internet or sitting down to eat.
- Plant a garden and tend to it every day.
- Stop at a local park on your way home from work every day and walk, jog, or bicycle around the park.
- Get your fiancé involved and go on weekly hiking excursions; pick a new spot every week.
- Get together with friends for weekly matches of volleyball, tennis, or badminton.
- Mow your lawn with a push mower or an old-fashioned motorless push mower.
- Try new outdoor activities such as rock climbing or canoeing.
- Take your regular exercise routine outside: Do Pilates in the early morning sun, yoga by the light of the moon, or kickboxing at sunset.
- Take your love dancing.

Whatever you decide to do in the great green outdoors, make sure it gets you moving and that you have fun doing it.

Prewedding Pampering

With the rise of the green movement, you may now find eco-spas and salons where you can get some prewedding pampering done. Look for local salons and day spas that offer organic body care products, natural spa treatments, and toxin-free hair and nail care. Ask if they adhere to green practices such as recycling, composting, and using sustainable products. The natural personal care line Aveda is introducing its line of concept spas in cities around the United States. Check out the websites *www .greenspanetwork.com* and *www.spaindex.com* to find both day spas and spa resorts that are eco-friendly.

If you are planning to get away for a few days to enjoy some prewedding pampering (or postwedding bliss), you may want to consider the Gold Lake Mountain Resort and Spa in Ward, Colorado. The eco-friendly spa and resort encourages recycling, composting and eco-friendly products. It uses organic cotton bedding, recycled paper products, and nontoxic paint, and its chefs are devoted to cooking with locally grown organic food.

Another getaway to consider is the Comfort and Joy Wellness Spa in Fairfax, Virginia. It is a socially responsible and eco-friendly full-service salon and spa that offers organic skin care, toxin-free hair and nail care, soy-based hair removal, nourishing body wraps, organic facials, massages, and a wide variety of natural and organic products.

When you test out new products, do so at least a week before the wedding. Never wait until the day of or the day before; you don't want to risk any allergic or adverse reactions that could leave you red, irritated, bumpy, or puffy on your big day.

If you don't have any green spas or salons in your area, maybe you could invite the girls over and have a day or night of organic cosmetic fun. Either make your own or purchase organic and all-natural products and give each other facials, manicures, and pedicures. You can download a brochure from *www.safecosmetics.org* that gives you details on how to host a healthy cosmetics party; it even has several easy-to-make recipes for natural beauty products.

CHAPTER 7

Eco-Invites

Approximately 350 million wedding invitations end up in American landfills every year. Invitations have become increasingly intricate with inner envelopes, outer envelopes, invitations, reception announcements, response cards, response card envelopes, and enclosures such as maps and registry information—and etiquette dictates a proper way to assemble that pile of paper. Fortunately, there are ways for you to create a greener invitation that (hopefully) won't end up in a landfill.

Recycled Paper

Your invitation is the opening act of your wedding. It is a preview of what is to come, a sneak peek into what your guests can expect. The invitation can set the theme and tone for your whole wedding. So how can you let guests know that you are having a green wedding?

FACT

According to Emily Anderson (*www.ecochicweddings.com*), more than 500,000 trees are destroyed each year for invitations, menus, table cards, and other paper items for weddings in the United States. To help lower this statistic, you can search for paper-free or recycled products.

One option is to print your invitations on pretty recycled paper. Many printers now offer recycled paper and card stock. Some green printers only use eco-friendly papers and inks. Of the Earth (*www.custompaper.com*) is one the best green paper/printing companies out there, with the biggest online selection. Some of its handcrafted paper is very pretty and embedded with flowers, which gives it a unique look and feel that your guests may not want to throw away.

ALERT!

Trees are the earth's principle means of processing carbon dioxide. The loss of trees and forests reduces our means of processing all the carbon dioxide that is released into the air. Global warming foes promote the planting of trees to offset the negative effects of carbon dioxide emissions.

Of the Earth offers recycled, handmade, tree-free, and plantable seed paper, invitations, ribbons, and paper accessories. You can custom design your invitation or choose from its overstock. You can pick the materials you want your invitations made from (flowers, seeds, etc.), and you have the option to purchase the invitations preassembled. For a discount, you can get all the materials you need and assemble the invitations yourself.

Twisted Limb Paperworks (*www.twistedlimbpaper.com*) has more than twenty wedding invitation designs that it offers on handcrafted and 100 percent recycled paper. It also sells thank-you notes, place cards, favors, guest books, menus, programs, and more. Green Field Paper Company (*www .greenfieldpaper.com*) offers tree-free and recycled paper options, and Acorn Designs (*www.acorndesigns.org*) has some wedding invitations printed with eco-friendly paper and ink. Earthly Affair (*www.earthlyaffair.com*) offers invitations printed on 100 percent postconsumer waste recycled paper and cotton paper. Your local printer may also offer green printing choices.

Invitesite (*www.invitesite.com*) offers many beautiful green, eco-friendly wedding invitations made from tree-free and 100 percent recycled fibers. It also sells do-it-yourself kits so you can design and print your invitations at home.

You can also make your own invitations on recycled paper or card stock with earth-sensitive inks made from vegetable oil, linseed oil, hemp seed oil, or soy bases. You can purchase kits you can use at home with your computer and printer. You could even try your hand at calligraphy and address your eco-invites with an old-fashioned flair using a quill or fountain pen (avoid disposable pens; they are just one more product that ends up in landfills in large quantities).

More than 300 million inkjet cartridges end up in landfills every year. When yours is empty, refill or recycle it. The Recycle for Breast Cancer program (*www.recycleforbreastcancer.com*) will send you prepaid envelopes, labels, or boxes so you can send in your empty ink cartridges. The organization also collects other electronic items, and all profits go to support the fight against breast cancer.

Recycled paper production saves trees, energy, and water. Recycling produces less pollution than processing virgin pulp. It also saves space by reducing the amount of paper that ends up in landfills.

By using recycled, handmade, and recyclable paper, you are saving trees from being cut down. Hopefully, by making your invitation unique and pretty, you may inspire your guests to hold on to your invitations instead of disposing of them in the trash. If you are still worried about the possibility that your guests may throw your invitations away, you can include a note that says "please recycle" with or on the invitation.

Tree-Free Paper Products

If recycled or handmade recycled paper isn't your thing, there are many more options. Did you know paper can be made out of many materials without harming one single tree? Before the nineteenth century, many types of plants and fibers other than trees were used to make paper. When industrial wood pulping technology was developed, forest resources were taken advantage of in the United States and the lumber business grew quickly. Today the lush forests are long gone, and even though many trees are planted specifically for the paper industry, they cannot grow fast enough to meet demand.

One out of every three trees that is harvested ends up as pulp for paper products. Even with all the alternative paper resources out there, forests are being consumed at rapid rates. The U.S. paper industry alone consumes more than 12,430 square miles of forest per year.

Loss of trees is not the paper industry's only ecological problem. While the impact on the world's forests is undeniable, the industry consumes vast amounts of energy and water to convert trees into paper. In addition, many chemicals that are used in the process end up in our air, water, and soil in large amounts, causing serious pollution.

When you mail out all those invitations, try to find old-fashioned moisten-and-stick stamps. New sticker-type stamps come on waxy paper that cannot be recycled. You can also ask for the invitations to be metered and stamped by a machine or by hand; just make sure the postage isn't being stamped onto peel-and-stick labels.

Tree-free paper is one eco-friendly alternative. The fibers from most plants can be made into quality paper products. Rapidly renewable resources such as flax and hemp can create quality paper. Experts believe the most effective and environmentally friendly resources for tree-free paper can come from otherwise discarded agricultural waste. Stalks and husks left after harvesting a main crop are perfect; corn, barley, oats, wheat, rice, rye, coffee bean skins, sugar cane husks, and even tobacco fiber can be made into paper. This method makes use of existing waste and turns it into something beneficial while saving natural virgin resources such as hardwood trees.

Some of the most popular alternative materials being used for paper-making today include the following:

- Bamboo is being used for everything from flooring to clothing and even paper. Bamboo paper and rice paper have been made on a small scale in Asia for centuries.
- Bagasse is the husk and pulp that remains after extracting juice from sugar cane; it can be processed into paper.
- Waste bark from banana trees can be made into paper. Banana leaf paper is known as abaca.
- Coconut husks can be processed into thick, textured paper.
- Corn plant stalks, known as corn stover, can be made into excellent paper pulp comparable to North American hardwood pulp.
- Cotton paper can be made from old cotton rags and other recycled cotton material, cotton processing waste, or even fresh organic cotton fibers.
- Paper can be made from bacteria- and odor-free elephant dung.
- Hemp paper is a superior quality product. It is said that Thomas Jefferson drafted the Declaration of Independence on hemp paper.
- Jute can be made into high-quality specialty paper.
- Kenaf is a hibiscus from Africa that has been used to make paper.
- Mango paper is made from the mango leaf and paper mulberry.
- Straw fibers are very similar to wood and make great paper. At one time, the United States produced straw paper, but the industry no longer exists.
- The petals and leaves from the tamarind tree can be made into paper.

Hemp is considered to be the best alternative to regular wood pulp paper. It is said that the world's first paper was made from hemp, and until 1883, 75 to 90 percent of the world's paper was hemp. The Gutenberg Bible, Thomas Paine's pamphlets, and Mark Twain's novels were all printed on hemp paper. Hemp paper is stronger than wood-based paper and will last centuries longer than regular paper. It does not crack, yellow, or deteriorate. Hemp paper does not require any bleaching and can be grown and processed with very little chemical use.

FACT

One acre of hemp can produce as much paper as four to ten acres of trees growing over a twenty-year cycle. While the trees have to grow for twenty to eighty years before they are mature enough to be harvested and turned into pulp, hemp can reach maturity in only four months.

Tree-free paper is not entirely a mainstream product yet, so it may be hard to come by at your local office supply store or printer. However, as with everything else, demand pushes supply up. As more people start asking for tree-free paper, mainstream stores will start supplying it to the general public. Until then, you can search in your local health food and natural supply specialty stores and online.

Plantable Paper

If you want a very symbolic invitation that won't end up in a landfill, send invitations made from plantable seeded paper. The invitations will bloom just like your love for your fiancé. Plantable paper embedded with flower seeds is a great eco-choice. Depending on the seeds, the flowers may last for weeks or months after your wedding and no paper waste is left behind.

Many plantable papers are made from recycled or tree-free fibers and are embedded with seeds so they are doubly and triply green. Not only were no trees harmed in the production of these papers, but beautiful flowers will grow from them once they are planted. Botanical PaperWorks (*www.botanicalpaperworks.com*), Tree Beginnings (*www.plantamemory*.*com*), and Ecoparti (*www.ecoparti.com*) offer plantable papers, invitations, and favors.

If you make your own recycled or tree-free handmade paper, you can add seeds to it at the end of the process while the slurry settles in the mold.

Creatively Green

If you are a craftsy person or someone who likes to experiment with new things, you might like to try making your own paper. You can make handmade recycled paper from old scrap paper or scrap fibers such as cotton—even dryer lint. Many types of plant fiber make usable paper, though using raw materials can be a lengthy and a somewhat more complicated endeavor than using scrap paper.

Homemade Paper

- ❤ lots of scrap paper
- ❤ a couple of wooden frames that should be a little larger than the size you want the finished piece of paper to be
- ❤ a window screen a little larger than the largest frame; it has to go over the frame and attach to it
- ❤ staples and hand stapler or staple gun
- ❤ old blender, preferably not one you'll want to use again for food processing
- ❤ a large rubber or plastic tub, big enough to immerse the frames in
- ❤ pieces of felt or wool larger than your frames, at least two per sheet of paper
- ❤ a sponge
- ❤ a rolling pin
- ❤ anything you would like to put into your paper—herbs, flowers, seeds, etc.

- ❤ cornstarch to mix into the slurry and make the paper easier to write on
- ❤ flat, edgeless cookie sheets
- ❤ optional items, including large cookie-cutter shapes, an apron, and extra towels and rags

You may have many of these supplies around the house. Papermaking supplies can also be purchased at craft and hobby stores. The frames and screen are called a mold and deckle, and the tubs are called vats. ❤

1. **Collect** a lot of scrap paper. Be aware that not all paper is a good choice for making your own recycled product. Newspaper will turn everything gray, and magazines are too glossy and will make everything gunky. Avoid any glossy or waxy papers such as gift wrap. Your best choices are junk mail, office, computer, and copy paper (colored paper is fine), and envelopes.

2. **Once** you have all your paper, rip it up into one-inch squares or shred it into small pieces. This helps break the fibers down and makes for easier processing.

3. **Once** the paper is all ripped up or shredded, soak it in a tub of warm water for at least two hours; soaking it overnight is preferable.

4. **To** make your mold, cut your window screen an inch or two larger than the frame, then stretch it over the frame and staple it to the back side. If you want your paper to have straight edges you'll want to use a second frame with no screen; this is called the deckle. The deckle sits on the mold and defines the shape of the paper. If you want the uneven edges that are characteristic of handmade paper, don't bother with the deckle.

5. **After** your paper is finished soaking, mix it up in your blender at a ratio of one cup of paper to 2–3 cups of water. Start with 2 cups; if the mixture is too thick and lumpy add another cup. You want a thick slurry, like a really thick smoothie consistency, not runny and watery. If you want to write on the paper, add a tablespoon of cornstarch. This process is called sizing and makes the paper less porous so it does not absorb the ink.

6. **Blend** the mixture on medium high until it has the consistency of thin oatmeal.

7. **Experiment** with colors by adding food coloring. Pour it in and mix very briefly. You can add flowers or other herbs or materials now or wait until you pour it into the mold and add by hand. Do not blend seeds in the blender. If you want to make plantable paper, wait until your pulp is ready.

8. **Once** your paper is blended into a nice slurry of pulp, fill your tub with about two inches of water for every blender-full of pulp.

9. **Pour** the pulp into the mold, then lower the mold into the tub of water at an angle and shake to distribute the pulp evenly over the screen. If you are using a deckle, place it over the mold now, gently shake it back and forth, and pull both the mold and deckle up out of the water tub gently. Let the water drain, allowing all the excess water to flow back into the tub.

10. **If** you don't dip the pulp into the water, this is the time to add materials such as seeds, flowers, and herbs. Mix them around or place them where you want.

11. **Use** a sponge, cloth, or towels to dry the excess water off the back of the screen.

12. **Lay** a piece of felt or wool on top of the paper on the screen and turn the whole thing over—mold and all—onto a hard surface such as a flat edgeless cookie sheet. If the paper doesn't come off easily, dry the back of the screen some more, tap it, or carefully peel the paper off.

13. **If** you have not already done so, add flowers, herbs, or seeds to the paper mixture. If you choose, make imprints in the paper by pressing plants, leaves, or even textured objects such as lace into the paper. Leave the objects there until the paper has dried.

14. **Cover** the paper with another piece of felt and roll over it with a rolling pin to bind the fibers together and to help imprint any designs. This will help your paper dry faster and flatter.

15. **Keep** adding sheets of paper to the pile as you make them; just separate each one with a piece of felt so they don't stick together.

16. **Sandwich** all the paper sheets together and keep them lying flat by piling books or boards on top of them. If you really get into the

homemade paper process, you could make a simple paper press from boards and C clamps. Kitchen cutting boards are also very effective for pressing the paper to keep it flat.

17. Leave the sheets alone until they are dry. Drying time can vary, but start by leaving the sheets overnight. Store the sheets so they remain flat until you are ready to use them.

This whole process can also be done with plant fibers, but plant fibers have to be cooked and processed, which can be extensively complicated.

The whole handmade paper making process may sound a bit hard and time consuming, especially for a busy couple planning a wedding. It may also take a lot of handmade sheets to have enough paper for custom invitations, but if you keep it simple and just send out postcard sized-invitations it'll be a lot easier if you make the paper yourself.

If you find you really enjoyed the papermaking experience and you'd like to get a little more creative, two books by Helen Hiebert are wonderful resources. Check out *The Papermaker's Companion: The Ultimate Guide to Making and Using Handmade Paper* and *Papermaking with Plants*.

Place Cards, Favor Tags, Guest Books, Etc.

Most of the paper products that are used in the name of weddings end up in landfills after the festivities are over—and they can just be eliminated. No one really needs a program to follow what is going on; it's a wedding ceremony, not a three-ring circus. You can skip the menus, too. Just say no to matchbooks and custom printed napkins. Place cards can be eliminated by letting guests sit wherever they want, and this is extremely easy if you have a small intimate affair. Favor tags are not necessary, but if you do decide to have them, let them do double duty as a favor tag and a place card.

Great green options for place cards and favor tags include using non-paper products such as leaves, twigs, or small stones. Names or sentiments can be written on the surface for the reception, and they can be returned to nature afterward—no garbage created.

If you do decide to use things such as favor tags or place cards, do them in the greenest way possible by using recycled, handmade, or tree-free paper for them. Many of the companies that offer eco-fabulous invitations also offer eco-accessories such as guest books, favors, favor tags, place cards, menus, and even ribbons.

Paperless

If you really want to prove your eco-centricity, go paperless. You don't need any of the fancy paper products wedding companies showcase. No, not even the invitations, not in today's electronic age.

Etiquette gurus may faint from the horror of it all, but you are a product of the green generation. The time-honored tradition of sending out printed invitations started before e-mail and the Internet even existed and before we knew of the long-term damage we were causing the environment. Today's bride and groom have electronic advantages that past generations couldn't even dream of. Someone on the other side of the world is just a click away; as soon as you hit "send," your invitation can be there, no postage or paper required.

You can cut down on paper invitations by e-mailing your save-the-date cards, or you can cut out paper entirely and send all the invitations themselves via the web. Several sites such as Evite (*www.evite.com*) and Sendomatic (*www.sendomatic.com*) help you create and send save-the-date cards and invitations online. You can also send out custom e-mails through wedding sites such as The Knot (*www.theknot.com*) and WeddingChannel (*www.weddingchannel.com*).

Evite and Sendomatic allow you to create invitations and announcements quickly and easily online, customize designs with your personal information, and even upload photos to include in your announcements or invitations. The sites also have many wonderful features that help you keep track of your address book, RSVPs, and much more.

The Knot and several other wedding planning sites also allow you to create a custom wedding website for free. Send everyone a link to your web page, and your guests can see all the information for themselves. Your page can include everything about your green wedding and all the information about when and where your wedding and reception will be. Many companies offer premium website design and hosting services for a price, but The Knot, WeddingChannel, mywedding.com (*www.mywedding.com*), and eWedding (*www.ewedding.com*) let you upload photos and lots of information completely free. Some sites allow you to keep the location and time password-protected so you don't get any unwanted crashers showing up at your intimate occasion.

ALERT!

According to the EPA, every year more than 900 million trees are cut down to provide raw material for paper and pulp mills to fulfill the demand of U.S. paper consumption. More than 90 percent of U.S. paper is made from virgin tree fiber.

Even in today's electronic environment, Grandma and Grandpa and some of your other guests may not have computers and e-mail. Don't let this obstacle derail your paperless dreams. You can call everyone whom you can't reach electronically. This is a personal way to invite your guests.

If you can't keep it completely paperless and must send out some paper invitations, be as simple and green as possible. You can always send a postcard on recycled or recyclable paper and request a phone or e-mail RSVP. Seal-N-Send (*www.seal-n-send.com*) offers all-in-one unique wedding invitations with removable response cards so there are no envelopes and no excess paper waste. Send a few of those to the guests who require old-fashioned paper invitations.

CHAPTER 8

Eat, Drink, and Be Green

Your reception will probably be the most expensive part of your big day, eating up as much as 50 percent of your wedding budget. Food alone can take 20 to 30 percent of that. The reception is the biggest and most expensive part of your green event, and it's also where you can have the most impact with your eco-choices. Whether you are having a small intimate eco-affair for twenty or a large eco-extravagant soirée for 120, the choices you make can all have a major impact on the environment.

Eco-Responsible Receptions

Everything from the simplest details to the most complex choices can have an impact on the environment in some way. For example, what if you are having a big reception and you decide to use disposable place settings, napkins, and utensils? Everything would end up in a landfill afterward.

You can stop the excess landfill pileup by choosing to use reusable plates and tableware that you rent or purchase for the occasion. Alternately, you can buy compostable, biodegradable, disposable table settings made from sugar cane fibers, natural corn and potato starches, or bamboo.

You can be both eco-friendly and casual. If formal dinnerware won't fit in with your green wedding, retailers such as Kokopelli's Green Market (*www.kokogm.com*) and BambuHome.com (*bambuhome.com*) can help. Kokopelli's Green Market sells compostable plates, bowls, cups, and cutlery, and BambuHome.com offers beautiful single-use products made from bamboo that are supposed to biodegrade in four to six months.

Experts may argue which choice is better; reusable dinnerware requires water and energy to wash while biodegradable and compostable products have to be disposed of properly. It comes down to personal choice and what is the most convenient for you. Either option is greener than regular wax-coated paper, Styrofoam, or plastic disposable plates and utensils.

There are many ways to have an eco-reception. Try incorporating some of these ideas into your event and into any prewedding parties:

- Ditch the disposables. Say no to plastic, Styrofoam, and waxy coated paper plates. This goes for anything that is a single-use product—not just tableware and eating utensils but also serving trays, punch bowls, dessert trays, and food warmers. Talk to your caterers to make sure they use reusable products.
- Rent or purchase reusable items. Most catering services offer complete table settings or have a recommended rental service they

suggest. You might even want to scour the thrift stores. You may find a variety of table settings that can be mixed and matched for an elegantly eclectic dinner service. If you don't need everything you bought, you can donate it to a good cause such as a homeless shelter, soup kitchen, battered women's shelter, or to a thrift store such as Goodwill or the Salvation Army.

- If you do opt for some disposable products, make sure they are made from recycled materials and/or that they are biodegradable or can be recycled or composted.
- Opt for a late evening or night-time reception and only serve drinks and cake. Other options include having a reception at a time of day where you are not required to serve a whole meal. At an afternoon reception, you could have just drinks, hors d'oeuvres, and cake.
- Consider organic, fair-trade, and local food choices when selecting a menu.
- A meatless menu is a very green choice. It can also help you keep costs down, because meat can add quite a bit to your bill.
- Keep it as simple as possible by having a buffet. Guests can serve themselves while they mingle, and you have fewer catering staff to pay for.
- Make sure your venue and caterer are as eco-friendly as possible. The Green Restaurant Association (*www.dinegreen.com*) has listings of green restaurants. While there is no similar list for caterers yet, ask ahead of time about your caterer's practices and make sure they recycle and adhere to other green standards.
- If you are considering a hotel for your reception location, visit the Green Hotels Association (*www.greenhotels.com*) to find a hotel that has implemented environmentally friendly practices in its daily business.
- For a great listing of green businesses for all your reception needs, visit Co-Op America's website (*www.coopamerica.org*) and check out its online version of the Green Pages to find screened and approved green businesses. If you want, you can also order a print copy of the Green Pages.

- Don't throw out leftover food. Send it home with guests instead. Have some packed up for you to take home if you aren't leaving right away for your honeymoon. You could also donate leftovers to a local shelter or soup kitchen; make arrangements ahead of time to make sure they will accept prepared food, then appoint someone responsible to deliver it after the reception.
- Encourage recycling and proper disposal of waste. Make sure your venue or caterer has containers set up to collect and separate recyclables. Make sure compostable items are composted. The goal is to keep as much out of the landfill as possible.

Earth-Conscious Caterers

You may find only a few strictly organic caterers in you area, though many caterers may offer organic options or entire organic menus. The popularity of organic menus for weddings and other special events is growing rapidly, especially now that celebrities and celebrity chefs are joining the organic crusade. However, it is still largely a niche market.

Several basic questions to make sure you ask your caterer include:

- Do you offer organic menus, menus with organic choices, or cuisine made with organic ingredients?
- Do you purchase locally grown foods from local farmers? Are the farms certified organic, or at least pesticide free?
- Are you experienced with vegetarian or vegan menus? What about raw selections?
- Do you use free range meats, meats raised without hormones or antibiotics, or sustainably harvested seafood?
- Are beverages and desserts organic, fair trade, or local?
- Do you provide reusable serving dishes, reusable real dinnerware, and cloth napkins and tablecloths? If you use disposable products, are they recyclable or biodegradable?
- What do you do with leftovers? Will you deliver them to a charity or do I have to make my own arrangements for that?

If the caterer does not offer organic options, consider asking whether you will be able to provide any of your own drinks or desserts. If so, will there be an additional charge for this?

However, you can judge caterers on many green levels, not just solely on the availability of an organic menu. Find out what their practices are. Do they recycle, support local farms and farmers, use local in-season products, buy organic produce, offer a wide variety of menus, or support fair trade practices? Organic is good, but supporting local farms and using fresh, locally grown, in-season produce can make a big difference as well. How green can it be if you want organic mangos in the middle of December in Maine? They might have been organically grown—thousands of miles away. The carbon emissions produced to get them to your wedding feast make them not such an eco-friendly choice.

ALERT!

Pretty much any recipe can be made organic. Just substitute organic ingredients for regular ones. Organic food now comes boxed, canned, and packaged just like everything else. Many big chain grocery stores have an organic and natural foods section, in addition to a selection of fresh organic fruits and vegetables in the produce section.

Also make sure to find out what your catering company offers in addition to the food and staff. Do they supply table settings, drinks, alcohol, linens, and the cake? Some caterers are all-inclusive, while others offer everything separately at set rates. Still others stick to the food and let you handle everything else through other vendors.

If you decide to request a special menu, ask if the caterer can do a taste testing or sampling of flavors. This will be particularly helpful if you are going with a vegetarian or vegan menu and you don't have much, if any, experience with the tastes and flavors of meat-free menu options.

Budget may play a big part in the final menu choice. Organic choices can cost more than a regular menu, but you may be able to save money if you cut out extras such as desserts (other than the cake), limit the number of hors d'oeuvres, or cut out meat and various side dishes.

Edible Organic Options

If you are not familiar with organic food, you may be wondering what the big deal is. Why is it a better choice for the environment? How is organic green?

Many hazardous chemicals such as DDT and hexachloro have been banned from use in the United States, yet the chemicals are still manufactured and are used in Mexico and throughout South America—prime sources for out-of-season produce in local grocery stores.

Every day, crops all over the world are sprayed with toxic chemicals. In the United States alone, more than 800 million pounds of pesticides and more than 54 million tons of synthetic chemical fertilizers are used on farmlands every year. These chemical-filled products pollute the ground and water, and traces remain on the food we eat.

The EPA published a report called *Unfinished Business: A Comparative Assessment of Environmental Problems* that stated the number-three risk for cancer is pesticide residues in food. Beware of foods that are particularly susceptible to contamination, especially when you eat the skin of the fruit or vegetable.

Organic fruits, vegetables, grains, and fibers are grown without the use of toxic chemicals. For a farm to be considered organic, healthy soil and crops must be maintained through natural methods; chemical fertilizers, pesticides, fungicides, rodenticides, and herbicides cannot be used. Varying stages and levels of organic certification are still being formed to regulate what can be considered organic. In 1991, Congress passed the Organic Foods Production Act as part of a national farm bill. However, many states also have their own independent certification standards.

To learn more about organic foods, visit *www.theorganicreport.com*, *www.foodnews.org*, *www.organicconsumers.org*, *www.organickitchen.com*, and *www.ewg.org*. To learn about the safety of the foods you purchase, visit *www.centerforfoodsafety.org*.

For a product to be certified organic, it has to follow guidelines of the National Organic Standards Act. In October 2002 the USDA became the official agency to supply this official accreditation through the National Organic Program. To be certified organic, any food or fiber had to be grown without toxic pesticides and fertilizers, synthetic hormones, sewage sludge, antibiotics, irradiation, or GMOs (genetically modified organisms).

Look for the "USDA Organic" label to find a certified product. Pay attention to what the label says: "100% Organic" means that all the ingredients are organic; "Organic" means that 95 percent of the ingredients are organic; and "Made with Organic Ingredients" means the product is made with only 70 percent organic ingredients. Meat can be organic as long as it follows the guidelines; living animals cannot be given antibiotics or hormones and must be fed with organic grains.

When you shop for meat and poultry products, look for labeling that says free farmed, free range, free roaming, or pasture raised. These choices ensure that the animals were raised in a comfortable environment and were allowed some freedom, rather than being shut up in small cages their entire lives.

It is possible to have a completely organic menu. Everything from your hors d'oeuvres to your cake and even your drinks can be organic. Beer, vodka, tequila, and wine are all being made in organic varieties. Some organic winemakers are Bonterra (*www.bonterra.com*) and the Organic Wine Company (*www.theorganicwinecompany.com*). Other organic alcohol varieties to consider include 4 Copas Tequila, Square One Vodka, Reyka Vodka, and Anheuser-Busch's new organic lineup that consists of Purus Vodka and the organic beers Stonemill Pale Ale and Wild Hops Lager. Other companies have announced plans to create new lines of green and organic alcohol beverages or to turn existing products green.

If you are looking for nonalcoholic organic drinks, you can choose from an array of organic juices and sparkling ciders. There are even some organic sodas. Blue Sky (*www.drinkbluesky.com*) offers several all-natural sodas, including organic sodas.

ALERT!

The organic foods industry in the United States is estimated to be a $9 billion per year industry, growing at a rate of 20 percent per year. Globally, the industry is practiced in about 100 countries; North America and Europe lead the continents in demand, but Australia and South America have more land dedicated to organic farming.

By choosing organic you'll help save the environment and quite possibly your own good health. To locate organic farms, restaurants, and stores that sell organic products, visit *www.eatwellguide.org*, *www.localharvest.org*, and *www.sustainabletable.org*.

If you can't find any local stores or organic farms in your area to purchase organic produce or other organic foods, you can always order online. Lydia's Organics (*www.lydiasorganics.com*) has a good selection of organic and raw foods, while Gold Mine Natural Foods (*www.goldminenaturalfoods.com*) has a pretty big selection of organic, raw, vegan, and other specialty foods. Eden Foods (*www.edenfoods.com*) and Walnut Acres (*www.walnutacres.com*) can direct you to the stores and online retailers that sell their products.

Vegetarian and Vegan Choices

Organic options are very green, although environmental experts and animal activists and organizations such as People for the Ethical Treatment of Animals argue that vegetarian choices are even better and vegan are the absolute best. They combine what's best for the environment, best for human health, and, of course, best for the animals.

An estimated 70 percent of all human diseases are connected to diet, including one-third of cancer types. Experts argue that a vegetarian diet reduces the risks for diseases such as coronary artery disease, high blood pressure, diabetes, and several types of cancers including colon, breast, prostate, stomach, lung, and esophageal cancer. Vegetarians are less likely to be obese than their meat-eating counterparts. Studies show that overweight people who switch to a vegetarian diet lose an average of twenty-four pounds in the first year; five years later, they're still able to maintain their weight.

Experts argue that our meat-based diets are partly to blame for the millions of people around the world who go hungry. Resources that could be used to grow food for people are being used to grow food to feed farm animals. Crops that could be used to feed the hungry are instead being used to fatten up animals for slaughter.

You may wonder what the differences between vegetarian diets and vegan diets are. Obviously neither includes meat, though some types of vegetarians eat dairy, poultry, and fish and just avoid beef and pork. A lacto-ovo vegetarian eats dairy products and eggs. A lacto vegetarian eats dairy but not eggs, and an ovo vegetarian eats eggs but not dairy. A pesci-vegetarian eats fish but not poultry. A semivegetarian may eat small amounts of poultry but follows a diet of primarily fruits, vegetables, grains, legumes, seeds, and nuts.

A strict vegan avoids all animal products, including anything made with fur, leather, or wool or any other animal by-products such as honey and gelatin. They also like to avoid anything that has been tested on animals.

If you look purely at the facts and statistics, eating an animal-free diet is better for the environment and your health, but it is going to be hard to get many people to give up steaks, cheeseburgers, and bacon, especially in a nation obsessed with the fast food culture. Doctors and scientists argue the benefits of vegetarian and vegan diets, though there are plenty of doctors that support eating meat and dairy products—in moderation. In the end it is a personal choice.

This is where having a vegetarian or vegan menu can really make a difference. You can give your guests the chance to experience a whole new world of tastes and textures, perhaps food they would never try on their own. You don't even have to tell them the hamburger is really a veggie burger or the milkshake is made from nut or soy milk unless they ask. Include traditional pasta or rice dishes made with meatless meat, and many people might not even notice the real meat is missing.

According to the late Dr. Benjamin Spock, a leading authority on children's health, "Children who grow up getting their nutrition from plant foods rather than meats have a tremendous advantage. They are less likely to develop weight problems, diabetes, high blood pressure, and some forms of cancer."

Not only will you be opening doors to a whole new world of tasty possibilities, you'll also be saving animals and helping save the environment. You'll be the head of your own eco-revolution, changing the world one meal at a time. To learn more about vegetarianism or to find tasty vegetarian and vegan recipes, check out *www.goveg.com*, *www.vegcooking.com*, *www.vegweb.com*, *www.vegkitchen.com*, and *www.vegetariantimes.com*.

If you would like to experiment with some vegetarian or vegan recipes at home, there is a wide range of books available. One great one is *Extra Vegan Za* by Laura Matthias, which is filled with many tasty and unique vegan dishes.

Raw Possibilities

If you want something truly unique and extraordinarily healthy, you may consider a completely raw foods menu for your reception. Raw food isn't just salads and veggie trays. A raw food diet is filled with fruits, vegetables, nuts, seeds, sprouts, and fresh living juices that are packed with enzymes and nutrients to promote optimal health. A raw diet is all about the enzymes in fresh foods. Enzymes are responsible for every metabolic action in the body; they enable cells to work and chemical reactions to happen. Temperature greatly affects enzymes in food. Cooking, baking, frying, and even freezing all deplete natural foods of enzymes, vitamins, and nutrients.

In a true raw/living foods diet no animal products—including meat, eggs, and dairy—are consumed. Raw foods are served raw, with no cooking and generally no heating above 110°F. Some foods are dehydrated or soaked in vinegar to ferment. Some are gently steamed or blanched for short periods at low temperatures to help break down the cellulose fibers to make them easier to digest.

A raw diet made from organic produce is arguably the most environmentally sound and health-conscious of all choices, but in today's fast-paced society who has the time to sprout, dehydrate, ferment, and "process" their own organic, raw, living foods? However, if you have an expert raw chef or caterer in your area who has experience with raw foods, this may be the perfect opportunity to try it out, either for prewedding parties or for your green reception.

A raw food menu has many options you would probably never imagine. In the book *Living Cuisine: The Art and Spirit of Raw Foods* by Renee Loux Underkoffler, there are more than 300 amazing recipes for raw foods. Her recipes include beverages, fresh soups, salads and salad dressings, appetizers, seed and nut cheeses, side dishes, main course dinners, burgers and other meatless patties, and a wide varieties of desserts.

Not one thing is cooked in any of those recipes. Everything is soaked, pressed, and processed either in a food processor or through dehydration. Any cookie, bread, grain, or crust food is always pressed and dehydrated. Some food is gently warmed, blanched, or steamed, but only enough to make it easier to eat while retaining all the natural enzymes.

You don't have to totally change what you eat, but it might be fun to try something new for prewedding get-togethers; if that goes well, you can make the decision to stick with it for the main wedding menu.

Shop Locally

According to *E/The Environmental Magazine*, the average dinner travels 1,500 miles before reaching your plate. Whether it goes from the farm to the grocery store or from the farm to the slaughterhouse to the packaging plant to the grocery store, that's a lot of traveling for one dinner.

The vehicles used to transport your dinner to your table release a great deal of carbon dioxide into the air. You also need to consider all the plastic, paper, and cardboard that is used for packaging, shipping, and selling your food. Most of that packaging just ends up in landfills.

ALERT!

According to Emily Anderson, author of *Eco-Chic Weddings*, for the average wedding that serves chicken or beef, approximately 9,625 square feet of forest are destroyed and 1,190 pounds of carbon dioxide are generated.

By shopping locally, you can avoid much of the pollution created through shipping, and you'll be supporting your local economy. Buy in-season produce from local farms, vegetable stands, and farmers markets or ask local grocery stores to buy from local farms. Not only will the food be greener, it'll taste better because it's fresher.

CHAPTER 9

Flower Power

Flowers are amazing gifts from nature, a delight to the senses and beautiful to look at and smell. Flowers and love have gone hand in hand since the beginning of mankind. For centuries, herbs and flowers have been carried or worn by brides around the world. Today, they play a central part in wedding décor. They are used in bouquets and boutonnieres, and they figure prominently in centerpieces and other decorative spreads. There are many green options for you to choose from when it comes to the greenery at your wedding.

Gloriously Green

Brides dream of being surrounded by beautiful flowers on their wedding day, walking down the aisle amid an amazing floral fantasyscape. But how green is that? The floral industry is very hard on the environment in terms of both the resources and the energy needed to cultivate the flowers. In addition, staggering amounts of pesticides are used to make the flowers appear perfect. However, with some creative thinking and eco-planning you can have a gloriously green wedding full of eco-bouquets and floral arrangements that are splendidly sustainable and awesomely organic.

Remember the essentials: reduce, reuse, recycle. Choose floral elements that follow three-R thinking.

- If you dream of being surrounded by flowers on your wedding day, a ceremony held in the middle of a blooming garden might be among your top options for a location. It requires less decorating for you and fewer flowers to buy.
- Renting large potted plants, flowers, and trees is another option. They can be used as decorations for both the ceremony and reception and they'll go on to be used over and over again.
- Consider living floral arrangements. An assortment of plants and flowers can be planted together in containers. These can be used as wedding accents and reception centerpieces and décor. After the reception is over guests can take them home and enjoy them indoors or plant them outside in a garden. The containers can also be donated to hospitals, nursing homes, and senior centers—any place that could use a little cheering up.
- Have the bridesmaids and flower girl carry nonflower elements such as decorative silk purses, vintage handbags, Southern style parasols, Spanish or Asian style silk fans, or baskets full of organic fruit that can serve double duty at the reception as décor and food.
- Use nonfloral centerpieces such as candles, bowls of pretty rocks, or baskets full of fruits, nuts, or vegetables. If you are having a theme wedding, incorporate reusable nonfloral theme elements into your décor.

- Keep it simple by only using flowers for what is really necessary: the bridal bouquet, boutonnieres, corsages, the altar arrangement (which can also serve as the bridal table centerpiece), bridesmaid bouquets, and flower girl basket.
- Reuse the bridesmaid bouquets at the reception. Invest in bouquet stands or clips that can be attached to tables.
- You can keep it extremely simple by using just one dramatic or exotic flower instead of a bunch of flowers as a bouquet. This could work for you and the bridesmaids or you could carry the flower and they could carry something nonfloral. Calla lilies are perfect for this purpose.

Harmful and Unnatural Floral Practices

There is nothing more natural and beautiful than a flower. Unfortunately, harmful practices make it very un-green to go to a regular florist and pick out beautiful flowers for your wedding. Cut flowers are one of the world's most pesticide-ridden crops. Since cut flowers are not considered to be an ingestible import, the USDA does not regulate the pesticide levels on them. Importers are free to load up on the chemicals to keep the flowers looking pretty and fresh. The flowers you choose can have a great impact on both social and environmental issues.

FACT

More than 50 percent of all cut flowers in the United States are imported, mainly from Central and South America. Colombia alone exports more than $630 million worth of flowers annually, a large portion of that going to the United States.

The toxic chemicals used on the flowers pollute the ground and water and become part of the never-ending cycle as birds and animals ingest the poisons and pass them on to other birds, animals, and even humans. The workers and handlers who are exposed to the toxic chemicals get sick and expose others to the pesticides through residual contact, which makes others sick.

Sooner or later all the harmful stuff that goes on in other parts of the world can make its way back to us. The pesticide pollution can make its way to food crops that are grown and shipped around the world or to crops that are grown to feed animals that become food for humans. Things that happen thousands of miles away can touch your life in ways you never thought of.

ALERT!

Most U.S. flower growing occurs in California, where flowers and ornamentals rank sixth among all crops causing pesticide illness, according to data from the California Department of Pesticide Regulation.

There are other problems within the floral industry that make what should be a very eco-friendly industry very bad for the environment. The dumpsters of floral shops are usually overflowing with flowers and greenery that should be composted or mulched and paper wrappers and cardboard boxes that could be recycled. Instead of being disposed of properly, everything gets mixed in with the junk that can't be recycled, such as floral foam, which is a petroleum-based product, plastic-coated wires, wire ribbons, and other florist waste. Pesticide-laden flowers end up in local landfills and pollute the soil and groundwater surrounding them.

All these practices have green—or at least greener—solutions. Find florists that utilize green options such as buying fair trade products, purchasing local flowers, using organic flowers, mulching and composting floral waste, recycling materials and packaging, and using natural, eco-positive products such as ribbons and paper made from tree-free, recyclable, and recycled materials.

The choices you make can make a difference, both good and bad. The good news is that you do have choices. Look for florists that follow green practices and purchase eco-sensitive materials.

If you can't find an eco-florist in your area, maybe you can encourage one to adopt more earth-conscious practices. If there are no local organic flower farms, point out to your florist that online organic retailers such as

Organic Bouquet (*www.organicbouquet.com*) and California Organic Flowers (*www.californiaorganicflowers.com*) will ship large quantities of flowers for weddings. Organic Bouquet also has a wholesale program that florists can sign up for. If that doesn't work, you can always have the flowers shipped directly to you and arrange them yourself (or get stylish friends and family to help).

The fair trade movement is slowly catching on in the United States. In 2000 fair trade sales in the United States totaled around $100 million; within two years it nearly doubled to $180 million. However, workers in many countries such as China and India—from which the United States receives a majority of manufactured products—still work for low wages in poor conditions.

Organic Flowers

Organic farming works with nature by using natural techniques and old-fashioned methods to utilize the land and protect the air, water, and wildlife. Organic farming does not use harmful and toxic chemical pesticides or fertilizers. Organic practices use all-natural techniques to grow healthy plants.

FACT

Organic agricultural practices became popular in the 1940s when J. I. Rodale, a farmer and publisher (Rodale Publishing), began to publicize the advantages and superior attributes of farming organically. He founded the Rodale Institute, which is still one of the leading centers of organic agricultural research in the country.

Organic floral farmers follow the same strict guidelines as organic food producers. Many farmers are wary because of the time, effort, and cost that it takes to become certified organic. It takes three years to transition from regular to organic farming and the costs can be high. Plus some don't believe that consumers really care whether or not products are grown organically, especially crops that are not food.

However, because of the growing awareness of pesticide pollutions and dangers, many consumers do want choices. They want all of their products to be free of dangerous toxins, including their pretty flowers. As more people push for healthier solutions, more farmers will switch to organic growing. Let flower shops know you want organic flowers. In turn, they'll look for organic suppliers, and as regular suppliers start losing customers they'll have to switch their practices to more environmentally acceptable solutions.

Local and Seasonal

The greenest option is, of course, buying local and seasonal flowers. Depending on where you live, different flowers may be in season at different times. If you live in a warm climate, some flowers may bloom all year long, while in colder climates they may only bloom at a certain time of year. However, some organic flower farms have greenhouses and keep fresh flowers blooming all the time.

Here are the most popular fresh flowers you are likely to find during certain seasons:

- **Spring:** allium, anemone, apple blossoms, cherry blossoms, daffodil, freesia, iris, lily of the valley, lilac, narcissus, peony, ranunculus, sweet pea, tulip, violet
- **Summer:** allium, amaryllis, aster, calla lily, dahlia, geranium, gladiolus, honeysuckle, hydrangea, liatris, orange blossom, peony, rose, sunflower, zinnia
- **Autumn:** amaryllis, anemone, aster, calla lily, dahlia, narcissus, marigold, sunflower, zinnia
- **Winter:** amaryllis, daffodil, hyacinth, mimosa, tulip, evergreens
- **Year-round:** alstroemeria, aster, baby's breath, bird of paradise, calla lily, carnation, daisy, eucalyptus, fern, freesia, gardenia, gerbera, gladiolus, iris, ivy, lily, orchid, rose, statice, stephanotis

If you have a green thumb, you may want to try your hand at growing your own flowers by planting them in your garden and coordinating the date of your wedding with the blooming time of the flowers. The easiest way to grow your own is to plant continuously blooming annuals in little pots that can be used as centerpieces or favors. Marigolds, petunias, and other spring and summer annuals continue to produce flowers throughout spring, summer, and even fall. They'll continue to bloom until the first frost as long as they are well taken care of. You could start them out as seeds in late winter or very early spring or purchase flats of tiny plants that can be transplanted into bigger decorative containers before the wedding.

It is also possible to grow certain bulb flowers any time of year by forcing the bulbs. However, that can take a lot of time and very extensive planning and coordinating to ensure that you have blooming flowers on the day of your wedding.

Growing your own flowers can be very tricky and subject to many variables including weather, insects, animals, and other things you have no control over. Flowers may wilt before the wedding or they may not grow at all. Unless you are very confident in your floral growing abilities, let the professionals handle this and just buy what you need. To find local organic growers in your area, check out *www.localharvest.org* or go to a search engine and search for organic or sustainable flower farms.

VeriFlora Certified Sustainably Grown

To know you are getting quality organic or sustainably grown flowers, look for USDA organic certification through Quality Assurance International. Also look for certification that the products are VeriFlora Certified Sustainably Grown.

VeriFlora is a sustainable certification program for fresh cut flowers and potted plants. The label that reads "VeriFlora Certified Sustainably Grown" is a guarantee that the flowers or plants you are purchasing have been produced in an environmental and socially responsible manner.

VeriFlora · is America's first comprehensive sustainability certification program for the floral and potted plant industries. The program has established procedures for verifying agricultural practices administered by

Scientific Certification Systems. To be certified, growers and handlers must meet or exceed performance criteria in seven areas: sustainable crop production, ecosystem protection, resource conservation and energy efficiency, integrated waste management, fair labor practices, community benefits, and product quality.

Silk and Dried Options

Some retailers may offer silk flowers as greener alternatives to regular pesticide-laden blooms. However, the vast majority of silk flowers are actually made from plastic, polyester, and other petroleum-based products—not very eco-friendly materials.

If you choose to use fake flowers, look for ones that are made with environmentally friendly materials such as organic cotton, real silk, hemp, bamboo, or handmade paper. The one good thing about artificial flowers is that they will last if you want to preserve them. If you would like to keep your bouquet, one made from artificial flowers will never wilt, fade, or die. You can display it in a case or curio cabinet for years to come.

ALERT!

An Italian tradition is to cover the front grill of the wedded couple's getaway car in flowers, which is said to pave the road to a happy marriage. The throwing of the bouquet also has superstitious origins; it's said to bring luck and protection for the newly married couple.

The goal is to keep material out of landfills. If you choose wisely, artificial flowers can be an option as long as you look for green materials, plan to keep or reuse the flowers, or donate arrangements to nursing homes or some other place that could use pretty, cheerful arrangements.

Dried flowers are a good green option, especially if you go with organically and sustainably grown ones. Many flower and herb farms will carry dried flowers or you can purchase fresh flowers and dry them yourself. However, do not use silica gels or unnatural products to dry the flowers.

Most flowers and herbs dry nicely by being hung upside down somewhere where they will not be disturbed. Baby's breath, delphinium, larkspur, rose (bud form dries best), statice, and tansy all look very nice when they are dried. Dried flowers that are commonly found in arts and crafts stores and floral shops have often been treated with loads of chemicals, both while they were being cultivated and afterward to preserve them for drying. Look for organic labels or labels that say "dried naturally" to make sure you are getting good, quality green products.

If you can't find any organic dried flowers locally, another option is, of course, ordering online.

Edible Flowers

You can let your flowers do true double duty by using edible delicacies as décor and food. Imagine your buffet table covered with delicate, edible beauties; trays garnished with gardenias, lavender, or sunflowers; salads filled with a variety of greens and colorful blossoms; your cake covered in delicious petals sparkling with organic sugar crystals.

FACT

Dandelions are edible. The common yellow flower that we think of as a pesky weed is actually considered to be an herb. It has been used throughout history medicinally; the Chinese have used dandelion to treat colds, bronchitis, pneumonia, ulcers, and obesity. There are many culinary recipes that include dandelions as well.

Many flowers are edible as long as they are grown organically and not treated with any other chemicals or pesticides. Any flowers you buy from a normal floral shop or grocery store flower section are not made to be eaten. They have probably been treated with all kinds of chemicals, preservatives, and even dyes. However, if you buy flowers from a certified organic farm it is safe to eat them. Always ask first, though; some flowers look very similar to each other and while one may be safe the other may be poisonous. For instance, regular violets are safe to eat but African violets, a common houseplant, are not. Also, don't ever eat wildflowers, especially ones by the side of the road; you never know what they have been exposed to.

Edible flowers can be used extensively in your bouquets, decorations, and food. Keep in mind that if you use flowers from plants that bear fruit— orange blossoms, lemon flowers, squash flowers—that will be one less fruit for each flower you pick. If you pick the flower, there will be nothing to bloom into the fruit or vegetable. If you want both flowers and fruit or vegetables to harvest, plant twice as many.

While many flowers are edible, the following is a list of some of the most common ones that you may find at a local farm or that you can grow yourself to be sure they are free of pesticides and other chemicals.

- Borage has small, light-purple flowers with a delicate vegetable flavor.
- Broccoli has small dainty white flowers with a slight broccoli taste.
- Calendula is also known as pot marigold. It is bright yellow to orange with daisy-like petals; it has a slightly bitter flavor. It is often used in place of saffron. Calendula is a great garnish on sweets.
- Chamomile is a well-known herb used for tea and many medicinal purposes; it has small dainty white petals with a yellow center. It looks like a tiny daisy. Chamomile is very mild with a sweet flavor that's perfect as a garnish for sweets or salads.
- Chives are hollow grass-like stalks that are often used in soups and on baked potatoes. They bloom with fluffy light purple flowers in spring.
- Day lilies can be eaten in bud or in full-bloom form. They have a sweet vegetable-like flavor and are great in salads. The lighter their color, the sweeter they taste.
- Gardenias have a very fragrant white bloom similar in appearance to a rose. They have a very mild flavor. They are excellent for bridal presentations with their big, fragrant blooms.
- Hibiscus flowers are flat and broad with red petals and a very sweet flavor.
- Honeysuckle has small white to golden fragrant flowers that smell and taste like sweet honey.

- Jasmine flowers are white to golden and very fragrant with a soft perfume-like flavor.
- Lavender is made up of lilac-purple flowers clustered on stalks. The flowers have a mild and sweet taste.
- Lemon trees produce small white blooms that have a sweet flavor.
- Nasturtiums grow in six colors: cream, mahogany, scarlet, cherry-rose, salmon, and tangerine. They have a very strong spicy flavor similar to peppers. They are great for salads.
- Orange blossoms are delicate, sweet-flavored white flowers.
- Pansies bloom in beautiful shades of blue, purple, maroon, yellow, and red. They look beautiful on desserts and are commonly used to decorate cakes and other sweet edibles. Pansies have a sweet flavor.
- Roses are the flower most often equated with love. More than 20,000 varieties of roses exist, both natural and man-made. Roses have a very fragrant flavor and should only be used sparingly.
- Sage is a common cooking herb with a strong aroma and flavor. Its flowers are blue-violet.
- Squash flowers (acorn, butternut, and zucchini) are rather large and are yellow to bright orange in color. Very tender and mildly sweet, they can be eaten as a bud or as an open flower.
- Sunflowers have beautiful petals in shades of yellow, gold, orange, and red. The petals are mild and sweet, and you can also eat the seeds, which have a nutty flavor.
- Tulips come in many colors and are members of the lily family. They have a beanlike flavor.
- Violets are beautiful deep purple flowers similar in appearance to pansies. They have a sweet and mild flavor. Do not eat African violets.

Herbs also offer pleasing texture and variety for both visual and edible appeal. Some herbs bloom with edible flowers that can be incorporated into your floral fantasy display. Some common herbs that are relatively easy to find fresh or to grow in a kitchen garden or window box are basil, chives, oregano, parsley, and several varieties of mint.

Fresh herbs and herb flowers frozen into ice cube trays make an elegant addition to punch bowls, pitchers, or glasses of tea, water, and lemonade. Some of the best herbs to add to ice cube trays are lavender, mint, fennel, sage, chamomile, and whole cloves. Cloves are particularly tasty with orange and apple drinks.

Meaningful Flowers

Throughout history, flowers and their colors have had special meanings. Long ago, brides carried herbs instead of flowers in their bouquets to ward off evil spirits, and they carried sage for wisdom, dill for lust, and rosemary for remembrance. Rosemary was also said to ensure faithfulness. Marigolds dipped in rosewater would later be eaten as aphrodisiacs.

Flowers later replaced herbs. Orange blossoms were put into bridal bouquets for happiness and fertility, ivy for fidelity, and lilies for purity. Wheat symbolized fertility. After the wedding, bouquets were dried and hung in the bride's new home.

Modern brides tend to carry flowers based on color and personal preference, but choosing flowers for their meaning is still popular. If you would like to be green with meaning and incorporate a little symbolism into your eco-bouquets, here are a few popular wedding flowers and their meanings according to the Society of American Florists:

- Baby's breath: festivity
- Calla lily: regal
- Casablanca lily: celebration
- Daffodil: chivalry
- Daisy: innocence
- Day lily: enthusiasm
- Gardenia: joy
- Iris: inspiration
- Jasmine: grace and elegance
- Magnolia: dignity
- Marigold: desire for riches
- Nasturtium: patriotism
- Orange blossom: fertility
- Orchid: delicate beauty

- Pansy: loving thoughts
- Passionflower: passion
- Rose (pink): friendship
- Rose (red): passionate love
- Rose (red and white): unity
- Rose (white): purity
- Stargazer lily: ambition
- Stephanotis: good luck
- Statice: success
- Sunflower: adoration
- Sweet pea: shyness
- Tuberose: pleasure
- Tulip (pink): caring
- Tulip (purple): royalty
- Tulip (red): declaration of love
- Tulip (white): forgiveness
- Tulip (yellow): hopelessly in love
- Violet: faithfulness

People in the Victorian era were fascinated by the meanings of flowers. Brides carefully selected flowers for their bouquets based on the meaning of the flower. They popularized the red wedding rose, which symbolizes true love.

There isn't a flower that says "I care about the environment" yet, but maybe one day soon there will be a flower that symbolizes the green bride.

Natural Options: Leaves, Twigs, Berries, and More

To cut down on the amount of flowers you need to use in your bouquets, arrangements, and decorations, you can use many other natural elements as filler or focal points. Not only will lessening the number of actual flowers you use help save the environment, it can save your pocketbook as well. Fresh flowers can be quite expensive; minimizing the number you use can save you a small fortune.

Many natural elements may be found in your own backyard or can be purchased very cheaply from local flower and herb farms. Many different things can be included in your bouquets and floral arrangements: leaves, twigs, berries, small filler flowers such as baby's breath, vines, ornamental grasses, herbs, and small fruits such as crab apples and grapes.

Small twigs can be tied in bunches and adorned with bright berries; berries also make lovely accents in bridal bouquets nestled among the pretty flowers. In the fall, bundles of leaves can be grouped together for stunning bouquets and table centerpieces, and crab apples and grapes can be grouped together with fall leaves for beautiful centerpieces. You could even work them into a harvest bouquet symbolizing abundance and prosperity. Natural vines can be used instead of wires to wrap stems and twigs together.

To get ideas for what kind of floral and natural decorations you may be interested in for your wedding, visit bridal shows, flip through seasonal decorating books, floral design books, floral magazines, and bridal magazines to get ideas. Stroll around craft shows, art shows, parks, or orchards—you never know what may inspire you.

CHAPTER 10

Green Decorations

The best option in green decorating is, of course, not decorating at all. That way, no resources are used and nothing has to be disposed of. However, many couples may not be so lucky as to find a truly beautiful location that doesn't need any added decorations. Stay on the eco-track by choosing fabulous green decorations that can range from natural elements such as twigs, rocks, flowers, and greenery to new and trendy green options such as artful centerpieces made from recycled glass, metal, or a variety of other items. Green décor can also take you back to a bygone era by utilizing vintage signs of the times.

Natural Decorations

You may want to let Mother Nature take center stage when you are decorating for your green wedding. It is a green wedding, after all, celebrating the beauty of the natural world and the desire to preserve that beauty for the future. Many natural elements can be transformed into elegant and stylish decorations. Use the seasons to get the most out of what is naturally available.

FACT

The term *bride* is thought to be Celtic in origin. It comes from Brigid, the name of an exalted goddess of Celtic lore. She was transformed to a saint with the rise of Christianity and became St. Brighid of Ireland, the patron saint of healers. It is thought that she bestows blessings on brides-to-be.

Using green objects is truly eco-friendly because no extra resources are being used, especially when you use found and wild objects straight from your backyard—wild grape vines, blooming crab apple branches, nuts and acorns, fruit, and rocks. Open your eyes to the abundance that is all around you. If you'd like to venture further from your backyard, just choose wisely and don't stomp all over someone's property or go hacking up their carefully tended landscaping.

ALERT!

Balloon releases used to be popular at weddings, but balloons are potentially harmful to wildlife. Unsuspecting animals can often eat balloons or get tangled in the ribbons, sometimes with fatal consequences. You can still enjoy balloons at your wedding—just hold on to them and make sure they are properly disposed of.

The other great thing about using décor straight from nature is that everything can easily be returned to nature if it isn't taken home or eaten. Vines and branches can easily be mulched, and any perishable food items can be composted. Rocks can be returned to the stream or put in a garden.

In the spring you'll want blooming branches and fresh flowers such as hyacinths, tulips, daffodils, and many varieties of bulb flowers. In the summer you'll be able to find many types of flowers, grasses, and early fruits and vegetables—mainly berries, acorns, green nuts, fresh vines, and branches full of green leaves. Late summer and autumn are the best times to use natural décor because of the sheer abundance of what is naturally available—apples, pears, plums, pumpkins, squash, gourds, tomatoes, assortments of leaves in brilliant fall colors, vines, grapes, and so much more. In the winter, evergreens are plentiful. Use these gifts from nature to adorn your tables and as material for wreaths, swags, and centerpieces.

Decorating the Table: Centerpieces and More

Many items can adorn a table at a wedding reception—centerpieces, favors, place cards, confetti, plates, napkins, glasses, and menus are just the beginning. For your green wedding, eliminate all the excess that would just end up as waste. You'll save yourself the hassle and money. Try to avoid using anything that cannot be reused or recycled. Go for the green and choose eco-smart centerpieces and other earth-friendly décor.

Centerpieces

Centerpieces are among those seemingly must-have wedding reception decorations. The most common types of centerpieces are those that incorporate flowers, candles, or a combination of both. You can quite easily use flowers and candles in many green centerpieces or you could consider more unusual green options for your eco-extravaganza.

Follow your three basic green guidelines (reduce, reuse, recycle) and you could come up with something no one else has done before. Some great green centerpiece ideas are:

- Pots of edible herbs or wheatgrass
- Pots of planted flowers guests can take home and plant
- Assorted topiaries, made from fresh or dried flowers, herbs, and other materials
- Natural wreaths laid flat on a table with a candle in the middle

- Single, large flower heads floating in shallow water-filled bowls
- Bulbs planted in tall vases
- Small containers grouped to form a larger central display; this works great with small square containers or vases that can be pushed tightly against each other
- Apples, oranges, pears, peaches, or other fruits in tall, clear vases
- Trendy and chic vintage items
- Anything you choose made from recycled materials
- Vintage candy dishes and bowls filled with yummy treats
- Rented, borrowed, or secondhand bowls with floating candles in them; these look very elegant when placed over a mirror tile because the reflective light is soft and romantic
- Rented, borrowed, or secondhand vases filled with a single flower
- A potted mini-tree that can be taken home and planted

The list could go on and on. Centerpiece choices can be as simple or as complicated and as varied as the couples choosing them.

Look for some meaning to put into your décor. For instance, in old Welsh tradition a man would give his love an intricately carved spoon, called a love spoon. Scottish men gave their brides a piece of the family tartan during the marriage ceremony. You can use your imagination to turn old family or cultural traditions into unique decorations.

Be extremely eco-fabulous and have your favors multitask as centerpieces. At each table, your favors could be artfully arranged in a container such as a basket, a bowl made from recycled glass, or a terra cotta flower pot. The container could be themed to go along with the favors or it could just be a complementary container to match the overall green theme and feeling of your wedding. The following ideas are eco-friendly centerpieces and favors:

- Small packets of organic, fair trade coffees or teas as favors in vintage coffeemakers, teapots, or oversized mugs that you found at thrift stores.

- Small bars of handmade organic soaps in unique soap dishes you found at yard sales or antique shops
- Vintage costume jewelry in old jewelry boxes
- Bamboo kitchen utensils in bamboo salad bowls, old mason jars, or old cookie jars
- Baskets with rolled kitchen towels or washcloths made from organic cotton, hemp, or bamboo
- Pretty paperweights made from recycled glass in a large bowl or on a platter
- Seed packets arranged inside flower pots
- Soy or beeswax candles in cute baskets adorned with natural ribbons or berries

Any little trinket that you decide to use as a favor can be placed artfully in or around a container and used as a centerpiece. Elegant arrangements of fruits or vegetables can serve double duty; let the guests take the fruits and veggies as favors when they leave.

Place Cards

While some people consider place cards to be an unnecessary and out-dated custom, you may be a traditionalist or you may just want to make sure that Aunt Wilma doesn't get stuck at a table with Cousin Fred. However, don't let paper companies or anyone else convince you that you need them.

If you decide to use place cards, let them be multipurpose. Let the place card and favor be one and the same. Some ideas for place cards that can be favors as well include:

- Seed packets with the guests' names written elegantly on the package
- A small potted plant with a guest's name on the pot
- Plantable place cards made with handcrafted seed paper
- A piece of fruit with a little card attached made from handmade, recycled, or tree-free paper
- A bar of handmade soap with the guest's name carved into it

- A handmade paper envelope containing bath salts
- A small package of handmade note cards tied with hemp, organic cotton ribbon, or twine
- A card made from handmade, recycled, or tree-free paper, announcing that charitable donations have been made to the bride and groom's charity of choice in place of favors
- Bags or envelopes made from sustainable materials filled with fresh or dried organic herbs
- Photo frames made of green materials

Any one of these items can be used as an elegantly green place card/ favor combo. Think outside the box and you may come up with more delightful eco-combos.

Edible Décor

Food is always essential at social gatherings, but you might never have considered using it as part of your décor. Edible decorations are a great way to ensure that nothing goes to waste. Whatever is left over can be taken home with you, sent home with guests, or donated to charities that could use the food.

These edible delights can be used as centerpieces, favors, place cards, and accessories at the dinner tables, bridal table, gift table, cake table, buffet table, guest book station, or any other place that looks particularly bare. Some edible ideas include the following:

- Fresh fruits and/or veggies
- Freshly baked loaves of bread
- Jars of jams, jellies, and preserves
- Homemade jars of pickles and other canned goods
- Bottles of organic vinegars and oils
- Bottles of natural honey or real maple syrup
- Freshly baked muffins or cupcakes
- Organic chocolates
- Homemade organic fudge

- Fresh nuts
- Bundles of fresh or dried herbs
- Organic or fair trade coffee or tea
- Containers of herbed cheeses or fruit cheeses
- Nut cheeses
- Jars of layered cookie, brownie, soup, or stew mixes

Let your imagination and your taste buds run wild and think of some delightful tasty treats that your guests are sure to love.

Candlelight Romance

Love is in the air, and nothing says elegance and romance like the soft, mesmerizing glow of candles. Choose candles made from natural soy or vegetable-based wax or natural beeswax. Regular wax candles made from paraffin are not a very green option because they are a petroleum-based product.

The tradition of using an aisle runner for the bride originated when roads were unpaved and often muddy. The aisle runner was used so the bride did not get her gown dirty. If you do not want an aisle runner that will just be thrown away at the end of the ceremony, consider outlining the aisle with reusable ribbons.

Many natural and health food stores—not to mention boutiques, craft stores, and malls—carry candles made from soy and beeswax. The concept has caught on quickly and now many online retailers offer wide varieties of soy candles. You can find a variety of soy candles at *www.beeswaxcandles.com*. For other environmentally friendly candle choices, check out *www.greenspacecandles.com* and *www.wayoutwax.com*.

You could even make your own soy candles. The popularity of soy candles has grown so much that many craft stores such as Michaels and JoAnn's sell soy wax and candle-making supplies and Amazon.com offers several soy candle-making kits. Container candles are the easiest to make, and you can put them in just about any container that won't melt or catch on fire. Glass, metal, or heat-resistant ceramic are the best choices. If you choose to use glass, it is best to select glass made for food, such as canning jars, sauce jars, and baby food jars because they can withstand heat. Avoid antique and very thin glass, which can break from the heat. Some great objects to recycle into candle containers include glass baby food jars, coffee mugs, and tea cups. Scour the thrift stores and see what you can come up with if you decide to make soy container candles.

Other soft lighting options include olive oil and hemp oil lamps. Not just any old oil lamp can be used with olive or hemp oil; they have to be designed a certain way and made for use with that specific oil. However, they can be rather hard to find. Some "green" home goods stores carry them, including Lehman's (*www.lehmans.com*) and Phoenix Rising (*www.phoenixrising-pt.com*).

When choosing to use candles or oil lamps to light up your event, make sure that the location allows them; some places do not allow any open flames. Also be sure that fire extinguishers are easily accessible, especially if alcohol will be available. You never know when someone might get a little tipsy and clumsy.

If your location does not allow the use of open-flame candles or lamps, you can get the same effect from beautiful battery-powered flameless LED candles. Many can be found in grocery stores or online. You can find a wide variety of flameless LED candles—even some that are rechargeable—at *www.smartcandle.com*. Strands of LED lights also offer beautiful energy efficient lighting. Get great deals on them right before or after Christmas when they go on sale.

Elegant Eras: Decades of Decorations

Planning on a theme wedding that flashes back to another place in time? Look for cool signs of the times that can be used as reception focal points to showcase your theme in unique ways. Thrift stores, antique shops, garage sales, and yard sales are all treasure troves. Turn the search into a treasure hunt that will be fun and stress reducing. If you love to shop, looking for vintage bargains and antique finds may be the highlight of your wedding planning.

Anything that is from the era or decade of your theme may be incorporated into your creative décor. Look for old kitchen items, glassware, vases, kitschy collectibles, purses and handbags, costume jewelry, small furniture, and even clothing accessories such as hats and gloves. You can also incorporate popular posters representing that era. Authentic or reproduction posters are fine, or consider ads, photos of popular movie stars, or even popular album covers.

Two great books that can help you plan a vintage wedding are *Vintage Weddings: Simple Ideas for Creating a Romantic Vintage Wedding* by Daniela Turudich and *Accessorizing the Bride: Vintage Wedding Finery Through the Decades* by Norma Shephard. They are extremely useful for researching wedding attire of different decades, but they also include helpful information, popular colors, and customs of the eras.

The Victorian Era

Victorian times were all about romance—hearts, flowers, cupids, lace, cameos—you can use all these lovely things for your vintage Victorian theme. Adorn your tables with lace parasols and fans, use pretty teapots and teacups filled with roses as centerpieces. Victorian valentines are relatively easy to find, with both real and reproductions available online. A great website for helping to plan a Victorian wedding is *www.victoriana.com*; go to the wedding area for lots of useful Victorian wedding information.

The 1920s

Flappers and female freedom were the theme of the 1920s. It was a new era—people were shedding the tight constrictions of the Victorian era and times were wild. Art deco was a big trend with bold geometric shapes and patterns that were used for everything from art to jewelry to interior design. Because of Prohibition, the gangster subculture full of bootleggers, mobsters, and speakeasies was prominent. Hollywood glamour was also starting to influence modern culture.

Elements you can use for your 1920s reception include old black and white photos of popular stars, ostrich feather fans, art deco posters, beaded glass curtains, long strands of beads, and anything reminiscent of speak-easies—cocktail glasses, martini glasses, old liquor bottles, wooden liquor crates, and long cigarette holders.

The 1930s

During the 1930s, weddings were mostly simple affairs because of the Great Depression. In the early '30s the art deco style was still very popular, but it settled into a softer, more feminine style toward the end of the decade. Hollywood was becoming very influential at a time when most could not even dream of the riches it depicted.

Popular movies of the decade included the original *King Kong*, *Dracula*, and *Frankenstein* along with *Wuthering Heights* and the all-time favorites *Gone with the Wind* and *The Wizard of Oz*. Movie stars included Clark Gable, Fred Astaire, Ginger Rogers, and Mae West. For inspiration, you can watch some of the classic comedies like *It Happened One Night* (which happens to be about a runaway bride), *My Man Godfrey*, and *Bringing Up Baby* to see screen legends like Claudette Colbert, Carole Lombard, and Katharine Hepburn in elegant, satiny gowns.

Lou Gehrig and Joe DiMaggio drew people to the baseball stadiums, while many people stayed glued to the radio for news and entertainment. By 1939, 80 percent of the U.S. population owned radios. Before television, the radio was the number-one source of news and entertainment. Popular things to use for your '30s theme would be movie posters, '30s-style kitchen collectibles and glassware, baseball memorabilia, and old-fashioned radios.

The 1940s

The 1940s brought World War II, and the popularity of the red, white, and blue soared. Patriotic and USO-themed merchandise was everywhere. The government wanted people to support the war efforts. Women were forced into predominantly male roles while the men were off at war. Women worked in factories, played baseball, and kept the United States running smoothly while the men were fighting.

Hollywood glitz and glamour kept everyone dreaming of better times. The '40s also brought televisions into homes, and saw the rise of comic book heroes and the beginnings of beatnik groups. People in the '40s enjoyed swing music and dance while wearing well-tailored clothing, zoot suits, and sexy seamed stockings. Pinup girls were also becoming cultural icons of the era. Betty Grable and Rita Hayworth were popular pinup favorites.

To celebrate the 1940s, you could go with the patriotic theme and decorate with war posters and flags, or go for a more upbeat theme (literally) and have it be all about swing—use musical instruments, music notes, old record players, radios, and vintage records as decorations.

FACT

A classic Hollywood favorite, *Casablanca*, was released in 1942. Humphrey Bogart and Ingrid Bergman starred as one of the most beloved couples in cinematic history. The specter of war loomed over the cosmopolitan African city.

The 1950s

Rock out your 1950s theme with poodle skirts, sweater sets, saddle shoes, and jukeboxes while drinking malts and eating burgers and fries. The guys could be decked out in bad boy leather jackets, cuffed blue jeans, and plain white T-shirts.

The '50s was the era of the malt shop and sock hops, a time of teenage abandon. Popular stars of the day were Elvis Presley, James Dean, Marilyn Monroe, Audrey Hepburn, and Grace Kelly.

Have a casual '50s theme by using all the above elements or go for Hollywood glamour or '50s mod. For Hollywood glamour, think of movies such as *Breakfast at Tiffany's* or anything with Audrey Hepburn, Marilyn Monroe, or Grace Kelly. For '50s mod, think of the style and interior designs of the era—boxy but sleek furniture, simple designs, refined elegance. Plastic products became very popular in the '50s along with kitchenware made from Melmac. The Barbie doll came out in 1959.

Stuff from the 1950s is pretty easy to find at almost any thrift shop or antique store or on eBay. You can also find cheap reproductions of black and white movie star photos and posters; just make sure to stay green by using things that you'll use again or that can be donated or recycled afterward.

1960s

Free love and peace symbols, hippie chicks and love beads. Totally groovy, man. Give a nod to our green forefathers who were ahead of the times in their tree-hugging ways by having a psychedelic '60s wedding.

Flower power and tie-dyed T-shirts, bell-bottoms and long flowing hippie dresses, and the music—oh yeah, the music. There was the British invasion and the unbelievable popularity of the Beatles. Woodstock was the cultural experience of a generation, and years later those who were born too late to experience it in person have seen film footage and wish they could have been there.

Popular television shows of the 1960s included *Bewitched*, *The Addams Family*, and *I Dream of Jeannie*. Be ultra unique and use a popular show of the day to inspire your wedding theme and décor.

Have fun with this theme, play the music, tie-dye the decorations, light some candles, and toss around some love beads. Get groovy with it. You can also go '60s mod; think James Bond. Grab some go-go boots, and slip on a short dress and a pillbox hat.

Thrift stores are full of old clothes and other memorabilia from the '60s, and your parents' closet or attic might even house a few forgotten memories. See what you can come up with for this ultrahip theme.

1970s

The beginning of the 1970s were still full of hippie influence, but that soon gave way to disco fever. Outdoor weddings and bright colors were popular in the '70s; of course, so were polyester bell-bottoms. Cool things to incorporate into a '70s-style retro wedding include lava lamps, platform shoes, disco balls, mood rings, beaded curtains, and maybe even eight-track tapes. Use record albums or any significant '70s stuff you may find for centerpieces and more. Serve fondue, or use old fondue pots as centerpieces; you're likely to find a lot of them at yard sales and thrift stores.

1980s

Ah, the '80s. Madonna, Prince, Duran Duran, MTV, and the Rubik's Cube. Many couples that are planning a wedding today were probably born in or were young children in the '80s. The '80s can be very nostalgic for some, while others may hate it.

The '80s are full of so much that it's hard to know where to begin. The '80s featured beloved toys such as Holly Hobby, My Little Pony, Care Bears, and Strawberry Shortcake. Movies were a big deal; *The Breakfast Club*, *Ferris Bueller's Day Off*, *Pretty in Pink*, and *St. Elmo's Fire* topped the blockbusters.

Pick something and run with it. Choose your favorite '80s movie, book, television show, or music video and use it as your theme. Chances are you may still have many precious things from your childhood laying around at home or at your parents' house that can be used as cool '80s theme-wedding decorations. If you don't have anything, don't worry; '80s retro stuff is literally everywhere.

When you search for cool era decorations, just remember to try to buy actual vintage items instead of reproductions. That way, precious resources and energy are preserved and those old things stay out of the landfills. If you do buy new items, make sure they are items you will use again or donate to charities.

Remember to Reuse and Recycle

Let all of your décor fall into the reuse and recycle categories and you'll be right on the green track. Reuse vintage items, creatively use previously used items, buy recycled and recyclable stuff, and recycle whatever cannot be reused.

Many caterers and wedding rental shops have good selections of rentable wedding décor both large and small—arches, trellises, cake table accessories, card box rentals, large candelabra, and many centerpiece selections. This is a great green option; there is less hassle and probably less expense for you.

If you don't want cookie-cutter wedding stuff, go ahead and think outside the box. Natural Spaces (*www.naturalspaces.com*) has some unique stuff made from reused and recycled materials. Fire & Light (*www .fireandlight.com*) and the Green Glass Company (*www.greenglass.com*) both sell very cool glassware made from reused and recycled glass. Some of their vases, bowls, and bottles would make very elegant additions as table centerpieces. If you are having a music theme wedding, check out Eco-Artware.com (*www.eco-artware.com*). It has taken old LP records and turned them into bowls.

Avoid disposable, wedding-themed, and one-time-use items such as disposable cameras and cake-shaped bottles of bubbles. Also stay away from plastic, Styrofoam, and other non-eco-friendly wares. These can't be recycled, and you don't want to think about them piling up in a landfill.

For some great do-it-yourself green ideas and tips, visit EcoArt Weddings (*ecoartweddings.com*). It is full of cute and trendy ideas for many DIY projects for your wedding.

If you want to be really green, think ahead to the home you'll have (or may already have) with your soon-to-be spouse. Are there any items you could use for your wedding that you could use again in your home? Do you need glasses, bowls, or vases? Buy some and then take them home after the wedding. Are you having a small reception? Perhaps you could buy several different tablecloths made from organic cotton or hemp that you would lovingly use again and again in your home. Maybe you are a gardener and you are having a garden theme wedding. Flower pots, buckets, pails, garden tools, even a big wheelbarrow (to put all your gifts in) are all things you'll reuse, so go ahead and splurge.

If you've chosen a theme for your big day, maybe you would like to continue that theme in your home. Use posters, photos, and unique collectibles for your green event, then reuse them in your home, perhaps in a room you also plan to decorate in that theme.

On the flip side, you may already have lots of stuff that can be used to decorate for your wedding. Chances are if you choose a theme it is something you both enjoy—say, old black and white Hollywood movies, classic literature, or classic rock. You probably already have a multitude of things that can be used at your eco-event. Just make sure you appoint someone to get all your treasures back to you afterward if you are not staying for the cleanup. Also appoint someone to make sure all recyclables go in their proper places and get taken to the recycling center.

CHAPTER 11

Fabulous Favors

Wedding favors began centuries ago. Rich European aristocrats would show off their wealth by offering opulent gifts to wedding guests. The extravagant gifts were originally small, fancy boxes, known as bonbonnières in France and bombonieres in Italy. They were often made of porcelain, crystal, or gold and encrusted with precious gemstones. Contained inside the box was a bonbon or other sugary treat. Today wedding favors are a multimillion-dollar industry all by themselves. Choose eco-wisely and hopefully your favors will be the treasured gifts they were meant to be.

Green Gifts That Grow

The greenest gifts are those that grow. What better way to share your love for each other and your love for the environment than by giving your guests seeds, trees, or plants they can enjoy for weeks, months, and even years to come?

Measure Your Options

The options for favors that grow are practically as limitless as the multitude of trees, flowers, and seeds you can find. However, you should consider several things when you choose a live favor. Is the plant species native to the area where you and the majority of your guests live? When is the optimal time for planting it in the ground? For instance, if you're getting married in October, you might not want to give a tree that should be planted in the spring. What is your budget for favors? Where will you store all the plants or trees until the wedding, and how easy will it be to transport all of them to the reception location? Also consider how hardy the plants are. You don't want to buy fragile plants that could perish at any given moment before the wedding.

Even though favors have become quite popular over the years, they are not required at your wedding reception. The food, the drinks, and the whole party you are providing is plenty. If you don't have the money to budget for favors or you think they are an unnecessary waste of energy and resources, you can choose to skip them.

Small trees, small potted plants, potted flowers, and lucky (curly) bamboo all make good green favors. Easy-to-grow potted flowers include marigolds, petunias, poppies, Shasta daisies, impatiens, mums, and small sunflowers. These flowers can be purchased rather cheaply; you can find a whole flat for around $10 and then transplant them into larger decorative pots for the reception. Buy them a month or so in advance to let the flowers take root in the new containers and fill out into pretty, full plants.

Homegrown Plants

You may want to support the grow-your-own food movement and give fruit or vegetable plants that grow well in containers such as berries, tomatoes, or peppers. Culinary herbs are rather easy to grow in small containers, and there are many to choose from, including basil, oregano, thyme, chives, and several kinds of mint.

You can start many flowers, plants, and herbs from seeds indoors if it is too cold to grow them outside, and you don't need anything fancy to grow them. A large windowsill or sunny area, several egg cartons, and lots of peat pellets will do the trick. Just water the peat pellets until they swell inside the egg carton holes, put the seeds deep into the peat soil, water them, and soon you will have flowers growing. Just remember to keep the peat moist and put a tray under the egg carton to collect excess water. If it gets warm, you can transfer the cartons outside. The plants can be transplanted into larger pots or containers once they grow large enough.

Trees are sometimes harder to start from seed, so you may want to purchase seedlings that are already well established. Tree in a Box (*www.tree inabox.com*) offers many styles for wedding favors and gifts, and the Arbor Day Foundation (*www.arborday.org*) has a wedding package that consists of your choice of redwoods, pines, or spruces. You can make a customized label with a personal message, and the tree comes in a tube that can be converted into a bird feeder.

ALERT!

Trees manufacture more than five pounds of pure oxygen per day, consume carbon dioxide to reduce the greenhouse effect, and provide natural cooling. They also collect pollutants from the air, provide homes for birds and animals, enrich the soil, and prevent soil erosion.

Bulbs and Seeds

Another beautifully green option is flower bulbs. You can give just the bulb itself in a nice little eco-package with directions for planting it or you can grow bulb flowers in containers or pots. Bulbs can be forced to grow out of season, but it can be a tricky process and very draining on the bulb. You can always experiment ahead of time to see what works for you. A very striking display is a bulb flower growing in a clear vase.

Seeds are a wonderfully green option. Some companies offer custom printed seed packets with all your wedding information on them. Favors with Seeds (*www.favorswithseeds.com*) specializes in creating all kinds of beautiful seed favors, kits, and seed packets.

FACT

While Kevin and Lori Graham were planning their own wedding in 1995, they realized they worked very well together. After the wedding, they created a low-impact business that offers earth-focused products. Of the Earth is now one of the largest retailers of handmade, recycled, and tree-free wedding invitations.

You can get the same effect by purchasing many regular seed packets and designing and printing your own custom labels at home on your computer. It's not that difficult or time-consuming, and you'll save a lot of money. Instead of buying individual seed packets, you could purchase a big bag of wildflower seeds and scoop handfuls into custom-made cloth or mesh bags or handmade paper envelopes and affix a cute tag or label with planting directions.

GreenWorld Project (*www.greenworldproject.net*) has a wide variety of reasonably priced live tree seedlings, wildflowers, and tree seeds in addition to custom printed wedding seed packets and other earth-friendly favors. If you are worried about seeds ending up everywhere, go for favors made from plantable, handcrafted seed paper. Plantable seed paper favors will coordinate beautifully if you sent out invitations made from handcrafted seed paper. Make your own or purchase seed favors from Of the Earth (*www.custompaper.com*), Botanical PaperWorks (*www.botanicalpaperworks.com*), Tree Beginnings (*www.plantamemory.com*), or Ecoparti (*www.ecoparti.com*). Pretty and useful plantable paper favors are a great eco-favorite.

Any of these beautiful green favor options can be elegantly displayed at each table setting or they can be grouped together as takeaway table centerpieces. Use individual square pots or vases for a centerpiece that fits tightly together. Experiment ahead of time to discover what arrangement pleases you the most.

Organic Goods

Edible favors are always a hit, especially if they're something yummy. Chances are food favors won't end up in the garbage; they'll end up in someone's belly. If you have leftovers that no one takes home, they can go home with you or you can donate them to a food bank.

The ancient Greeks and Romans celebrated special occasions with honey-sweetened almonds, and the introduction of sugar cane in the fifteenth century allowed confectioners to offer sweet almonds, also known as confetti. They were often given in groups of five to represent happiness, longevity, wealth, children, and health. It is also said that the number five is indivisible—just like the couple.

There are many organic treats you can give as favors—anything from candy to wine. Does your grandma make the tastiest homemade jam? Maybe she can make a huge batch of it with organic ingredients. You can buy tiny canning jars that, once filled, can be sealed until you are ready to use what's in them. Small decorative bottles can be purchased for homemade vinegars, oils, or syrups. If you aren't handy in the kitchen, don't despair! Health food stores and many Internet shops sell organic goodies in bulk that can be used for fabulous eco-favors.

Here are some great organic choices that can be used as delicious favors:

- Homemade canned goods: jams, preserves, jellies, pickles, relishes, salsas, old-fashioned canned vegetables and fruits, applesauce
- Bottles of real maple syrup or real honey
- Flavored honeys or syrups

- Herbal vinegars
- Herbal oils
- Bags of fresh or dried herbs
- Bottled herb blends for cooking
- Fruit, herb, or nut butters or spreads
- Organic chocolates
- Organic or fair trade coffee and/or teas
- Bottles of custom labeled organic wine

Whether you make your own or purchase yummy organic treats, edible favors will surely be a hit with your guests.

Eco-Favors

Some eco-favors may not be flashy, but they can be extremely practical and therefore very green. Green is all about being useful—particularly when it comes to reusing materials. Give your guests favors they will use; as a bonus, they will showcase what you and your wedding are all about.

FACT

A CFL (compact fluorescent light) bulb will last six to ten times longer than a regular incandescent light bulb and save at least $45 worth of energy in its lifetime. Australia and other nations have even banned incandescent bulbs altogether. In the United States, manufacturers are selling greater numbers of CFL bulbs, and Wal-Mart has even coordinated with General Electric to produce a low-cost bulb.

You could give each guest reusable tote bags, CFL light bulbs, green cleaning supplies, organic bath and body products, organic soaps, or even carbon offset certificates. Rechargeable batteries and battery chargers, mini LED flashlights, a strand of LED lights, or other energy efficient gifts also make great eco-favors.

Beauty Without Cruelty (*www.beautywithoutcruelty.com*) sells travel-size bottles of organic hair, bath, and body products that are just the right size for fabulous eco-friendly favors. If you want to experiment with making your own personal care products, you can give each guest a sample of home-made organic bath salts, bath bombs, or custom blended massage oils that you package in vintage or recycled bottles or jars.

Recycling one ton of paper instead of creating one ton of new paper from virgin wood pulp can save 4,100 kW hours of electricity—enough electricity to heat a home for six months. It saves 3.3 cubic yards of landfill space, uses 50 percent less water and 64 percent less energy, and creates 74 percent less air pollution.

You can also consider giving guests organic cotton, hemp, or bamboo washcloths or kitchen towels, or bamboo kitchen utensils. Including a little brochure (printed on recycled paper, of course) with a list of green living websites and local stores that offer green products is a thoughtful touch. Depending on the size of your wedding, you might even be able to give gift certificates or coupons to one of the stores. A list of do-it-yourself green cleaning recipes might inspire your guests to think green—and it will make them think of you every time they use it.

Vintage Favors

To keep up with the theme of your vintage wedding, you may want to incorporate little vintage accessories as eco-fabulous favors. If you want to go for an authentic favor for your era, think cake boxes. For the first half of the twentieth century the most common favor at a wedding was the cake box. Each guest was sent home with a slice of cake or a mini cake in a pretty decorated box. Today you can often find plain cake boxes, and you can decorate them yourself. If you want to offer your guests something more than a prettily packaged slice of cake, look for anything that can be purchased in large quantities at flea markets, thrift stores, antique shops, or even on the web.

You might be able to find costume jewelry pieces, hatpins, hair pins or clips, cuff links, tie tacks, buttons, or vintage hankies. Vintage ornaments would be wonderful for a winter wedding around the holidays. Books—especially old poetry books—are a creative choice. Put a custom label on the inside of each book to thank your guests for attending. The books could even be grouped together in the center of the table for an unusual center-piece. Other vintage favor ideas might be old cosmetic compacts, business card holders, and other small trinkets that are commonly found in antique shops.

ALERT!

Search through your old family photo albums for vintage wedding photos. It would be a wonderfully personal touch to incorporate vintage wedding memories from your own family into your big day. Go through the photos with your older relatives, and ask them questions about their own weddings.

If you only have a few photos, postcards, or other vintage ephemera, try copying them onto recycled paper or card stock and use the images to make tags or bookmarks. The images could even be used on your invitations. You can also look into downloading vintage photos and other images from the web and printing them out for your paper décor and favors. Use scraps of vintage fabric, lace, ribbons, and even old wallpaper to make bookmarks. For a romantic Victorian theme wedding, Victorian teacups, valentines, or postcards are very decorative. You can fill old bottles or jars with candy, bath salts, or oils. Take a stroll through your local flea markets, antique stores, and thrift shops to get ideas for unique favor ideas.

Handmade Favors

Making your own favors can be a truly rewarding experience. Imagine walking around your wedding gathering where everyone is oohing and ahhing all over the fabulous favors and being able to smile and proudly say, "I made that."

The following four books are full of inspirational wedding crafts:

- *The Artful Bride: Wedding Favors and Decorations: A Stylish Bride's Guide to Simple Handmade Wedding Crafts* by April L. Paffrath and Laura McFadden. This resource is full of charming and unusual ways to decorate your wedding, and it includes some cute favor ideas.
- *Wedding Papercrafts: Create Your Own Invitations, Decorations and Favors to Personalize Your Wedding* from the editors of North Light Books. This is an excellent resource that's full of beautiful and stylish ways to make your own papercrafts. The directions can easily be altered to include eco-friendly materials.
- *Making Glorious Gifts from Your Garden* by Marie Browning. This is a must-have book for the do-it-yourself bride who is into gardening and culinary delights. It is full of step-by-step directions for drying flowers, pressing flowers, dehydrating fruits and vegetables, making fragrance crafts, baking delicious culinary treats, and brewing bath and body recipes, body oils, floral waters, sachets, potpourri, and all-natural cleaners. While it is not a wedding book, any of these ideas can be used to create splendid wedding décor and favors.
- *Wedding Decorations on a Budget* by Miriam Gourley. This book is extremely good if you are planning an outdoor or garden-theme wedding or an informal, romantic, or Victorian-style theme.

Need some quick inspiration for favors you can make yourself? Here's a list of relatively easy-to-make crafts that can be customized to fit your theme, color scheme, and budget:

- Handmade paper crafts such as note cards or stationery
- All-natural soaps
- Bath salts, bombs, scrubs, or oils
- Potpourri
- Scented sachets
- Handcrafted soy or beeswax candles
- Craftsy photo frames made from scraps and found materials such as twigs

- Fire-starter bundles, great for late fall or winter weddings
- Key chains made from found and recycled materials
- Homemade tasty treats: candy, chocolate suckers in unique shapes, cupcakes, cookies

If you aren't so craftsy, get savvy friends and family involved to help make your green event extra special and unique. Or you can always check out sites such as Etsy (*www.etsy.com*) and eBay (*www.ebay.com*) to see what is available. Plenty of crafters sell their wares on those sites. Visit local craft shows to help support a local crafter or artisan.

The traditional favor of choice at Spanish weddings is a small vase filled with orange blossoms, which symbolize happiness and fulfillment. The Dutch give out a treat called bridal sugar, a sweetmeat candy. Five pieces are given to guests in a tulle bag. The five pieces represent love, loyalty, happiness, virility, and prosperity.

Attendant Gifts

You want your attendant gifts to be bigger and better than the favors you give to everyone else, but you still want them to follow the theme of your wedding. Skip the cookie-cutter attendant gifts such as money clips and engraved business-card holders in favor of more eco-friendly gifts. Besides, no one ever uses the faux crystal ring holder anyway; why not give something that's both practical and environmentally friendly?

You could give attendants a basket full of green household supplies—green cleaners, organic cotton, hemp or bamboo towels and washcloths, bamboo kitchen utensils and cutting boards, or recycled glassware.

Alternately, you could opt to give each attendant a basket full of organic goodies—cookies, coffee, tea, cocoa, fresh fruits, jams and jellies, or a wide variety of other organic treats. Your attendants could receive full-size versions of the miniature favors everyone else gets. June Taylor Jams (*www .junetaylorjams.com*), Green Mountain Coffee Roasters (*www.green-mountaincoffee.com*), and Food for Thought (*www.foodforhought.net*) all have great gift basket selections that would be great for your attendants. If you have intellectuals in your group, a journal made from recycled or handmade paper or a nice stationery set made from high-quality tree-free paper might be just the ticket. Ex Libris Anonymous (*www .bookjournals.com*) has notebooks made from recycled books.

Female attendants might enjoy baskets full of organic pampering; include bath and body oils, lotions, bath salts, bath bombs, soy and beeswax candles, organic chocolates, and organic tea. Give the male attendants gifts made from recycled materials—belts or photo frames made from recycled bicycle tires or chains. Music buffs would love a big bowl made from an old vinyl record. Natural Spaces (*www.natural spaces.com*) and EcoArtware.com (*www.eco-artware.com*) are full of unique items that may be perfect for one or all of the members of your bridal party.

ALERT!

EcoArtware, founded in 1999, is an exclusive web gallery of unique environmentally friendly gifts. It sells natural, recycled, sustainable works of art made by artists who are passionate about the environment and their creative work. Its products are designed to be impressive without overtaxing the earth.

Each attendant may enjoy a nice T-shirt made from organic cotton, hemp, or bamboo. Check out Bamboosa (*www.bamboosa.com*), Hemp Traders (*www.hemptraders.com*), or Rawganique.com (*www.rawganique .com*) for many different styles and colors to choose from. You can give all the attendants the same thing or customize each gift so you know you're giving each attendant something he will use and enjoy.

Charitable Giving

Make your favors really meaningful by purchasing them from charities or from organizations whose proceeds are donated to charities. You can forgo traditional favors and simply make a donation to the charity of your choice. Instead of favors, give each guest a card (on recycled paper, of course) telling them that you have made a charitable donation in her name. Explain what charity you chose and why.

Instead of printing hundreds of favor cards, posting just one big sign is a great way to conserve paper and other resources. Post the sign near the entrance or near your guest book so that everyone will see it. You could also choose to have your deejay announce your donation.

You can purchase gift memberships and give-a-tree cards at the Arbor Day Foundation. Endangered Species Chocolate (*www.chocolatebar.com*) sells a variety of products, including individually wrapped bite-size chocolates and large chocolate bars. Ten percent of its net profits are donated to support wildlife species and their habitats. In addition, Endangered Species Chocolate sponsors and partners with many organizations to conserve and protect wildlife. It also works with community outreach programs in Indianapolis, Indiana, contributing around 100 hours per month of community service.

The I Do Foundation (*www.idofoundation.org*) lets you choose a charity to donate to, and favor cards are printed and sent to you for your guests. The World Wildlife Fund (*www.worldwildlife.org*) offers couples the chance to donate in lieu of traditional favors, and you can download table tent signs for the reception that you can print from home.

There are many charitable organizations that you could donate to instead of purchasing favors. Pick something that you are passionate about. If you are interested in the environment, the Nature Conservancy (*www.nature.org*) is dedicated to environmental conservation. Through that organization you can adopt an acre of rainforest in Costa Rica or rescue a coral reef. You can also purchase gifts and gift memberships.

If you are interested in wildlife preservation, the National Wildlife Federation (*www.nwf.org*) or World Wildlife Federation (*www.wwf.org*) are superb places to donate money. At either organization you can get a membership, give gift memberships, or adopt an endangered animal. The Heifer Fund's (*www.heifer.org*) mission is to put an end to world hunger and poverty. It tries to reach its goal through many programs and projects around the world.

FACT

America's Second Harvest network supports around 50,000 charity agencies that operate more than 94,000 programs throughout the United States, including food pantries, emergency shelters, soup kitchens, and after-school programs. Every year they provide food assistance to more than 25 million people in the United States, including more than 9 million children and more than 3 million senior citizens.

No matter what charity you choose, it is meaningful and it matters. Every little bit counts. You might even want to check your area for local charities and organizations that could use your help. Charity.com (*www.charity.com*) and JustGive.org (*www.justgive.org*) are two good online resources to help hook you up with a charity. Think about local homeless shelters, soup kitchens, battered women's shelters, and food banks. America's Second Harvest Network (*www.secondharvest.org*) distributes more than 2 billion pounds of donated food and groceries every year.

"Think globally, act locally" is a great green motto to live by. It is often those in our own backyard who could get the most from our help.

CHAPTER 12

Eco-Responsible Photography

Your wedding day will be one of the most important and most photographed days in your life. You want to make sure that all of your important moments are captured so you will always have the opportunity to look back on images of your precious day and smile. In this chapter you'll learn what green photography really is and how you can incorporate it into your wedding day. By choosing a photographer who follows green practices, you can have the photos of your dreams with minimal impact on the environment.

The Problem with Traditional Photography

Photographs may be an important part of humankind, a way of remembering and preserving, of creating and envisioning—but some of the basics of photography are not environmentally friendly. Many of the chemicals used to develop photos are toxic, most photo paper is not recyclable, and the amount of resources and energy that goes into making and powering cameras, batteries, lighting, and all the other equipment can be tremendous.

According to Ecology.com, the world's consumption of paper has grown more than 400 percent in the past forty years. Today 35 percent of the trees that are cut down around the world—approximately 4 billion per year—are used in the paper industry.

The actual act of taking a photo is not a highly consumptive process, especially in natural light. It requires little other than the camera and the photographer. However, developing the photographs uses the most energy, resources, and possibly hazardous chemicals.

Some of the highly toxic chemicals that are used in the developing process include silver and silver nitrate, diaminophenol hydrochloride, ethylene diamine, formaldehyde, iodine, lead oxalate, hydroquinone, mercuric chloride, acetic acid, ammonium hydroxide, and bromine. These chemicals can cause damage through inhalation or contact with skin. If they are not properly disposed of, they end up in landfills and sewage systems, contaminating soil and groundwater. The good news for photographers who still process in darkrooms is that there are now safer chemicals such as Kodak's Xtol, one of several new ascorbate (vitamin C) developers. Silvergrain Photography (*silvergrain.org*) has several nontoxic solutions.

What Is Green Photography?

Photographers who say they are green or that they offer green photo packages mean they use only digital photo processes. They shoot with digital cameras, and they offer all photos to be proofed digitally. They only print what is requested. This means they are eliminating the use of regular film and the harmful chemicals that are used to develop it. They also cut out paper waste by giving you digital proofs.

Say no to disposable cameras. They produce quite a bit of waste. Even though manufacturers claim that almost all the parts are recyclable, the majority of the cameras still end up in landfills. You also have to develop every single camera, and you have no way of knowing whether the photos are actually good until you have them developed.

Some people will argue that most photographers use digital technology now but they don't label themselves as being green. Digital photographers are quick to label themselves as being green to get a piece of the big eco-pie, but practicing green photography means a lot more than just a digital camera and digitally stored photos.

Ask all your guests to take photos with their digital cameras and camera phones and e-mail them to you or post them on photo-sharing sites on the web. You only have to print the ones you really want. You'll save money and resources.

Eco-minded photographers are embracing the new products and technology that make their career and the earth a little greener. New technology makes being green easier than ever, especially for shutterbugs. Even though some photo paper cannot be recycled, it can be made from recycled materials. Red River Paper's Green Pix photo paper is made from 100 percent postconsumer material, and Viastone makes paper from minerals instead of paper pulp.

An up-and-coming technology that may prove to be a very green option for photographers is Zink. Zink paper has color crystals embedded inside, and the use of special printers activates the ink. This will cut down on ink production and wasteful packaging.

Rechargeable batteries, energy-efficient lighting, and solar-powered battery packs are some of the examples of how new technologies are producing better, greener options every day. Green photographers are embracing these new ways in addition to implementing other eco-responsible practices into their businesses and their lives.

The Digital Age

Digital technology has made photography an art that is readily accessible to almost everyone. There is no need for hazardous chemicals and darkrooms to develop photos. All you need is a good photo printer or a trip to a photo kiosk, and you can crop and edit your own images in a snap.

The digital age has made it easier than ever to take, process, and edit photos. Anyone with a decent camera and a computer can create some beautiful photographs. However, make sure you hire a professional to capture your images perfectly for your wedding. This is one area you shouldn't skimp on. You can't go back and recapture the moment.

In addition to hiring a fabulous photographer for your great green wedding, get friends and family involved to make sure every aspect of your big day is captured for you to remember. Remind everyone to bring along their cameras. Encourage tech-savvy friends to get creative with photos and prints. Have some switch to black and white or sepia camera settings to get interesting and dramatic photos of your wedding day.

Make sure your wedding photographer is on the same green page as you by offering digital proofs and online viewing and ordering. Make sure nothing gets printed except what you specifically choose.

If you want the convenience of single-use cameras at your wedding, consider a camera rental service such as CameraRenter (*www.camera renter.com*). You choose how many digital cameras you would like to rent, and they come in the mail. Guests take photos with the cameras on your big day, and then you send the cameras back. CameraRenter creates a custom website with all your photos and videos for easy viewing, sharing, downloading, and print ordering. It also offers options such as custom-created movie DVDs of your event.

Before digital technology made digital proofs a reality, every single photo was printed out for the couple to view and pick from. The bare minimum number of photos a wedding photographer takes at a wedding is around 500. Most photographers take well over 1,000 photos per wedding. If a couple decided not to purchase their proofs, all those photographs were dumped in the garbage.

What to Do with Digital Photos

After the wedding, the photos can be e-mailed to you or uploaded to photo-sharing sites such as Snapfish (*www.snapfish.com*), Shutterfly (*www.shutterfly.com*), or Flickr (*www.flickr.com*). You can easily share, e-mail, and edit these photos. You can add them to your own personal websites and only print the ones you really like. You can even create beautiful photo albums, collages, and many other custom photo keepsakes and gifts. Don't forget to create backups of all your photos on CDs or DVDs. Make a copy that can slide right into your wedding keepsake album so it doesn't get lost in the pile of other photo disks.

Shutterfly and Snapfish can help you plan your wedding right from the start with engagement announcements, save-the-date cards, and personalized invitations. Snapfish even has a wedding planner book that you can personalize with a favorite photo.

After the wedding, you can use all of your wedding photos—yours and all the ones your guests share online—to create beautiful photo memory books, albums, calendars, thank-you cards, postcards from your honeymoon, framed photos, photo collages, and many other fun photo gifts and accessories. On the photo-sharing sites, you can also make an archival backup DVD of all your photo memories and create a custom multimedia photo/movie DVD with special effects and music. Create your wedding photo albums on any photo-sharing site and all your friends and family can see it. They also have the option to order prints of any photos they may like or make their own memory books or accessories from your special day.

Sharing photos via a site is so much easier than e-mailing everyone photos one by one. All you have to do is upload the photos one time then send e-mails with the web page link to anyone and everyone whom you would like to share your album with.

Digital technology combined with the resources of the Internet has created the opportunity for anyone to become a photo artist and create spectacular photo albums, books, and custom-printed materials that once only professionals with expensive equipment and know-how could make. You can upload your photos from home, get creative, then have your projects mailed right to your door.

Eco-Responsible Photo Practices

Even though digital technology has vastly reduced the amounts of toxic chemicals used to develop photos as well as the need to print photos that just end up in the garbage, it creates a different type of strain on the environment. Digital practices require a lot of energy to power all the electronic equipment and resources to create new equipment. In addition, if old or broken equipment is not disposed of properly it can cause severe environmental damage.

Greener Photographs

Besides using digital cameras and digital sharing methods, photographers can be more eco-responsible in many ways:

- Conserve electricity by powering down equipment when it is not in use.

- Unplug unused equipment such as battery chargers when they are not being used.
- Purchase high-capacity rechargeable batteries.
- Take advantage of natural light as much as possible and consider using LED and CFL lighting when appropriate.
- Switch to LCD computer monitors and television screens, which use less energy than regular or plasma screens.
- Use solar-powered battery chargers and battery packs.
- Consider powering the entire office through solar panels.
- Print photos on handmade and recycled papers.
- Showcase print photos in albums made from recycled and hand-made materials.
- Go electronic for communication and advertising.
- Reuse and recycle everything possible.
- Make sure old electronics and batteries and chemicals are disposed of properly.

Eco-Examples

There are many ways photographers can green their business and their lives. Each will have his own passions and his own ways of being as green as possible.

Grazier Photography, a Boston-based husband and wife team, announced in the beginning of 2008 that they were going green. They felt that becoming a green photography business and offering a green wedding package was a natural progression in their lives since they already use digital photo technology, work at home, recycle, and purchase locally grown and organic food.

Now in addition to their regular eco-responsible ways, Grazier Photography is offering green wedding packages showcasing beautiful albums, including the company Couture Books, made from 50 percent recycled content. They also invest 5 percent of every wedding package into carbon offsets and actively support charities such as Habitat for Humanity, the National Wildlife Federation, and Oprah Winfrey's School for Leadership.

His and Her Photography based in Portland, Oregon, claims its mission is "to provide artistic and creative photography to our clients while engaging in ecological and socially responsible business practices." His and Her Photography supports these eco-responsible claims by using local resources, investing in renewable energy projects, powering the studio with wind energy, and shooting entirely with digital cameras powered with rechargeable NiMH batteries.

Many photographers and other business owners take being green very personally and strive to live a more meaningful, responsible lifestyle. They recycle all paper, packaging, and ink cartridges. They reduce and reuse, and they pass along their beliefs and strive to inspire others.

ALERT!

It is very important to dispose of digital cameras and other electronic waste properly. Electronics can contain toxins such as mercury and lead that can be released into the air, ground, and water. An estimated 1.5 million tons of e-waste is thrown away every year. Some companies will take back old products to be recycled, and many areas have local e-waste recycling programs.

The Green Photographer

As technology continues to progress, more businesses are becoming capable of switching over to green practices. Photographers seem to be leading the way and leaving behind a smaller enviro-footprint.

Every day more photographers green their studios, adopt eco-wise business practices, and go green in their everyday lives. Not only have they gone digital and begun trying to recycle everything, they are shopping local, buying organic food, working in home offices, and driving fuel-efficient vehicles. They donate their money and sometimes their time and talents to charitable causes.

Kristina Carter of Vrai Photography in Illinois believes that "being green isn't just about recycling or going digital." She says that it is a mindset and a lifestyle that she is happy to share with her clients—so much so that in early 2008 she gave away a bridal photography package to the greenest couple that entered her contest. She decided to have the contest as a way to reach out to "brides who want to do things that are environmentally supportive for their wedding."

Anne Ruthmann of Anne Ruthmann Photography in Indiana is "passionate about preserving the beauty and diversity of our planet." She also gave away a bridal photography package in early 2008 for one lucky couple who took "into consideration the impact their wedding would have on the environment." She picked three finalists and let her blog readers choose the grand prize winner.

Not only are these photographers incredibly giving, they are very green both in their life and business decisions. They represent the photographers who are changing their thinking, changing their practices, and therefore changing the world to make it a better place for us all.

FACT

More than 2,700 photographs are taken every second. All around the world people are snapping photos that add up to well over 80 billion images a year, according to estimates published by the United States Department of Commerce. As more and more digital cameras and camera phones are made, the number of images taken will continue to grow rapidly.

You can find green photographers through green wedding planning sites such as Portovert (*portovert.com*), Everything Green Weddings and More (*www.everythinggreenweddings.blogspot.com*), Green Elegance Weddings (*www.greeneleganceweddings.com*), Green Weddings and Events (*www.greenweddings.net*), and at Co-Op America's National Green Pages (*www.coopamerica.org/pubs/greenpages*). Check local phone books and online classifieds such as Craigslist. You can even search for green photographers by simply typing the phrase into a search engine along with your location. If you cannot find a green photographer, at least find one that offers all-digital packages. Look for a photographer who uses digital cameras exclusively and will give you all-digital proofs. Make sure nothing is printed until you place an order for specific photos.

Photography Choices

You want a photographer who is green, but you also want one whose artistic style matches your own. Photographers shoot in many styles. Some shoot candid photos, while others only shoot posed photos. Some offer a more photojournalistic style, which is kind of arty and focuses on more candid shots than posed ones. Many photographers also offer a variety of image options including black and white and sepia shots. Black and white photos can add a touch of elegance and drama to photos, where sepia prints impart a feeling of nostalgia. If you are having a vintage theme wedding or are incorporating vintage elements, sepia prints add a bit of whimsy and class.

Most couples prefer to have a combination of posed shots and candid photos. That way they are sure to get as many memories captured on film as possible. Check out the photographer's portfolio to determine what kind of photos she is capable of taking. If you see nothing but posed shots, that's a sign you won't get many candid shots of your wedding.

Once you pick a photographer, how are you sure she is going to capture everything you want on film? For one thing, communication is essential. Ask if there is a standard checklist followed for capturing photos. If there isn't such a list, create one of your own. If there is, check to make sure it includes all the photos you want; add anything that is missing. If you have any special requests, be sure to let the photographer know ahead of time.

This is a rather standard list of shots that most photographers take at weddings:

PHOTOS TAKEN BEFORE THE CEREMONY

- ❑ Photo of the wedding dress draped over a chair or hanging up
- ❑ Bride looking into the mirror
- ❑ Bride with her mother
- ❑ Bride and bridesmaids applying makeup, putting on jewelry, or arranging hair
- ❑ Bride pinning corsage and boutonniere on mother and father
- ❑ Bride hugging parents

- ❏ Groom tying his tie
- ❏ Groom before the ceremony
- ❏ Groom pinning corsage and boutonniere on mother and father
- ❏ Groom hugging his parents

PHOTOS TAKEN DURING THE CEREMONY

- ❏ Outside of ceremony site
- ❏ Guests arriving at ceremony
- ❏ Parents being seated
- ❏ Grandparents being seated
- ❏ Maid of honor walking down the aisle
- ❏ Bridesmaids walking down the aisle
- ❏ Flower girl and ring bearer walking down the aisle
- ❏ Groom walking into the ceremony
- ❏ Groom waiting for bride at the altar
- ❏ Musicians
- ❏ Officiant
- ❏ Altar, canopy, or huppah
- ❏ Closeup of bride before she walks in
- ❏ Bride and father walking down the aisle
- ❏ Groom seeing the bride as she walks in
- ❏ The back of the bride as she walks down the aisle
- ❏ Father giving the bride away
- ❏ The audience from the bride and groom's point of view
- ❏ Any special ceremonies, unity candle lighting, family medallion, rose ceremony, or other personal moments
- ❏ Closeup of vow exchange
- ❏ Distance shot of vow exchange
- ❏ Exchange of the rings

- ❏ Closeup of the rings on bride's and groom's hands
- ❏ The kiss
- ❏ Bride and groom walking down the aisle as husband and wife
- ❏ The receiving line after the ceremony
- ❏ Bride and groom outside of the ceremony site
- ❏ Guests throwing confetti or birdseed or blowing bubbles
- ❏ Bride and groom hugging and mingling with guests
- ❏ Bride and groom signing the marriage certificate

POSED WEDDING PHOTOS USUALLY TAKEN BEFORE THE RECEPTION

- ❏ Bride alone
- ❏ Bride with maid of honor
- ❏ Bride with bridesmaids
- ❏ Bride with groomsmen
- ❏ Bride with entire wedding party
- ❏ Bride with parents
- ❏ Bride and groom together
- ❏ Bride and groom with families
- ❏ Bride and groom with entire wedding party
- ❏ Bride and groom with flower girl and ring bearer
- ❏ Groom alone
- ❏ Groom with his parents
- ❏ Groom with best man
- ❏ Groom with all the groomsmen
- ❏ Groom with entire wedding party
- ❏ Groom with all the female attendants

Let the photographer know ahead of time if you have any special situations so everyone can be ready for the pictures. She needs to know if your parents are divorced and do not want to be in any pictures together. If you want any additional photos of you with people who mean a lot to you, ask. Write down all your special requests and make two copies—one for you and one for the photographer.

COMMON PHOTOS TAKEN AT THE RECEPTION

- ❑ Outside the reception site
- ❑ Bride and groom arriving at the location
- ❑ Bride and groom greeting guests
- ❑ Table centerpieces and setting
- ❑ The bride and groom's table
- ❑ The guest book
- ❑ The cake
- ❑ The cake table
- ❑ The cake topper
- ❑ The groom's cake
- ❑ Gift table
- ❑ The wedding toasts or speeches
- ❑ Bride and groom drinking champagne
- ❑ Bride and groom's first dance
- ❑ Bride dancing with father
- ❑ Groom dancing with mother
- ❑ Bride and groom cutting the cake
- ❑ Bride and groom feeding each other cake
- ❑ Groom removing the garter from his bride
- ❑ Groom tossing the garter
- ❑ Bride throwing the bouquet

- ❏ Women scrambling for the bouquet
- ❏ Garter- and bouquet-catchers' dance
- ❏ Dollar dance
- ❏ Any other special traditions carried out at your reception
- ❏ Picturesque shots of the bride and groom in the garden, gazebo, or other romantic place at the reception site
- ❏ Candid shots of the bride and groom mingling with guests and of guests mingling with each other
- ❏ The getaway vehicle
- ❏ The bride and groom leaving the reception

By choosing the right photographer, you are ensuring that all the special memories of your big day are recorded. Photographs preserve memories and record important times in our lives that we never want to forgot. One of the great joys in life is to be able to look back through a photo album, smile, and remember.

Whether that photo album is on a computer screen or bound in a beautiful album made from recycled paper, choose eco-wisely for fabulous memories with no guilt and a minimal footprint.

CHAPTER 13

Vendors That Share
Your Vision

The winds of change are blowing toward a new environmentally positive outlook, especially in regard to business practices. Existing companies are adding green products to their available merchandise, and new eco-minded businesses are popping up every day. As the "green collar" market continues to expand, it will become easier to find enviro-friendly services or products. Many companies have realized that the green wedding trend is here to stay and are offering all-natural, organic, sustainable, and fair trade wedding items from your veil to your shoes and everything in between and beyond.

Eco-Responsible Vendors

By now you've probably researched companies that offer eco-friendly locations, elegantly green attire, ethical jewelry, natural health and beauty products, handmade paper invitations, green printing services, organic food and beverages, pesticide-free flowers, eco-décor, fabulous favors, and eco-responsible photography.

In addition to these vendors, there are others you might want to work with as you prepare for your wedding day—musicians, deejays, wedding ceremony officiants, wedding coordinators, seamstresses and tailors, bakers—the possibilities go on and on. Any and all of the people you come in contact with or do business with can be green, eco-responsible, or socially ethical in their lives and business practices.

The popularity of green continues to grow and more people are becoming aware of how important environmental issues are. More consumers are becoming eco-minded, and they want to make socially and ecologically wise purchases. This is forcing companies to rethink their ways and incorporate more eco-responsible practices into the workplace in a wide variety of ways, from recycling and buying recycled products to purchasing strictly organic and fair trade.

ALERT!

In 2006, the sales of green/eco-friendly products topped $228 billion in the United States. Because of the vast growth, many companies are more than eager to hop on the green bandwagon and start reaping the benefits of the new trend.

Eco-minded businesses such as Seventh Generation, Bi-O-Kleen, Of the Earth, Burt's Bees, EcoArtware, Greenline Paper, and many others walked down the green path before it was ever cool and trendy to do so. Now that green is going mainstream you will be able to find eco-products in many more locations, from your market to big box stores such as Wal-Mart.

Ethical Practices

While being environmentally responsible is fabulous, there are a lot of other things to consider when you choose the companies and people you will work with. There are so many companies out there that do good things for other people; they donate money, time, and services to community programs and charities around the world.

Finding Responsible Vendors

Co-op America has an entire Green Business Network that lists green businesses in its National Green Pages (*www.coopamerica.org/pubs /greenpages*). These companies have been screened to make sure they qualify for membership in the Green Business Network, which is the oldest, largest, and most diverse network of ecologically and socially responsible businesses in the United States. There are thousands of green businesses listed in the Co-op America publication and online database.

FACT

According to consumer research, approximately 43.8 percent of consumers want to use more natural cleaning products—but only if the products work adequately. The problem has been that many all-natural cleaners don't seem to clean as well as chemical-laden ones. Now companies are trying to combine cleaning power with safe, natural alternatives.

To qualify as a green business, a company must operate in ways "that solve, rather than cause, both environmental and social problems." Green businesses work under principles and practices that improve the quality of life for customers, employees, communities, and the environment.

If you can't find any businesses listed in your area that are considered to be green, look for small business owners that are listed with the Better Business Bureau or go through word of mouth, online listings, and web searches.

Think nontraditionally. Go to your local farmer's market or visit a craft show. Many people do things as hobbies so they never even think about advertising or they don't find a need to.

The Internet has made it possible to have a green store or eco-business without the need for a physical storefront. Not only is this less overhead expense for them, it cuts down on the consumption of resources and energy.

ALERT!

People in the United States make enough garbage every day to fill 100,000 garbage trucks; 15,000 tons of that (a whopping 32 percent of the total) is packaging materials. Only about one-tenth of all solid garbage in the United States gets recycled.

While many online retailers may also have a business open to the public, many work from home. This makes their work greener. They don't have to travel back and forth to work, they don't have to maintain two locations, and they can do much of their work electronically through the web and over the phone. This is very green, but these business owners may not even consider themselves to be green because they are just doing what is natural for them.

Highlighting Responsible Vendors

Tara Lynn designs natural fiber gowns custom made for brides. In addition to using organic hemp, silk, and cotton fabrics, the company is committed to making a difference. It recycles everything it can, powers its studio through solar energy, donates 5 percent of its profits to environmental organizations, and gives garments to local nonprofits once a year for auctioning. Order from this Vermont-based business at *www.taralynnstudio.com*.

CocoaVino (*www.cocoavino.com*) has both online and real-world storefronts. A relative newcomer to the green business scene, it creates unique chocolate favors that have been a big hit in Brooklyn, New York, where the company is based. CocoaVino was founded in February 2005 by two graduates of the French Culinary Institute of New York, Alisha Lumea and Avril Pendergast-Fischer. They create exquisite chocolates made from wines, liqueurs, fruits, and other ingredients that are sustainable, fair trade, organic, and often regionally grown. In addition to using eco-minded ingredients, CocoaVino's kitchen and offices are powered by wind energy, its shipping boxes are made from 100 percent recycled materials, and its packing peanuts are made from 95 percent cornstarch.

Pear and Peony was started by two graphic designers in Northern California, Aimee Aikens and Kirsten Yeates, who wanted to create beautiful, soulful designs. Everything they sell is assembled or made by hand. Their products are all environmentally friendly, they purchase renewable energy certificates, and their office is powered by green energy.

In addition to finding vendors whose values align with your own, make an effort to hire vendors whose personalities are compatible with yours. The more closely you work with your vendors, the more imperative it is that you be able to get along with them.

Ethical Weddings (*www.ethicalweddings.com*) is a strictly Internet-based business. It was founded in 2005 by Katie and James Fewings while they planned their own eco-minded wedding. After realizing how much it was going to cost to get married, they figured they should invest their money wisely in something positive and worthwhile. They did extensive research into fair trade, organic, recycled, and sustainable materials and decided to make all the information available on one site to help couples around the world plan their own green wedding. Ethical Weddings is based in the United Kingdom, but it has company listings for around the world and its articles and advice are applicable to everyone.

There are people and companies like this everywhere, all over the Internet and maybe in your town. Some of them don't even advertise themselves as being green businesses; they just do what they do because they believe in it and enjoy it.

Simply Sustainable

You don't have to live in New York, Los Angeles, or green central Boulder, Colorado, to find eco-minded businesses. There are green businesses even in the smallest towns—they just may not advertise themselves as such.

Chances are that living in a small town or out in the country will provide you with resources the big city green bride may not have access to. You are surrounded by people who live simple sustainable lives instead of the fast-paced hustle bustle of the big city.

Think of the small farm at the edge of town that sells fresh goods from a stand by the road, or the old woman down the hill who makes the best homemade strawberry preserves ever. What about the weed lady who grows her own fresh flowers and herbs all year long in her yard and her greenhouse? What about the mother of three up the street who can stitch a prom dress or an evening gown in a matter of days?

Look around you. The people and businesses you see every day may be exactly what you want; you just have to open your eyes and see them in a new light. They may not be trendy, fancy, or New York/L.A. high style. But that's kind of the point, isn't it? Green is simplicity at its best.

Shop local to support your local economy. Enlist the services of small businesses; employ local artists and craftspeople to use their unique outlook and artistic expression to create a one-of-a-kind wedding for you. Look for local musicians who create music the old-fashioned way: unplugged. Search for town tech-geeks who have the largest capacity MP3 player available with a sound system they can hook up to it. They can create a custom playlist for you without the need of a deejay. Until you are planning a wedding, you really don't notice the wealth of resources available within arm's reach.

Eco-Wise Wedding Planners

A wedding planner is one of those extra things you may or may not consider depending on your budget, your personality, and other factors such as whether you want to do everything yourself or feel comfortable putting arrangements in someone else's hands. Whether called a wedding planner, a bridal consultant, a wedding coordinator, or your personal wedding expert, a wedding consultant can be a huge asset to invest in.

FACT

A survey performed by SuperWeddings.com found that 72 percent of recently married brides who did not use a wedding planner's services for their wedding wished they had. If they had to do it over again they would hire a wedding planner to help them.

A wedding planner can offer a wide variety of services, from simple consultations that point you in the right direction to full service that has the coordinator there every step of the way. Most wedding planners offer varying levels of services or coordination packages that will depend on your needs and desires.

Here are just some of the services a consultant may provide for you:

- Help you create a budget, stay within the budget, and track payments made to vendors.
- Help you choose the theme, style, and décor for your wedding and help coordinate everything to stay within that scheme.
- Help with time management; create checklists and timelines to keep you and the wedding planning on track.
- Set up appointments with other vendors, attend the appointment with you if you wish.
- Negotiate prices and contracts with vendors.
- Stay in contact with vendors and oversee their work.
- Coordinate rehearsal and rehearsal dinner.
- Provide you with valuable advice, including etiquette answers and knowledge of how things are traditionally done.
- Oversee the wedding day, making sure everything and everyone is in the proper place on schedule.

- Intervene in case of mishaps and last-minute problems; brides often never know of problems because the coordinator handles everything.

ALERT!

According to Angel and Company Wedding Planners, the average wedding takes more than 250 hours to plan. If you decide to go with a wedding planner, try to find one who has experience planning green weddings, who will likely have some creative ideas and will already be in touch with green vendors you can trust.

A wedding consultant can save time, worry, stress, and money while making the wedding planning and the wedding day itself go much more smoothly. Many wedding planners are starting to realize the need for green services and are specializing in providing a couple with the eco-wedding of their dreams. They integrate green business practices into their own company as well as working with others who are dedicated to providing ecologically and socially responsible weddings.

Green wedding consultants can point the way to green services and green vendors that you might not have been able to find on your own. They can save you time and money while giving you exactly what you want, in a great green way.

Don't Get Greenwashed

How do you know if you are really getting a good environmentally friendly product or shopping with an eco-responsible retailer or vendor? Not all claims are regulated or controlled. To an extent, you just have to do your research, ask questions, and read labels. Many companies are not held accountable or investigated to see if their green claims are true; however, Co-op America does have a set of guidelines any business listed within its Green Pages has to abide by. Other programs also certify the green, eco, and organic claims.

Green Seal is a private, nonprofit organization that sets standards and awards its label to products that meet and exceed its environmental criteria. Its label appears on a wide range of products from copy paper to cleaning products. Scientific Certification Systems (SCS) certifies environmental product claims for biodegradable products, certified organic ingredients, pesticide residues, recycled fibers, water efficiency, and sustainable forestry. The Chlorine Free Paper Consortium certifies paper products that have been made without the use of chlorine, and the Chlorine Free Products Association certifies paper mills that are chlorine free and that make chlorine-free products. The Global EcoLabeling Network lists programs that offer eco-labeling all over the world, and the European Union EcoLabeling Program is working to unite the eco-labeling systems around Europe.

Your local city, county, or state government may also certify businesses as environmentally friendly. Check to see if such a program is in place in your area. If it isn't, you can write to your representatives to recommend they initiate a program.

EcoLogo gives its label to products it proves are environmentally responsible. It is the only North American standard accredited by the Global Eco-Labeling Network. It has more than 120 standards that it uses to evaluate environmental issues. Everything is examined—the product's contents, the manufacturing process, and even how the product will be used by consumers. Its website includes a complete list of all the companies and products it has certified. The list includes automotive products and services, building and construction products, cleaning and janitorial products, containers, packaging, bags, electricity products, fuels, office furniture and supplies, printing products and services, and pulp and paper products. Even services and events can get the EcoLogo seal of approval.

The LEED green building system is a program through the U.S. Green Building Council that certifies buildings to be green based on five points: sustainable site development, energy efficiency, materials selection, water savings, and indoor environmental quality. The Forest Stewardship Council accredits organizations that certify wood from responsible forests. Two FSC certifiers are Smartwood and Scientific Certification Systems.

The Green Restaurant Association provides businesses with education and training so they can become green companies. It educates green restaurants about ten environmental guidelines: energy efficiency and conservation; water efficiency and conservation; recycling and composting; sustainable food; pollution prevention; recycled, tree-free, biodegradable and organic products; chlorine-free paper products; nontoxic cleaning and chemical products; green power; and green building and construction. It also provides the restaurant staff with its book *Dining Green: A Guide to Creating Environmentally Sustainable Restaurants and Kitchens*. A list of green eating establishments is available at *www.dinegreen.com*. You can check them out when you consider reception and rehearsal dinner locations.

Another way to look for authenticity in green claims and labeling is just to do your research and ask questions. Do the owners or workers participate in environmental activities? Do they give to charity? Do they do volunteer work? Are they members of environmental or other organizations? Are they backed by well-known organizations? Trust your gut and you'll be sure to find the right businesses, products, and services that meet and exceed your green standards.

CHAPTER 14

The Do-It-Yourself Green Wedding

More couples are deciding to arrange aspects of their wedding themselves. Some brides make their own favors, while some grooms landscape yards. There are even brides who have sewn their own wedding gowns, grooms who have built backyard gazebos, and couples who have renovated entire buildings to house the ceremony and reception. A DIY wedding is a great way to save resources and energy, not to mention money. The best part is that you'll be adding an intimate touch and a loving personalization.

14

Get Crafty

There was a time when a wedding was an extremely intimate affair, but in recent years weddings have become very public and more of a show. What should be the focal point of the wedding—the joining of two people in love—has been overshadowed by the emphasis on the wealth of the families who are throwing the celebration.

The Crafty Couple

Many of today's couples combine both private and public elements by customizing their ceremonies with personalized vows and special music and by getting friends and family members involved. They also add a bit of glamour with extravagant centerpieces and breathtaking flowers. Some couples combine these elements in creative ways by embracing their wedding day as truly theirs and hand-making many elements, from décor to favors.

ALERT!

Be careful not to spend too much time and money on a project. In some instances it may be easier and a lot cheaper just to buy something or pay someone else to do it. You are already very busy; don't stretch yourself too thin by taking on too many tasks that could easily be handed over to someone else.

Green couples really seem to be in touch with the DIY wedding by planting flowers or growing fresh herbs in pots to give away as favors, or by making handmade paper for their invitations.

Making beautiful handcrafted elements for your wedding as a couple is a wonderful way to bond and spend quality time together while planning your big day. It is also a great way to relax and de-stress in the midst of planning a large event. Chances are you are extremely busy, hustling around between appointments, fittings, and normal day-to-day living. Crafting is a way to slow down and concentrate on absolutely nothing but the task at hand.

You can make almost anything and everything for your wedding: announcements, invitations, guest books, centerpieces, favors, flowers, and other décor. If you or your fiancé are skilled craftsmen or woodworkers you may even make larger items such as an arbor, trellis, or huppah.

The Sky's the Limit

You can find inspiration in many locations. There are books and web-sites devoted entirely to DIY weddings such as *www.do-it-yourself-weddings.com* and *www.diybride.com*. DIY Network (*www.diynetwork.com*) also has a bridal section on its website. Michaels has a page devoted to weddings (*www.michaels.com/weddings*) that's full of creative ideas and supplies for making your own wedding invitations, pew bows, stenciled aisle runners, favors, and even your own veil and tiara.

The DIY Bride: 40 Fun Projects for Your One-of-a-Kind Wedding by Khris Cochran (the founder of *www.diybride.com*) is a fabulous resource with really unique and craftsy projects. Some top choices are the ribbon-bound guest book, the split bamboo centerpieces, the cupcake tower, the rhine-stone monogram cake topper, the faux metal pew cones, and the vintage necklace tiara. Those are just a few of the very chic DIY bridal projects in this book. Some projects are already green; some can be made green with just a few adjustments, such as making sure all the paper and card stock is made from recycled or tree-free fibers.

Make It a Family E-ffair

There's no shortage of advice and ideas from family and friends when you are planning a wedding. Invite them to help out with your projects. If some of those family members and friends are creative, art savvy, or truly talented, then by all means get them involved.

Many families are full of creative and talented individuals who could work wonders on some special part of your wedding. Aunt Sarah the culinary craftswoman may be the perfect choice to cater a scrumptious meal for your intimate reception, Grandma the confectionary wizard could bake the wedding cake of your dreams, and your nerdy cousin Joe could be a digital photographer. Other friends and family members could be recruited for simple tasks such as tying ribbons, filling flower pots with dirt, or tearing and cutting scrap paper to make your handmade paper invitations.

Making Glorious Gifts from Your Garden by Marie Browning is full of recipes and wonderful how-tos for many DIY items, especially edibles. This is a must-have for a DIY gardener/crafter/culinary wonder.

Most tight-knit groups of friends and relatives will freely offer help when it comes to planning a major event, but if you do have to coax someone into helping, do it nicely and offer food. Turn it into a party. Instead of asking them to come over and roll silverware in napkins, tell them you're having a little get-together with pizza and beer. Mention that you'll be doing some wedding crafts, but emphasize the party aspect.

Easy crafts almost anyone can make are:

- No-sew scented sachets can be made with scraps of fabric and shaped into squares, hearts, or pillows or even rolled like a neck roll. Glue three sides together with a hot glue gun, stuff it with potpourri, and glue the final side together. Add cute embellishments such as ribbons, lace, buttons, cording, or whatever you have.
- Terra cotta pots can be painted and filled with potting soil after the paint dries. Add fresh herbs, plants, or flowers. You could also fill the pots halfway with sand to anchor a candleholder, then fill the remaining area with potpourri. These make pretty centerpieces.
- Scented bath salts are really easy to make. Just buy a bulk container of plain sea salt that's meant specifically for baths and scrubs and add a little bit of scent. Mix it all up and then scoop portions into individual bags or jars. Try to keep the scent to something relatively neutral or universally pleasing such as vanilla or a mild citrus scent.

- Container candles are also easy to make. Melt wax and pour it into a container with a wick. Some DIY candle-making can be pretty complicated, but container candles are probably the easiest to make without the need for a lot of extra equipment.

No matter what you decide to handcraft, if you have a lot of favors to make it's definitely worth it to round up some help.

Incredible Edibles: Recipes and Ideas

Everyone loves food. By using food as décor, you're sure to make your wedding a hit. From fresh fruits and veggies to baked goods and jars of homemade canned goodies, food items can be artfully arranged into stunning décor. Canning and apothecary jars can be grouped into centerpieces and stylish arrangements by mixing up several different styles and sizes of jars. Envelopes and pouches of fresh or dried herbs can fill baskets, cans, or jars or be strewn across tables. Fresh fruits and colorful veggies look beautiful in tall clear glass vases.

People love to hear wonderful things about the food they make. If you know someone who makes amazing salsa or delightful jam, you could ask for the recipe or even flatter them into offering to make a large batch for your big day.

Unique Choices

Get creative with food and reap the rewards. One great thing about edible favors and decorations is that you probably won't have any left to worry about; your guests will be more than glad to take it home. If by chance there is any left, donate it to a local shelter or food pantry that could really use it.

Message Bread

Baked goods can be arranged in old-fashioned wicker baskets or pretty cloth-lined bread baskets, or they can be placed on rising tiered serving plates for an eye-catching display. If you really want to wow your guests, give them baked message breads. These mini bread rolls have a piece of paper inside like a fortune cookie. You can inscribe the paper with little sayings, quotes about love, or designs with symbolic significance. These little baked goods are something that will surprise your guests and keep them talking for some time after the reception. You'll probably get more than a few requests for the recipe and directions for how to make them.

Message Bread

Makes 20

- ❤ 1⅔ cup all-purpose flour
- ❤ 1 teaspoon baking powder
- ❤ ⅓ cup fresh grated Parmesan cheese
- ❤ ½ cup butter
- ❤ ¼ cup water
- ❤ 1 egg yolk
- ❤ 1 tablespoon heavy cream
- ❤ 1 tablespoon sesame seeds
- ❤ 1 tablespoon poppy seeds
- ❤ Real parchment paper that can be baked
- ❤ Nontoxic felt pen

These mini bread rolls can be made sweetly with sugar and icing or herb cheesy with Parmesan cheese, herbs, poppy seeds, and sesame seeds. ❤

---

1. **Gather** your ingredients and make the parchment cutouts first. You'll want to cut them into 2" × 3" rectangles and write your little sayings on each one. Once you have your messages ready, you can start on the bread.

2. **Mix** flour, baking powder, salt, and cheese in a mixing bowl.
3. **Heat** butter and water, add to the bowl, and blend well.
4. **Place** dough in a warm area for one hour.
5. **On** a floured surface, roll the dough into a ½" thick rectangle.
6. **Using** a pastry wheel, sharp knife, or pizza cutter and a ruler, cut out twenty 3" × 4" rectangles.
7. **Place** each message on top of the dough rectangle and roll into a cylinder shape, then twist the ends.
8. **Beat** egg yolk and cream, then brush the rolls with the mixture. Sprinkle the tops of the rolls with the sesame and poppy seeds. To give them more of an herb flavor, add a little bit of garlic and Italian herbs to the mixture before brushing it on and skip the seeds.
9. **Bake** for 25 minutes at 375°F.
10. **Cool** on a wire rack. Tie the ends with ribbon for a cute and whimsical addition.

Alternate Toppings

To make a sweet version of the message bread, exchange the grated cheese with ⅓ cup sugar and add 1 teaspoon vanilla extract to the butter and water mixture. Skip the herbs, garlic, and seeds and add icing after the bread cools.

Simple Strawberry Freezer Jam

You don't have to know the first thing about canning to make this easy recipe successfully.

Simple Strawberry Freezer Jam

2 quarts

♥ 2 quarts fresh organic strawberries, washed, with tops removed

❤ 8 cups of organic sugar

❤ 2 packages of powdered pectin (1.75 ounces each)

This is a quick and easy recipe that can be made in advance and then put into little jars for the day of the wedding and given out as favors. It can be frozen for up to a year or refrigerated for three weeks. ❤

---

1. **Crush** strawberries in blender or food processor.
2. **Pour** strawberries into a large bowl and add sugar. Let stand for about 10 minutes.
3. **Combine** pectin and 1½ cups of water in a saucepan and bring to a boil. Let boil for about one minute, stirring constantly.
4. **Add** pectin to strawberry mixture and stir until sugar dissolves.
5. **Pour** into freezer-safe containers and cover. Let sit at room temperature for 24 hours.
6. **Store** in refrigerator for up to three weeks; freeze for up to one year.

ALERT!

It's All in the Presentation
Before the wedding day you can place your fresh strawberry jam into mini canning jars or cute little apothecary jars. Display them on tables or in a large cloth-lined basket for a very elegant country look.

Finding Inspiration

The Internet and your local library are full of recipes and resources. Take advantage of both if you want to make some incredible edibles for ultimately green décor. Be sure to tap into your family and friends' culinary skills and secret recipes for yummy treats.

If you're not sure which edible treats will make wedding-friendly decorations, here's a partial list of treats that can be transformed into elegantly edible décor with just the addition of a few decorative labels or fashionable accessories:

- Bottles of herbed and flavored vinegars or oils. Use a variety of bottle shapes and sizes to add visual texture.
- Tiny jars of spice mixes such as garden blend, garlic and herb, Cajun spice, and chili seasoning. Make sure to include a label with ingredients or directions on how to use.
- Jars of fruit or herb butters
- Flavored honey or syrups
- Jars of flavored sugar
- Baskets full of baked goods such as mini loaves of bread, muffins, cupcakes, cookies, and brownies
- Tins of specialty teas
- Jars of dry goods mixes, such as a jar layered with all the dry ingredients for oatmeal cookies, chocolate chip cookies, or even Grandma's famous brownies (secret ingredient included); include a tag with directions on what to add and how to mix and bake. You can also make jar mixes for things other than sweet treats—for instance, chilies, soups, stews, and even cornbread.
- Bags filled with mixes for biscuits, scones, or muffins
- Plates filled with fresh strawberries dipped in chocolate

The edible options are endless. Pick something you are passionate about that you think your guests will enjoy.

Bird Lovers' Paradise

If you are a bird lover or if you just enjoy the appeal of our flying friends' accessories, a bird lover's theme can be very green and very easy to pull off. A bird lover's theme wedding is also very accommodating and can be coordinated with a wide range of styles: eco-elegance, charming country, cutesy craftsy, nature's bounty, or even exotic paradise.

Your décor, centerpieces, and favors can all center around birds and bird accessories: birdhouses, birdbaths, birdcages, bird nests, bird feeders, birdseed, and of course birds and their feathers.

Birdhouses, bird feeders, and birdcages, both new and used, can all be found in numerous locations. Stroll through any resale shop or thrift store and you are likely to find at least one handmade birdhouse or old birdcage. Any of these can be transformed into something beautiful for your bird lover's theme wedding. Birdhouses can be cleaned up and freshened with a new coat of paint. Birdcages can be cleaned and finished with white spray paint. Cover them with some vines, twigs, or ribbons to turn them into a show-stopping card collector or gift-table centerpiece.

If you love the bird theme but don't want to make everything, check online for cute and craftsy ready-made bridal birdie accessories at *www .annwoodhandmade.com*. Ann makes little birds and bird cake toppers from scraps of vintage fabric and lace. Check out *www.blissweddings market.com* for mini bird nests filled with sugar-coated almonds. They would make great favors for your bird-inspired wedding.

Large birdhouses make beautiful centerpieces, and mini birdhouses make charming favors. You can hang birdcages in the reception area with vines trailing from them. Birdbaths make elegantly charming decorations, and birdseed can be put into little bags or envelopes and given as favors.

Make Your Own

It is amazing how many ordinary things that are normally tossed into the trash or recycling bin can be turned into birdhouses and bird feeders. Coffee cans, milk cartons, juice bottles, 2-liter soda bottles, plastic soda and water bottles, and even pinecones and old logs can be turned into feeders for the birds.

To turn any container into a bird feeder, clean it out thoroughly, remove all labels and stickers, and make large enough holes in the side of the bottom of the container for birds to get in and get the seed. These bird feeders can be decorated however you want and given away as favors.

Decorative birdhouses can easily be made out of scrap wood. If you are making houses you hope actual birds will nest in, here are a few guidelines for making a bird-worthy house:

- The birdhouse roof should hang over the entrance hole to keep out rain and provide shade.
- There should be small ventilation holes in the birdhouse where the roof meets the walls and underneath the overhang so air can circulate.
- Small drainage holes should be in the bottom of the house so any water that gets in can drain out.
- Either the back wall or front should be engineered to swing open or up so the house can be cleaned out after each nesting season.
- The ideal circumference for most entrance holes is about 1½". This way birds can get in but larger predators can't.
- The distance from the bottom of the house to the entrance hole should be about 5"; this keeps baby birds in the bottom of the nest protected.
- The base nesting area should be big enough to contain five baby birds and the mother comfortably.
- The birdhouse should have a built-in means to be mounted or hung, or it should already be attached to a pole that will be placed in the ground.

ALERT!

Birds need a place to escape from land development and urban sprawl. Putting up birdhouses can give them safe places to nest in addition to creating a bird-friendly environment for you to enjoy watching wildlife. Make your area even more bird friendly by filling your yard with a variety of vegetation, and add bird feeders and birdbaths to your landscaping.

If you are going to make birdhouses to attract specific types of birds you may want to do a little research. Some birds are picky when it comes to where and how they nest. A good book to check out is *Build Your Own Birdhouses* by John Perkins, complete with unique designs and floor plans for many types of basic and bird-specific houses.

Everyday Items Transformed

You may have a treasure trove of items lying around your house collecting dust that can be transformed into amazing wedding décor. With a little imagination, paint, glue, ribbons, or other craft accessories and some old-fashioned elbow grease, you can turn everyday items into extraordinary elements for your wedding.

Glass Bottles or Jugs

Large glass receptacles such as wine bottles, liquor bottles, and juice jugs can be turned into elegant lamps that can be used for centerpieces and accessorizing wedding décor. A regular empty bottle can be transformed into an oil or electric lamp; just make sure to clean it out really well. You can purchase kits from *www.vinoglo.com* that contain everything you need to make a bottle into a romantic oil lamp—the wick, oil, and glass hurricane-like globe. No tools are necessary.

FACT

Reusing old items for wedding decorations is a wonderfully green way to reduce and reuse. You are reusing what is readily available and you are reducing by not having to purchase brand new materials. Additionally, you reduce the amount of stuff that normally might end up in landfills.

If you want to turn a bottle into an electric lamp, you'll need a bottle lamp kit that can be purchased at most local hardware stores or at *www.natural craft.com*. The kits usually contain all the hardware needed; no electrical knowledge is necessary. You will need a tool that can cut a hole in the glass large enough to pull the electrical cord through and you will have to purchase or make a lamp shade that coordinates well with your new bottle lamp.

To really transform the bottles you can add pretty decorative touches such as painted designs to match your wedding theme and color scheme, or decoupage photos or cutouts. Another creative touch that will really stand out is etching a design into the glass. This works best on a plain un-textured surface.

Glass Etching

- Etching cream (available at most craft stores)
- Tracing paper
- Carbon paper
- Adhesive-backed shelf paper or premade vinyl etching stencils
- Tape
- Scissors
- Craft knife
- Cotton swabs
- Steel wool
- Paper towels
- Newspaper
- Protective goggles and gloves
- Warm water

Take precautions by wearing goggles and gloves to protect your skin and eyes at all times. Cover all surfaces well so that nothing gets damaged by the etching cream, and work in a well-ventilated area because of fumes. Always use an aluminum or stainless steel sink because etching cream chemicals will damage porcelain and enamel finishes. ❤

1. **Trace** the design onto the tracing paper, then place carbon paper on top of the vinyl shelf backing, carbon (transfer) side down. Place the tracing paper on top of the carbon paper and trace the design again. You can also draw directly onto the vinyl with a marker.
2. **Cut** the design out of the vinyl, leaving a 1" border around the design. Peel away the paper backing. Determine the best location before removing the backing.
3. **Place** the vinyl on the desired area of the glass and smooth it on, pushing out any air bubbles and ripples in the vinyl. If it is a rounded surface, pleat the outer edges, trying to keep the inner design as flat as possible.

4. **Use** the craft knife to cut out the design area. Only cut the part you want to be etched. For example, if you wanted a grape pattern you would cut out the grape. Make sure the border is still attached firmly to the vinyl once the design is cut out.

5. **Heat** the etching cream by soaking the jar in a pot of warm water. Wearing your gloves and goggles, use a cotton swab to apply the etching cream in a thick layer over the exposed design. Use the cotton swab to gently pop any air bubbles in the cream.

6. **Leave** the cream on according to the directions on the jar, usually about five to six minutes. Gently rinse off the cream with low-pressure running water (be careful not to splash) and pat dry with paper towels.

7. **Pull** off the vinyl stencil, and you have etched a design in glass.

ALERT!

Variations
This process can be used on glass tumblers, jars, bottles, vases, and pitchers—anything you find that could use a creative touch. If you don't want to try cutting your own stencil, there are a wide variety of premade etching stencils. All you have to do is peel and stick, then follow the directions for the etching cream.

Canisters, Cans, and Metal Tins

A plain metal can may be transformed into a candle holder. Food canisters, cocoa tins, and coffee cans all can be turned into decorative containers. Clean up any plain can and turn it into something beautiful. Small flat cans such as tuna, chicken, and cat food tins make nice holders for votives or small floating candles. Larger cans, such as soup cans, work well with pillar-style candles.

Clean the cans thoroughly and make sure the labels and any label remnants are removed. Paint them with spray paint (Krylon offers a low VOC spray paint that is 100% acrylic latex) in a well-ventilated area over newspaper or drop cloths. It is usually easiest to spray the inside first then flip it over and spray the outside. It may take a couple of coats to get a thick even finish.

Once they are dry, you can embellish the outside of the cans with your choice of items: paint designs with acrylic paints, attach fabric cutouts, glue on lace or ribbon borders, add vintage buttons, or attach sea shells or decoupage paper cutouts.

> It used to be hard to transform plastic containers into anything craftsy since normal paint never stuck well to plastic surfaces, but now Krylon makes Fusion for Plastic spray paint. Almost any old plastic item such as a watering can, patio furniture, or plastic paint cans can have a new life just by adding a new coat of paint.

Large containers such as bulk-size food cans, big coffee canisters, or paint cans may be transformed into spring-time buckets filled with flowers, spring goodies, or favors. Metal cooking cocoa tins can be turned into little banks and given away as favors. You can paint sayings on them such as "a penny saved is a penny earned," "a penny for your thoughts," or "rainy day fund."

Cardboard and cardboard-aluminum mix cans with lids can be painted or wrapped in fabric and transformed into cute storage containers. Turn a few into decorative centerpieces and fill them with handmade soaps, little bags of potpourri, or envelopes of dried herbs for your guests to take home.

Plain Glasses, Bottles, and Glass Jars

Empty baby food jars, spaghetti sauce jars, olive oil bottles—all these can have life beyond what they were made for without going through the recycling process. Jars can be remade into candle holders or even into jar candles if you decide to melt some wax and try candle-making yourself. Be sure they're the right kind of glass for this purpose so they don't shatter when heated. Designs can be etched, painted, or decoupaged onto the glass to breathe new life into them and to make them oh-so-pretty for your green event.

What's Old May Be Useful

Keep your eyes open for the amazing things that can be made from normal everyday items you might think are trash. Plastic pop bottles become bird feeders; scrap wood becomes birdhouses; castoff chair legs, architectural finials, and spindles become candlestick holders. Cutouts from old calendars and wrapping paper add texture to plain boxes and crates, and wallpaper scraps can become elegant gift boxes. Use your imagination, visit craft websites for inspiration, or hit the library for craft books. You'll find many new ways to use old things, quite a few of which can be incorporated into your big green wedding.

CHAPTER 15

Green Giving

Being green can encompass so much more than just saving the environment. Consider green giving. Make your wedding day meaningful by supporting a worthy cause while you plan your big day and your life together afterward. This can be accomplished by supporting companies that are doing good things for their workers and their community, purchasing from businesses that donate part of their proceeds to charity, shopping directly from a charitable organization, registering for gifts from green stores, or requesting that donations be made in lieu of gifts.

Green and Eco-Friendly Registries

Even if you do not need or want a lot of new things, registering for at least several items that the two of you pick out together is a good idea. It is symbolic to choose things for your new life together. It is also a great bonding experience. Afterward you can look at it and think "that's ours," not "mine" or "yours." It's good to have things that belong to the two of you together.

Create a Registry

Take stock of anything you might need or want, from towels to hiking gear, and register for it. Creating a gift registry with exactly what you want is good in a couple of ways. Guests will know just what to get for you. There will be less impact on the environment because there won't be duplicate or unwanted gifts you have to return, ship back, or worse—give away or send to the trash.

Request minimal packaging and no gift wrap to keep your gifts really green. That way there are fewer wasted resources, less to recycle, and definitely less to end up in the trash. If many of your guests are in the same area as you, consider registering at a local store that gets its items primarily from your geographical region.

For a green couple there are many ways to register in eco-friendly fashion.

One way is to create an online registry through the I Do Foundation (*www.idofoundation.org*). Large retailers have partnered with the I Do Foundation and will donate up to 10 percent of the value of the purchases from your registry to the charity of your choice. Home Depot, J. C. Penney, Target, Gaiam, and Amazon.com are just a few of the stores you have to choose from. It is easy to create a registry, and you can even create your own personal web page that gives all the details of your wedding events and links to your registries.

Another green registry option is creating a registry at a store that sells green merchandise. Choose eco-minded and socially responsible goods. There are many eco-fabulous retailers online that have wedding and gift registries. These web stores may carry a variety of things. You can find stores that sell household products made from organic, recycled, and fair trade items or furniture made from reclaimed and sustainable materials.

Some great green choices for your wedding registry are:

- Greenfeet (*www.greenfeet.com*)
- Rawganique (*www.rawganique.com*)
- 3R Living (*www.3rliving.com*)
- Re:modern (*www.re-modern.com*)
- Green Nest (*www.greennest.com*)
- Gaiam (*www.gaiam.com*)
- Natural Spaces (*www.naturalspaces.com*)
- GreenSage (*www.greensage.com*)
- Green Living (*www.green-living.com*)
- Global Exchange (*store.gxonlinestore.org*)

You can register for sustainable household goods such as bamboo salad bowls and cutting boards, mini kitchen composters, garbage cans made from recycled tires, glassware and tableware made from recycled glass, art made from everyday recycled materials, organic bed linens made of cotton, hemp, or bamboo, luxurious organic terry-cloth robes and towels, and so much more.

Alternative Gift Registry

A really unique website to register at is *www.alternativegiftregistry.org*. At the Alternative Gift Registry you can let everyone know exactly what you want, even if it is something that cannot be bought in any store—such as Grandma's famous chocolate chip cookie recipe, Aunt Hilda's secret chili ingredient, or a night on the town with your best friends.

This gift registry lets you request personal things that cannot possibly be assigned a price. You can also request regular items that you can link to outside the site, and you can list local craftspeople, artisans, and even local boutiques or farms that you would like your guests to purchase your gifts from. In addition to that, you can also request that your guests donate to certain charities instead of buying gifts for you.

Supplies from Charitable Organizations

While planning your big green day, consider shopping for wedding supplies at eco-friendly retailers and charitable organizations. The I Do Foundation has partnered with Carlson Printers to donate a percentage of your invitation order to the charity of your choice. Many organizations offer favors and favor donations. There are also thrift stores that give their sale profits to good causes, such as Goodwill and the Salvation Army. When you are on the hunt for retro goodies and vintage inspiration, make sure to visit your local charity-run thrift shop to make the most of reusable style and green dollars.

If you are planning to make some renovations to your home or create some craftsy goodies for your wedding, check out your local Habitat ReStore. Operated by Habitat for Humanity, ReStores are retail outlets that sell used and surplus building materials, furniture, and interior design and décor accessories.

FACT

Some Habitat ReStores raise enough money to build ten or more additional houses than they normally would in one year. There are ReStores in forty-six states and nine Canadian provinces. For more information and to find a ReStore near you, go to *www.habitat.org/env/restores.aspx.*

A ReStore is the perfect place to shop if you are planning on building something big such as an archway, trellis, or gazebo for your backyard wedding. All proceeds from ReStore sales go to building Habitat for Humanity homes.

Many couples move into a new home once they are married or even while they are engaged. If you are feathering your nest while planning your wedding, shop eco-wisely. Look for green products and items made from eco-friendly and sustainable materials. Also be sure to buy quality products that are made to last, not disposable stuff that will need to be replaced in a short amount of time.

Charitable Donations

Instead of going all out and buying many things for your wedding that you really don't need, consider donating that money to charity instead. Instead of all those favors, place cards, confetti, and candles, donate a little something to the charity of your choice. The money will be well worth it. Charitable contributions can also be about donating yourself, your time, or your special talents or services. There are many ways you can contribute.

You can also donate your old stuff to charity. If it still has reusable life in it, chances are someone will take it. Getting ready to start a new life together is the perfect time to clean out some of the old cobwebs and get rid of clutter that has been piling up. There are charities that take anything and everything, and there are others that deal with only specific items.

Now is the perfect time to clear out your closets, dust off those shelves, and clear the path for a new life. Combining all your stuff into one space might require you to do this even if you don't want to. If it has life left in it, don't throw it out. Donate it, give it to a thrift store, or have a yard sale and donate the money you make from that to charity.

The following charities accept donated items to help support their causes:

- Give the Gift of Sight (*givethegiftofsight.org*) accepts old eyeglasses and eyeglass cases. They can be dropped off at any LensCrafters, Pearle Vision, Sears Optical, Target Optical, Sunglass Hut, or Lions Club.
- There are many organizations that take cell phones, including Call-2Recycle (*www.rbrc.org/call2recycle*) and Cell Phones for Soldiers (*www.cellphonesforsoldiers.com*).
- Reader to Reader (*www.readertoreader.org*) accepts donations of books.

- Hungry for Music (*hungryformusic.com*) accepts donations of musical supplies, books, instruments, sheet music, and even musical toys and distributes them to underprivileged children.
- Dress for Success (*www.dressforsuccess.org*) accepts women's business attire—suits, blouses, blazers, jackets, and shoes—that is in good condition and appropriate to wear to interviews.
- Goodwill and Salvation Army stores will usually accept just about anything that is still in decent shape.

There are several sites that can direct you to a worthwhile cause including Charity Guide (*www.charityguide.org*), Network for Good (*www.networkforgood.org*), Charity.com (*www.charity.com*), JustGive (*www.justgive.org*), Charity Navigator (*www.charitynavigator.org*), and the Better Business Bureau (*www.give.org*). Find something you are passionate about. There is so much to choose from—animal issues and animal rights, children's services, disease, the environment, homelessness, women's rights, poverty. You name it and there is an organization championing it that could use your help.

Charity Registries

Some organizations have created wedding registries for couples who would like to have their guests donate to a charity instead of or in addition to purchasing gifts. The I Do Foundation, in addition to their partner store registries, allows you to create a registry that consists of one or several of your favorite worthy causes that you would like your guests to contribute to.

JustGive.org also has a charitable wedding area that you can customize into your own unique charity contribution center. The World Wildlife Fund also has a wedding registry for nature-loving couples. At Heifer.org you can personalize your registry and decide which programs to help fund.

By encouraging your guests to donate to charity, you are showing the world that you care. Through one momentous occasion such as your wedding, you can inspire hundreds to donate money and perhaps even their time to a meaningful cause. They will tell others about it and inspire them to donate or create a charitable wedding registry of their own because they want to make a difference as well. One small action can cause hundreds and thousands of positive actions.

Get Involved—Volunteer

Make it all matter a little bit more by donating your precious and extremely valuable time. Volunteer alone, volunteer together, or get friends and family to tag along and volunteer as a group. Add to your ultragreen wedding by having charitable fundraisers or volunteer get-togethers as part of your prewedding parties. You could even include volunteering as a part of your bachelor or bachelorette party. Get your bridal party together and spend a day volunteering at a local Humane Society or animal shelter; hand out food at a food bank; give blankets, gloves, and hats to the homeless on a cold day; ladle out hot food at a soup kitchen; spend the day planting trees or flowers at a local park or school.

Finding Volunteer Opportunities

Organizations always need more volunteers than they can get. Schools, libraries, hospitals, senior citizen centers, children's organizations—so many need volunteers. ServiceLeader.org (*www.serviceleader .org*) has many great tips and ideas for volunteering. Network for Good (*www.networkforgood.org*) will help you search by state for volunteer opportunities.

Have a bridal shower or prewedding bash that is for a good cause:

- Have every woman invited to your bridal shower bring along an item of business clothing to donate to Dress for Success.
- Ask everyone to bring canned or boxed foods to donate to the local food bank.
- Get your entire wedding party together and spend the day working on a Habitat for Humanity house.
- Donate a Saturday morning to your local library and read to kids.
- Have an old-fashioned quilting bee. Project Linus (*www.project linus.org*) accepts new, handmade, washable blankets that can be given to children ages newborn to eighteen.
- Have a big barbecue/yard sale. Have everyone bring a dish to pass and something to sell in the sale. All money earned from the sale gets donated to the charity of choice.

- Have a wildlife party. Everyone who comes donates money at the door. All the money raised gets sent to your favorite wildlife organization.

If you feel as if you are being too pushy or feel that friends and family aren't into the volunteering thing, that's okay. You can volunteer on your own time without anyone else. There are many, many opportunities available.

Volunteer Vacations

Volunteer vacations are an excellent way to do good things while trying something new. A volunteer getaway is a way to experiment with public service and perhaps discover a passion for something you may want to explore in more depth: cataloging art in a museum, renovating and restoring a French castle, going on a real archaeological dig, rescuing and studying sea turtles, or even restoring railways around the world.

Inspire change. Just a little can inspire a lot. Post links, buttons, and banners that link to your favorite charity, environmental organization, or activist website on your wedding website. Visit *www.bethechange.org* for inspiring stories, quick ideas, resources, and ways to encourage more random acts of kindness and change.

It can be a way to live out your dreams and to visit somewhere you've never been before, all while helping others and doing something good. A volunteer vacation is a great way to share an experience with members of your bridal party or a unique way to bond with your fiancé before the wedding. If you don't have any time before the wedding, a volunteer vacation might make a dream honeymoon.

For a volunteer vacation, you may only have to pay for transportation to and from the location. Many organizations provide room and board for volunteers, while some may only charge nominal fees like $10 a day or $150 a week to help cover costs for food. Other organizations may make you pay for everything. If you choose a volunteer getaway make sure you get all the details ahead of time so that there are no surprises.

There are many charitable organizations and U.S. groups that accept volunteers, such as the U.S. Fish and Wildlife Service (*www.fws.gov*), the U.S. Bureau of Land Management (*www.blm.gov*), the U.S. Forest Service (*www.fs.fed.us*), and many national and state parks.

Greenpeace (*www.greenpeace.org*) accepts volunteers for environmental activism, the National Audubon Society (*www.audubon.org*) takes volunteers all over the United States for habitat restoration, the Sierra Club (*www.sierra club.org/outings*) plans outings that help clean up and preserve wilderness areas, and the Earthwatch Institute (*www.earthwatch.org*) and the Nature Conservancy (*www.nature.org*) take volunteers on many types of expeditions.

Appalachian Trail Conference (*www.atconf.org*) volunteers work along the Appalachian National Scenic Trail in various locations from North Carolina to Maine doing such tasks as building new trails and constructing shelters. You could help build and maintain forest trails in Colorado with the Colorado Trail Foundation (*www.coloradotrail.org*).

Go international. If wildlife is your thing, participate in the study of dolphins, manatees, howler monkeys, sea birds, whales, or sea turtles in the Bahamas, Belize, or the Peruvian Amazon through Oceanic Society Expeditions (*www.oceanic-society.org*). Research humpback whales in Hawaii or Australia with Pacific Whale (*www.pacificwhale.org*) or help preserve sea turtles through the One World Work Force. Do maintenance work in Peru with Peruvian Safaris (*www.peruviansafaris.com*). Help save big cats at the Peace River Refuge and Ranch in Florida (*www.peaceriverrefuge.org /volunteer.html*) or travel to Namibia or Kenya with the Cheetah Conservation Fund and learn about cheetahs in the wild (*www.cheetah.org*).

You are sure to be amazed at all the adventure possibilities that are available for you to participate in. These are a very small fraction of what is available around the world. Check out *Volunteer Vacations: Short-Term Adventures That Will Benefit You and Others* by Bill McMillon. Make sure you get the newest edition, because he updates it quite regularly. Also check out the websites *www.volunteertravel.com*, *www.charityguide.org /volunteer/vacations.htm*, and *www.volunteer.gov/gov* for tons of volunteer opportunities and volunteer vacation information.

CHAPTER 16

Environmentally Friendly Transportation

Motor vehicles account for a huge portion of the carbon dioxide emissions that contribute to global warming, and they also release other toxic pollutants into the atmosphere. Growing awareness of this is forcing vehicle manufacturers to become greener, and people are making more environmentally friendly choices when it comes to their transportation, not just for their weddings but for everyday living. The high cost of gasoline and increasing awareness of the political ramifications of dependence on foreign oil makes gas-guzzling SUVs less attractive, and more and more drivers are turning in their SUVs for more fuel-efficient cars. Be creative and you can have fun and functionally green transportation without giving up on style.

Arrive in Eco-Style

You can have uniquely green transportation for every aspect of your wedding—for the commute between ceremony and reception locations (if there is one) or for your departure as the newly married couple. Eco-friendly vehicles such as hybrids and electric cars are practical for getting from one place to another. You can also consider vehicles that run on alternative fuels such as biodiesel and E85.

Hybrids run on a gasoline engine and an electric motor. The electric motor is powered by a battery that recharges itself by capturing the energy that is released whenever the brakes are applied. According to *www.hybridcars.com*, United States oil consumption could be reduced by 1.5 million barrels a day if fuel efficiency were increased by just five miles per gallon.

For all your guests and everyone in your wedding party, you could arrange for carpooling or shuttling from one location to another. Consider shuttle buses that run on biodiesel, or offer guests information on renting hybrid vehicles. If the ceremony and reception sites are close together, just walk from one venue to the next. To keep things even greener, have the ceremony and reception in the same locale.

The United States uses more oil than any other country in the world, and two-thirds of it goes right into our gas tanks. Every gallon of gasoline burned releases twenty-five pounds of greenhouse gases into the air.

Many rental companies are now offering greener choices. Enterprise Rent-A-Car has a large fleet of FlexFuel vehicles in addition to the many hybrids in its rental fleet. It also offers a carbon offset program to its rental customers. Other rental companies around the world are offering a wide variety of more environmentally friendly rentals. Fox Rent A

Car (*www.foxrentacar.com*) offers several hybrids, and EV Rental Cars (*www.evrental.com*) in California and Arizona rents the Toyota Prius, Toyota Highlander hybrid, and Honda Civic hybrid.

QUESTION?

If natural gas is a petroleum product, how is it any better than regular gasoline?
Natural gas burns cleaner than regular gasoline and produces 20 to 30 percent fewer carbon dioxide emissions than regular gasoline. It is not perfect, but it is a more eco-friendly alternative.

Even limousine rental companies are expanding their green efforts and offering a greener variety of luxury. EVO Limo in California (*www.evolimo.com*) rents limos powered by compressed natural gas, which is a clean-burning fuel. Its SUVs are certified ultralow and super-ultralow emissions vehicles, and they have plans to introduce zero emissions vehicles that operate on hydrogen fuel cells and electricity. NYC Green Car (*www.nycgreencar.com*) offers a luxury car service committed to using only hybrid vehicles. Other companies in New York offer hybrid car services, but NYC Green Car was the first to offer only hybrids. Its fleet is full of Toyota Camry and Lexus hybrids.

Every day more companies are realizing that they have to be more environmentally friendly and offer responsible options for their customers. The following green transportation pioneers operate out of different parts of the United States; check your local resources to see whether companies in your area offer green transportation.

- Eco-Limo (*www.eco-limo.com*) in Los Angeles and San Francisco offers several green rental options.
- Elite Green Car (*www.elitegreencar.com*) in Atlanta will chauffeur you in a Lexus RX 400.
- Green Limousine (*www.greenlimousinecolorado.com*) offers biodiesel Ford Excursions in Colorado.
- Green Car Limo (*www.greencarlimo.com*) in California is stocked with hybrid rentals.

- LimoGreen (*www.limogreen.net*) in New York has a fleet of natural gas–powered Lincoln Towncars.
- Bauer's Limousine (*www.bauerslimo.com*) in Northern California offers many green options, including electric buses.

Custom-built hybrid limos are available through some companies, and in the near future the ultimate in luxurious rides may come in a green model. Bentley has announced plans to develop an eco-friendly limo. With a little bit of effort, a few phone calls, and maybe some web surfing, you should be able to find a green vehicle so you can ride around on your wedding day in eco-style.

Hybrids

If you are like the average person, you are probably confused about all the types of vehicles that are out there now. Hydrogen fuel cells, electric-powered batteries, hybrids—which is best for the environment? Here's a brief primer on hybrid technology.

If you are in the market for a greener car for everyday use or just for your wedding, the two greenest vehicles of 2007 were the Honda Civic GX and the Toyota Prius. Other vehicles that made the top ten greenest cars of 2007 were the Nissan Altima Hybrid, Toyota Yaris, Toyota Corolla, and Toyota Camry hybrid.

Hybrid vehicles are powered by a combination of electric batteries and regular gasoline. The electric motor assists the gasoline engine in acceleration and hill climbing, allowing the vehicle to conserve energy and waste less gas. The electric motor takes over completely when the car is stopped, which means no gas is wasted while the car idles. Hybrids are the most commonly driven environmentally friendly cars.

Electric-powered vehicles are extremely efficient and do not put out any greenhouse gas emissions. According to Hybrid Technologies (*www.hybridtechnologies.com*), driving a vehicle powered by electricity from the U.S. electric grid is cleaner than driving vehicles powered by oil.

Hydrogen fuel cell technology is promising, but currently the kinks are still being worked out; some hydrogen is produced from fossil fuels. Fuel cell vehicles that are powered by pure hydrogen emit no pollutants or greenhouse gases, but fuel cells consume four times as much electricity per mile as an electric battery and fuel cell fueling systems are complicated when compared to a battery plug-in for electric vehicles. Driving range is also a problem, as it's usually only half the distance of an electric battery's.

FACT

In 1900 there were only around 8,000 cars and 150 miles of paved road in the United States. By 1910 there were more than 500,000 cars, and by 1950 that number had increased to 40 million. In 1950, people in the United States owned approximately 75 percent of the world's automobiles.

Hybrids seem to be the best of both worlds by providing more power and driving range than all-electric vehicles while still reducing smog and greenhouse gas emissions. They save resources by not using as much gasoline as regular petroleum-powered vehicles since they also rely on the electric battery.

Alternative Fuels

There are several types of alternative fuels available today, and many more are still in the research and development stages. Right now the main alternative fuels that you may find at gas stations are E85 and biodiesel. They are the two most promising types of alternative fuels since both can reduce our dependence on oil, lower greenhouse-gas emissions, and be produced domestically from a number of different natural sources. Ethanol, the base of E85, is also biodegradable and does not contaminate water.

E85 is 85 percent ethanol and 15 percent petroleum fuel. Ethanol is produced from corn and other natural crops and it burns cleaner than gasoline, producing fewer greenhouse-gas emissions. Right now there are not any commercially created vehicles that run entirely on ethanol. FlexFuel vehicles are designed to operate on ethanol blends such as E85 or on regular gasoline. One drawback to E85 is that it reduces fuel economy by about 20 to 30 percent, which means that a car will travel fewer miles on a tank of E85 than on a regular tank of gas.

In the 1800s Henry Ford designed a car that ran only on ethanol. In 1908 he designed a Model T that operated on either ethanol or gasoline. During World War II, the United States used ethanol when gas was in short supply. However, gasoline was both inexpensive and readily available in the postwar era, so ethanol faded from thought.

Biodiesel is a natural fuel derived from vegetable oils and animal fats. It can be made from soybean oil, canola oil, sunflower oil, and recycled cooking oils. Biodiesel produces fewer air pollutants than regular petroleum-based fuel. Biodiesel is the most thoroughly tested of all alternative fuels and shows a lot of promise. It performs as well as regular diesel while emitting little to no greenhouse gases, and it can be used in vehicles that run on regular diesel without the need for any special equipment or conversions. Homemade biodiesels are not registered by the EPA and may violate vehicle warranties. Vehicles do need modification to operate on homemade biodiesel.

Dr. Rudolph Diesel intended the diesel engine to be able to run on a variety of fuels. When he demonstrated it at the 1900 World Exhibition in Paris, it was fueled by peanut oil. Diesel engines were used in ships and railway locomotives in the early twentieth century, but it was not until 1936 that Mercedes-Benz introduced them in passenger cars.

Natural gas and propane are current alternative fuels, but they are fossil fuels, though they both generate less air pollution and greenhouse gases than regular gasoline. Other biofuels are currently being developed; woody crops are being converted into butanol and oily crops such as jatropha show promise for diesel.

Eco-Savvy Alternatives

Think of arriving at your wedding in a horse-drawn carriage like a fairy-tale princess or leaving your reception by sailing off into the sunset. These are extremely romantic and extremely green methods of transportation. You could opt for some unique eco-friendly transportation choices—roller skates or inline skates, skateboards, electric scooters, bicycles, boats, carriages, and skis, snowshoes, or dogsleds for winter weddings.

Bicycles

Bicycles are very eco-friendly and can be a very cute way to arrive at your wedding or depart after the reception. They come in all different shapes, sizes, colors, and styles. You could ride on a bicycle built for two or get driven off in a rickshaw carriage.

You can burn as many as 750 to 1,000 calories per hour riding a bicycle, but that has to be some hard continuous riding. Most normal bike riding will burn 500 to 600 calories in an hour. Riding a bike is good for the environment, and it may help you shed some excess pounds.

Bicycles are very eco-friendly. Bicycling instead of using motorized transportation reduces greenhouse gas emissions, fossil fuel usage, air pollution, traffic congestion, and noise pollution. It decreases the amount of resources used to manufacture and recycle vehicles.

If you are planning on arriving at your wedding location on a bicycle, consider changing into your wedding attire at the venue or practice riding the bicycle in your attire or something similar ahead of time. Brides will have a difficult time keeping their dresses out of the way. If you are planning on bicycle departure, you could just change your clothing into something more casual before leaving the reception location.

A rickshaw carriage will solve the attire problems while still taking advantage of the eco-option of the bicycle. The happy couple can just climb into the carriage and be driven off by the rickshaw driver. Rickshaws are quite popular in other countries such as China, Japan, India, Greece, and Australia, and you see them occasionally in tourist areas of the United States. You might be able to find one for rent or even for purchase in your area or online.

FACT

If the average person stopped driving two days a week, she could save about 143 gallons of gas in a year. If just 1 percent of all licensed drivers drove two fewer days per week, they could save 273 million gallons of gasoline.

Sail Away

Is your wedding on a lake, pond, or even an ocean? Consider arriving or leaving via the water. Any nonmotorized boat is wonderfully green; canoes, rowboats, sailboats; even an Italian-style gondola can be a unique, romantic, and eco-friendly way to get around.

If you are sailing away in a small boat, you might want to practice getting in and out of the boat without tipping it and landing in the water. Making a literal splash might be comical, but it's probably not the grand exit you had in mind.

Horsepower

There's always good old-fashioned horsepower to get you where you want to go. No, not the kind under the hood of a gas-guzzling muscle car—real horsepower, the kind that can pull a Cinderella-style carriage.

Nothing says romance or old-fashioned style like a horse-drawn carriage. There are many types of horse-drawn carriages and sleighs, from simple hayride-style wagons to elaborate carriages straight out of a fairy tale. Make sure you get a look at the exact carriage or sleigh you are renting so there are no nasty surprises on your big green day. Also make sure that the horse farm is a reputable one and is known for treating its animals well.

Offsetting Carbon Emissions

You cannot escape carbon emissions when you plan your wedding. You will need a vehicle to transport yourself or other items to make sure they arrive at the wedding site. Think about how much energy it will take to make sure your wedding runs smoothly—electricity for the deejay, catering, lighting, and air conditioning or heating system. In addition, your out-of-town guests may have to travel long distances to attend your nuptial celebration. Fortunately, there are many ways you can offset these emissions.

ALERT!

A report released by the IPCC in February 2007, which was based on the work of more than 2,500 scientists from over 130 countries, states that humans have caused all or most of the planet's warming. Global warming caused by humans has been termed *anthropogenic climate change*.

Consider buying local foods and products because the items simply have to travel less distance to get to you. Encourage your guests to carpool or arrange shuttle service for them. One easy way to cut down on your guests' emissions is to hold your wedding at the hotel they are staying in. Ask your vendors what they do to make their businesses more sustainable.

Purchasing carbon offsets is another way to mitigate the harm emissions cause. By purchasing carbon offsets, you help the environment, reduce your footprint, and do your part to slow global warming. A carbon offset is a certificate that represents the reduction of one metric ton of carbon dioxide emissions. One metric ton equals 2,205 pounds of carbon dioxide, the major cause of global warming. Carbon offsets fund projects such as wind farms and tree planting, which reduce the amount of carbon dioxide in the air. They also support renewable energy and energy-efficiency projects.

Carbonfund.org (*www.carbonfund.org*) and TerraPass (*www.terrapass.com*) allow you to put money toward renewable energy or reforestation projects. Both have online wedding calculators to see how many carbon offsets you should purchase to have a zero-footprint wedding. CarbonFund.org has a ZeroCarbon Wedding package that offsets a minimum of eight tons. You can purchase additional carbon offsets to add to the package. If it's too expensive for you to assume responsibility for offsetting all of your guests' carbon emissions, you can let them know you would appreciate a contribution to a carbon offsetting organization instead of a wedding present.

CHAPTER 17

Postwedding Cleanup

Living by the three Rs is important, and if you planned your wedding in a green manner the amount of waste you have to dispose of should be minimal. But as you look around you after the wedding and reception and see everything that is left, you'll probably wonder how much would be left over if you hadn't planned an eco-friendly wedding.

It's Over. Now What?

Hopefully your guests, friends, and family took a lot of stuff home with them, but now what do you do with what's left? Natural elements such as twigs, branches, tree limbs, straw, hay, grasses, vines, and flowers can all be returned to nature. Large items can be shredded or put through a chipper and turned into mulch that can be placed in a garden. Other natural items such as rocks or sand can be returned to where you found them or placed in a garden.

Think of creative ways to keep mementos or create gifts for family and friends from some of the things you have left over. Leftover craft scraps, invitations, table tent cards, favors, ribbons, lace, place cards, and other materials can be turned into beautiful scrapbook pages, memory shadow boxes, and even time capsules that you can seal and open up five, ten, or twenty years later on your anniversary. If you plan to do a time capsule, get guests involved by having them predict what your lives will be like in the future—how many kids you will have, where you will live, or what careers you will be in. If they are not in touch with their psychic sense, they can always write wishes and personalized notes to place into the time capsule.

FACT

Two great books that give you creative ideas about ways to use stuff in new ways are *Don't Throw It Out: Recycle, Renew and Reuse to Make Things Last* by Lori Baird and the editors of *Yankee* magazine and *Beyond Recycling: A Re-users Guide: 336 Practical Tips to Save Money and Protect the Environment* by Kathy Stein.

After you've gathered up all the little things you can use for more craft projects and sent the nature items to their new home in a garden somewhere, you have to tackle the big stuff. Reuse it, recycle it, donate it, or just send it to the landfill. Determine what goes where and send it on its way so you can start enjoying married life.

Proper Waste Disposal

Every locale has different rules, laws, and processes when it comes to waste disposal. Some just collect everything and haul it off to landfills. Some cities offer curbside recycling, while others expect you to do all the work yourself and haul it to the recycling center.

You'll want to know the methods available in both the place you live and the location of your reception. If your reception site doesn't offer to recycle everything and does not have curbside pickup, you might want to take recyclables home with you. It might be less of a hassle to recycle from home than taking them somewhere to drop off. It all depends on what is most convenient for you.

QUESTION?

Why is plastic bad for the environment?
Plastics are made from nonrenewable petroleum resources. They require a lot of energy to produce, and many toxic chemicals that pollute air and waterways are used during plastic production. Most plastics are recyclable but many never get recycled. Only 3 percent of the 60 billion pounds of plastics produced each year in the United States gets recycled.

When you dispose of leftover wedding stuff, your goal is to keep as much out of the landfill as possible. Separate everything and dispose of things properly to accomplish this. Once you are done, the only things being carted off to the landfill should be soiled tissues and food waste that cannot be composted.

Recycle What You Can

Grab everything that has usable life left and put it to the side. Put everything you plan to take home with you in one bin and everything that is still usable but that you don't particularly want in another bin or box. This could be leftover centerpieces, glass bowls, candles, candle holders, baskets, and photo frames. Make sure you grab any memorabilia you wish to hold on to, such as the guest book, toasting goblets, your bouquets, and even your aisle runner and table centerpiece. Put it all in your to-keep box.

In 1950 glass beer and soda bottles were refilled around ten to thirty times each. Coke bottles averaged about fifty refillings per bottle. By 1991 less than 9 percent of America's bottles were refillable. Yet throughout Europe and South America, and even in Canada, refilling glass beverage bottles is still quite common. Refilling saves more energy and money than recycling and it reduces waste.

All other materials that are left sitting around or piled up should be put into proper recycling containers or garbage bins. Check to make sure you know what can be recycled in your area. For example, some paper recyclers will accept newspapers and magazines while others only accept office-type paper and junk mail. Check with the local program administrators to find out how recyclables should be separated. Some recycling facilities take everything commingled and do the sorting at the facility either by hand or through complex machine-operated sorting systems.

What can recycled plastic be turned into besides more plastic containers?
Plastic bottles can be "spun" into fleece fabric (EcoSpun) and carpet fibers along with many other new and innovative materials. Just thirty-six recycled bottles can create one square yard of carpet.

After the wedding and honeymoon, go through your wedding-related items and determine what you are going to keep and what can be given or thrown away. You may have newspaper clippings of wedding-related articles, stacks of bridal magazines, fliers, posters, streamers, paper decorations, leftover invitations, favor cards, place cards, and seating charts. Save some things to put in memory books and scrapbooks and send the rest to the recyclers.

Here are some recycling basics:

- Newspapers should be separated into their own container. Remove glossy inserts, ads, and magazines and put them in another bin.
- Magazines, colored paper, envelopes, printed fliers, invitations, note cards, table tent cards, seating charts, programs, menus, computer paper, maps, and posters can go into one bin, but do not include cardboard, laminated paper, waxy coated papers, stickers, rubber bands, or plastic wrap.
- Do not put paper plates, food-covered napkins, food wrappers, or anything with food residue into the paper recycling bin.
- Corrugated cardboard gets separated into its own pile.
- Some centers accept plastics mixed together, but others ask that they be separated by type. Plastics should have a number on the bottom, so you'll know how to separate them and whether they are recyclable in your area.
- Most temporary plastic food containers such as those in TV and microwavable dinners are not recyclable.
- Polystyrene cups, food trays, and egg cartons do not biodegrade, but many centers are starting to recycle them. Keep them in their own bin.
- Glass is divided by color—clear, brown, and green.
- Mirrors and light bulbs should not be placed with regular glass products.
- Compact fluorescent light bulbs can be recycled at IKEA stores if you have one in your area.
- Aluminum cans, foils, and foil packaging are highly recyclable. Food cans should be rinsed and have labels removed.
- If you have any paint cans, they need to be kept separate from other aluminum cans and the labels need to be left on them.
- If you have copper, bronze, or brass to recycle, keep them separate from the aluminum.
- If you have electronic materials to dispose of, do it properly. Consider donating to various organizations or learn the proper way to dispose of e-waste in your local area.
- To find a recycling center near you, call 1-800-CLEANUP.

If you have to haul everything to the local recycling center, enlist a responsible source to take everything there so you can go on and enjoy your honeymoon. Find an eco-minded friend or relative to take care of this for you so that you know it will be done by someone who appreciates the need to be green.

FACT

Paper can take up as much as 50 percent of landfill space, which is a real waste because most paper can be recycled. For every ton of paper that is recycled, you can save seventeen forty-foot Douglas fir trees.

Biodegradable Products and Composting

The Federal Trade Commission defines biodegradable as a substance that has been proven to break down completely and return to nature within a reasonably short period of time. Biodegradable products and packaging are wonderful; however, the problem with them is that a product needs adequate exposure to natural elements to biodegrade. It has to be out in nature exposed to sun, rain, water, and the elements. Biodegradable products that get stuffed in trash bags and sent to the landfill will not biodegrade the way they are meant to.

Get It Sorted Out

Ideally, your reception site has a composting program in effect and will take care of everything for you. The biodegradable substances left over from your wedding should go into compost bins or piles instead of garbage bags destined for the dump. If you went out of your way to purchase biodegradable products such as plates and silverware made from cornstarch, potatoes, sugar cane, or other natural biodegradable, compostable materials, make sure they go where they were meant to.

It might take a bit of effort and even a little gross factor to make sure everything ends up where it should (you can always convince responsible people to do it for you if the reception facility doesn't). Garbage will have to be divided into what will be recycled, composted, and sent to the dump. Plates will have to be scraped off because no meat, dairy, bones, or fatty greases should be put into a compost bin. Fruit, vegetable, and other scraps can go into compost as well as any natural décor you have left over such as leaves, flowers, twigs, or other organic materials.

Even in nature it takes some things a long time to biodegrade, so they are better off being recycled. Regular paper can take two to five months to biodegrade, plastic-coated paper milk cartons take five years, nylon fabric stays around for thirty to forty years, aluminum cans can last eighty to 100 years, and glass can take longer than a million years to break down.

DIY Composting

If your reception site does not compost biodegradable materials, you can do it yourself. Basically, you put all-natural scraps and organic matter into a big pile to break down and turn into nutrient-rich soil that's perfect for gardens. Ideal items for compost include leaves, pine needles, grass, yard and plant trimmings, fruit and vegetable peels, crushed eggshells, tea bags, coffee grounds and filters, sawdust, cornstalks, paper, wood chips, hay, and straw. The key to composting is to get the right mix of different types of scraps to keep the ratio of carbon and nitrogen in balance to allow for proper decomposition. You also need to keep it moist and rotated to allow for all-over decomposition.

There are many types of composting structures. The simplest method is to create a pile, but you can get elaborate and build a large three-chambered structure. There are bins, barrels, and drums in many home improvement and garden centers and at many online retailers. These bins are great for those who do not have a lot of yard space or who want things to compost quickly.

Composting is a great way to give back to nature and provide healthy nutrient-rich soil for future organic goods to grow. It continues the circle and closes the loop. If you would like to learn more about composting, there are many resources available on the web or in your local library. You could also check out local gardening groups and clubs.

Recycling saves precious resources and reduces energy consumption. Every glass bottle recycled saves enough energy to power a 100-watt light bulb for four hours. By recycling just one aluminum can you can save enough energy to power a television for three hours, and by recycling a one-gallon plastic milk jug you could have enough energy to power a 100-watt light bulb for eleven hours.

Donate What You No Longer Need

If it still has usable life left in it, donate it somewhere. Look for local charity organizations that could use baskets, glass bowls, dishes, tablecloths or whatever you have left over that you don't need to take home with you.

Clothing

Your huge stack of bridal magazines and books can be passed on to a friend or relative who is planning a wedding. Check if your local library would like them. Libraries often accept donations of books and magazines that are in good shape.

Brides in the United States buy more than 7.5 million bridal magazines every year. The average bride will purchase four to six bridal magazines while planning her wedding, and there are countless numbers of free local wedding-related publications to pick up.

Anything else you find you have left over that is nonfood and nonperishable can be donated to local Goodwill or Salvation Army stores. You can even offer items through your local online Freecycle (*www.freecycle.org*) chapter. There might be someone in the group who is getting married and could use 100 glass votive candle holders or fifty glass bowls for floating candles.

CHAPTER 18

Great Green Honeymoons

Now that you've had a spectacularly sustainable wedding, what's next? Why, going on a great green honeymoon, of course! Your honeymoon should be an expression of your values and ideals, just like your wedding. Whether you want high adventure, a romantic retreat, or a tropical paradise, choose wisely and make eco-responsible choices to make your honeymoon as green as your wedding. In this chapter you'll learn all about ecotourism, green lodging possibilities, and green travel.

Ecotourism

You've heard all the catchphrases—ecotourism, green travel, sustainable tourism, green honeymoons. There are many shades of green, from green lodging to eco-adventure trips to volunteer vacations. All of the green travel possibilities are based on the values and ideals of preserving, conserving, and protecting the natural and cultural environment of the locations you visit.

Here are the definitions of several terms you may see while planning your honeymoon:

- **Ecotourism.** This word gets thrown around a lot in the travel industry, and many people try to take advantage of what it really means. The Ecotourism Society defines it as "responsible travel to natural areas which conserves the environment and improves the welfare of the local people." Unless your trip actually helps conserve and preserve, it is not a real ecotour. The money you pay for your lodging and activities should go to the area and the people you visit, not into the pockets of some big corporation.
- **Adventure Travel.** This is another term that is often misrepresented. It actually means an unusual experience that includes some level of risk or difficulty. Adventure travel may or may not be green. It will all depend on what you do and where you go. Backpacking in the mountains, rock climbing, and white water rafting can be green as long as you tread lightly and leave the natural locations unharmed.
- **Nature-Based Tourism.** This is a highly used phrase that can mean anything from camping in nature to viewing penguins from a ship to staying in a lodge in the middle of a tropical jungle. It is not necessarily green, although it could be.
- **Sustainable Tourism.** This is a form of tourism that does not reduce resources and will ensure that future visitors will be able to enjoy the same experience you do. This means you are not disrupting or damaging the wildlife, the natural habitat, or the beauty of the area.
- **Responsible Tourism.** These travels focus on "leave no trace" ethics. You want to preserve nature, not destroy it. A camping trip, hiking tour, even horseback riding along trails is fine as long as you leave the area as you found it.

- **Cultural Tourism.** This is a trip that will have you interacting with and observing the native people of an area. You will be able to learn about their culture and participate in their activities, perhaps even live as they do. In simple ways, you participate in cultural tourism by shopping and eating at the local market or by learning about traditional dress and customs, maybe taking a pottery class from a local artisan.

- **Green Tourism.** This term is often used along with or instead of *sustainable tourism* or *ecotourism*, but it is most accurately described as tourism that includes any facility or activity that operates in an eco-friendly manner. Staying at a bed and breakfast that is powered by solar energy and uses only all-natural cleaning products and serves organic meals can be considered green tourism.

- **Multisport Adventures.** While a sport vacation may not necessarily be green, it certainly can be. Those who operate outdoor recreational activities are often concerned about preserving nature and may have very green business practices.

- **Service Trips/Volunteer Vacations.** These are trips you can take that will have you working for a good cause. The Sierra Club offers hands-on service trips for a wide variety of skill and physical levels. You can build and maintain trails, help archaeologists, repair meadows, and work in parks and wilderness areas. Some volunteer organizations only require you to pay for your transportation, while others require minimal fees for food and lodging. Most programs give you nights off and at least one day a week off to have time to explore the area and take in the sights and local culture.

When you are looking for an area or location for your honeymoon, get the answers to these important questions before you make your choice:

- Will the money you spend go into the local economy? Will it help support the people and the natural elements in that location?
- Is the lodging location or tour company respectful of the local culture and environment? Is it active in conservation efforts?

- Are the activities you plan to do safe for the environment? Will they leave everything as you found it?
- Are you comfortable with the location? Does it represent your values and what you want in a honeymoon?

It all boils down to finding a honeymoon destination and experience that will be enjoyable and memorable for both of you. Before you start planning, discuss what you both want from your honeymoon. Is it romance and relaxation? Pampering and fun in the sun? Frolicking in the beauty of nature? A truly meaningful getaway that is enjoyable for you and helpful to others? Mix it up and blend the ideas together. There is nothing that says you can't have it all, even if you have to go to more than one destination.

Once you decide what kind of trip you want to take, you can start looking for a destination and appropriate lodging.

Green Lodging

There are several types of green lodging available, and many locations are taking steps to become more eco-responsible. Some locations participate in extensive recycling programs, while others have implemented the use of renewable energy sources to provide power. Some have remodeled with environmentally friendly supplies, and other locations use all-natural cleaning products.

Eco-lodges

One green lodging choice is known as an eco-lodge. A real eco-lodge is set in a natural environment that allows visitors to experience the area's authentic local setting, cuisine, community, and culture. It is not really comfort-based, and it may not offer many amenities—possibly not even such creature comforts as electricity or running water. It is all about nature and leaving the smallest impact possible on the natural setting. Some eco-lodges have no electricity, while others use only solar, wind, or other natural energy.

One eco-lodge in North America is the Cree Village Ecolodge (*www .creevillage.com*) on Moose Factory Island in Ontario, Canada. Its owners, the MoCreebec people, took special care to design a facility that could be built with environmentally friendly materials. MoCreebec values and culture are a central part of the lodge.

Eco-resorts

An eco-resort blends the natural elements of an eco-lodge with luxury comforts such as electricity, running water, satellite television, wireless Internet, and even luxury spa treatments and activities. An eco-resort combines sustainability and comfort to create a fabulous green getaway.

The negative effects of tourism are taking a toll on the environment. Beaches are eroding, fragile ecosystems are being threatened, and carbon dioxide emissions from airplanes and automobiles are contributing to global warming. Almost 1 billion tourists travel around the globe every year.

Green Hotels

Green hotels are doing their best to be eco-friendly. Hotels, inns, and bed and breakfasts are earning the green label by incorporating eco-changes into their business. Thyme in the Country (*www.thymeinthe countrybandb.com*) is a bed and breakfast in upstate New York that has organic gardens, solar panels for renewable energy, energy efficient appliances and heating, and natural cleaning products. Its swimming pool is salt-filtered and its land includes a wildlife-filled pond and beautiful meadows where you may see the cow and chickens roaming about. It offers vegetarian and nonvegetarian meals of local, seasonal, and organic foods along with fair trade coffees and teas.

The Inn at Weathersfield (*www.weathersfieldinn.com*) in southeastern Vermont is a country inn that has taken great strides to become green and has succeeded beautifully. In addition to reducing its energy consumption, it composts, recycles, and uses environmentally friendly cleaning products.

Arbor House (*www.arbor-house.com*) in Madison, Wisconsin, uses energy-efficient appliances and nontoxic, organic, and recycled products. It offers organic and natural unbleached linens and organic mattresses.

Finding Eco-Friendly Lodging

What should you be looking for in a green hotel, inn, or B&B? The following are just some ways locations are becoming greener:

- Participating in recycling programs; having recycling stations in guest rooms or where guests have access to them
- Using all-natural cleaning supplies
- Offering organic, local, and fair trade menus
- Installing low-flow, water-conserving showerheads, toilets, and faucets
- Using recycled paper products and paper-free invoicing and billing
- Providing reusable materials instead of single-use disposables
- Providing guests with bicycle rentals or carpooling/company shuttle bus transportation
- Building and remodeling with green materials
- Using low- or no-VOC (volatile organic compound) paint
- Providing bamboo, hemp, or organic cotton linens
- Using energy-efficient appliances, sensors, and timers for thermostats, and CFL bulbs
- Powering with renewable energy such as solar or wind

Many locations are making changes from simple sustainable choices to extensive green renovations. You can find many of these at *www .greenhotels.com.*

Spa Retreats

Would you love to be pampered and taken care of on your honeymoon? Are you looking for a romantic retreat that can be luxurious while still being green? Would you like to nourish your body while caring for the earth? Your dreams are within reach. Green spas are popping up all over the world.

Two of the most popular eco-spas are the Daintree EcoLodge and Spa in Australia and the Maru Spa in the Bora Bora Lagoon Resort in French Polynesia. Closer to home you'll find the Gold Lake Mountain Resort and Spa in Colorado or the Gaia Napa Valley Hotel and Spa in California. All these spas offer state-of-the-art, eco-friendly locations and top-notch green spa treatments.

What can you expect from an eco-spa? An eco-spa should blend the elements of sustainable products, low-impact facilities, and nourishing, natural spa treatments. Products should be vegan, natural, or organic and special treatments can include massages with all-natural organic oils, detoxifying cedar enzyme baths, nonwax or soy-based hair removal, aromatherapy steam rooms, nourishing body wraps, and toxin-free hair and nail care.

Look for fabulous spas at *www.greenspanetwork.org* or *www.spaindex.com*.

Eco-Responsible Travel

Automobiles are among the biggest producers of carbon emissions worldwide, but airplanes are right behind them. How is it possible to see the world without damaging it? There are ways to green your method of transportation and cut down on guilt even when you require an airplane to get to your destination.

To cut down on carbon emissions, cut out the far-away travel. Spend your honeymoon close to home exploring all the great places nearby. Do some research to find the best local restaurants, lodgings, national or state parks, and cultural events. Your dream honeymoon location may be just around the corner.

Airplanes

If flying is your designated mode of transportation, you can purchase carbon offsets or search for an eco-friendly flight company to minimize your negative impact on the environment. British Airways has adopted ways to reduce carbon emissions by increasing fuel efficiency. Other airline companies are purchasing carbon offsets. Many companies are researching new materials and designs to make planes more eco-friendly. The biggest problem is the fuel. Biodiesel for airplanes is showing great promise. In October 2007, Green Flight International successfully completed the world's first jet aircraft flight powered by 100 percent biofuel.

Richard Branson, CEO of Virgin Atlantic Airways, has pledged to invest in researching clean fuel sources. He has partnered with Boeing and the engine maker GE to develop biofuels that can be used in commercial aircraft. They plan to test soy, newspapers, and vegetable-based biofuels in Boeing aircraft.

FACT

The aviation industry is responsible for releasing about 572 million tons of carbon dioxide into the atmosphere annually. That equals around 2 percent of total global carbon emissions. The European Union plans to include the industry in its effort to reduce carbon dioxide emissions beginning in 2011; industries such as steel and power generators are already required to reduce their emissions.

Trains

Train travel is much more eco-friendly than air travel—taking a train causes ten times less damage than taking an airplane, according to Greenpeace. Another one of Branson's companies, Virgin Trains, is now offering green train travel options in Europe. It offers sustainable and recycled materials in its trains.

A train trip might be the eco-way to go. Just make sure that if the trip is a long one you book a private room. You wouldn't want to spend a couple days of your honeymoon in public seats without any quality alone time.

Cruise Ships

Cruise ships, no matter how romantic they may appear, are extremely bad polluters. Ships dump enormous amounts of waste into the oceans every day. There are more than 200 commercial cruise ships that carry millions of passengers around the world. In just one day, a typical cruise ship can generate 25,000 gallons of sewage from toilets; 143,000 gallons of sewage from sinks, galleys, and showers; more than seven tons of garbage and solid waste; 15 gallons of toxic chemicals; and 7,000 gallons of oily bilge water. Learn more about the environmentally hazardous ways of cruise ships at Oceana (*www.oceana.org*) and the Bluewater Network (*www.bluewaternetwork.org*).

If you are thinking about taking a cruise for your honeymoon, you might want to think again, or search for one that is compliant with eco-friendly practices, such as Carnival Cruise Lines, Costa Cruises, or Cruise North Expeditions.

Green Travel Tips

There are many ways to green your travel even if your transportation or location is not particularly green. From purchasing carbon credits to offset air travel to picking up trash in tourist locations, you can make your honeymoon an eco-trip.

To make sure you're not wasting any resources, implement the following tips:

Green Your Home
- Turn off your air conditioner or heater, or put it on the lowest setting possible if you have animals or plants to protect.
- Turn your water heater all the way down.
- Unplug all of your appliances that will not be in operation while you are gone—televisions, cable boxes, stereos, microwaves, toasters, computers, printers, and so on.
- If you have a newspaper subscription, set it to vacation.

- Get programmable lighting for a few lights or lamps. This keeps your house from looking deserted and is much more economical than leaving your lights on the entire time.
- Pack your own toiletries and leave the complimentary guest toiletries in your hotel room unopened.

Green Your Lodging
- Let your lodging location know that your sheets do not have to be changed every day.
- Keep track of your towel and hang it up to dry; you can reuse it a couple of times before sending it to the laundry.
- Turn off all the lights, appliances, and air conditioning or heat when you leave your room to conserve energy.
- Reduce the length of your showers to preserve water.
- Participate in the area recycling program and make sure all waste is disposed of properly.
- Don't take unnecessary paper products, return newspapers to the lobby, and put brochures and maps back on the racks when you are finished with them.
- Go paperless for tickets and billing.
- Avoid room service or carry-out options; at the very least, avoid Styrofoam containers and ask for paper or aluminum foil.

Green Your Vacation Habits
- Do not purchase products such as tortoise shell, ivory, animal skins, or feathers. They may be from endangered species or killed specifically for tourist souvenirs. Also avoid starfish and turtle shells; even sea shells are questionable.
- Take photographs to keep as memories. Do not take sand, shells, or other natural souvenirs from natural or historical locations. If you must have a memento, purchase something socially and environmentally responsible in a gift shop, such as something made by a local artist.
- Never litter. Leave the place cleaner than you found it. If you see trash, pick it up and dispose of it properly.
- Support local conservation programs.

- Instead of renting a car, travel the area by public transportation or bicycle or walk to locations that are close by. If you must use a motor vehicle, see if the hotel offers a van or transportation services that will shuttle guests to locations. If you must rent a car, choose a small fuel-economic one or a hybrid.

- Support the local economy. Eat in small restaurants, delis, and open cafes and shop in small, locally owned shops and stores. Avoid chain stores and corporate places like McDonalds that tend to pop up all over the world in large tourist areas.

- Treat nature with respect. When hiking, bicycling, or walking, always stay on the trails and pathways. Stay away from wildlife and don't try to feed animals.

- When diving or snorkeling, do not touch coral reefs, stir up sediment, or touch any of the underwater plants or creatures.

- Respect the local people. If they speak another language, try learning a few words and phrases before you go on your trip. At least make an effort to know the basics so you can communicate more easily.

The best thing for you to remember on your trip is an old saying: "Take nothing but photographs and leave nothing but footprints."

CHAPTER 19

Staying Green after the Honeymoon Is Over

Now that you have had a fabulous green wedding and a great green honeymoon, what's next? Why, continuing on the green path, of course! In this chapter you'll learn how to take everything you learned while planning your green wedding and apply it in your everyday eco-living choices. Continue to reduce, reuse, and recycle and continue to purchase recycled and recyclable products that are earth-friendly and safe. Live green, shop green, and be actively green.

Continuing on the Green Path

Being green is not an all-or-nothing endeavor. Just like planning your wedding, every little bit counts and adds up. It is a process, a way to slowly evolve. No one expects you to throw out all of your old stuff and buy all new eco-friendly materials. In fact, that really defeats the purpose because it is wasteful and sends perfectly good stuff off to the landfill.

If everyone in the world consumed resources and energy the way the average American does, at least four additional planets worth of resources would be needed to support the earth's 6 billion residents. The average North American consumes ten times as much as the average person in China and thirty times as much as the average person in India.

No one expects you to change your ways overnight, but by being conscious of your actions and making responsible choices, you are well on your way to living a greener life. One day being green won't even be a conscious decision; it'll be just another thing you do naturally every day.

Simple Ways to Incorporate Green Living

Many people live green and they don't even know it. They conserve resources and save energy as a natural way of life. Living a green life does not have to be complicated; it can actually be quite easy, even fun.

Some simple ways to include green living in your everyday life are:

- Use reusable cloth bags when shopping instead of getting disposable plastic or paper bags every time.
- Get your name taken off direct mail advertising lists.
- Ride a bicycle or walk to nearby locations instead of taking your car.
- Carpool or take public transportation to reduce carbon emissions.

- Plant a tree. Even better, plant a whole orchard. Make it count even more by planting trees that produce food, such as apple trees or even nut-bearing trees.
- Give back to nature by planting a garden and making your yard wildlife-friendly.
- Get involved in your community, volunteer, and join local activist groups that share your beliefs.
- Purchase a reusable water bottle, such as a Sigg, instead of purchasing expensive bottled water.
- Purchase recycled and tree-free paper products.
- Refill your ink cartridges a couple of times before recycling them.
- Properly dispose of all waste.
- Recycle everything that you can.
- Go digital; be as digital as possible by taking and storing photos digitally and downloading songs, TV shows, and movies instead of buying DVDs and CDs.
- Avoid disposable products. Use reusable bags, towels, and plates instead. If you must get disposable products, get items made from postconsumer waste recycled fibers and/or biodegradable/compostable products that you will put in your compost.

The most effective ways to be green are through energy and resource conservation. Save energy with these easy habits:

- Install compact fluorescent lights (CFLs). These bulbs last six to ten times longer than incandescent bulbs and use much less energy, saving you money as well.
- Switch to LED lights for flashlights and strands of lighting such as Christmas lights and other decorative lighting. This can save you a bundle because they use so much less energy and last more than twenty years, and you don't have to worry about them heating up and causing a fire.
- Unplug appliances and gadgets when you aren't using them. They still drain electricity even when they're off. Turn off power strips when you aren't around.

- Fix all leaky faucets and pipes. This will save water and cut costs on your bills.
- Install low-flow showerheads and faucets and dual-flush water conserving toilets. The initial investment is minimal and will save you a lot in the long run.
- Invest in rechargeable batteries.
- Wear clothing more than once before washing it. Only do laundry when you have a full load.
- Only run the dishwasher when you have a full load.
- Wash clothing in cold water instead of hot.
- Purchase Energy Star appliances.
- Consider going solar.

The United States Postal Service delivers more than 87 billion pieces of direct mail every year. Take your name off lists, opt out of credit offers, and get only the catalogs you actually want to reduce your paper waste. Take care to recycle the unwanted items that still find their way to your mailbox. For more information, visit *www.dmachoice.org*.

There are so many ways to live a simple, green, sustainable life. If you would like more ideas and ways to live a green life, visit the numerous websites devoted to green living. Start with *www.idealbite.com* and its fantastic tip library. Additional resources include *www.greenlivingjournal.com* and *www.greenlivingonline.com*.

Shop Green

People in the United States are consumed with the need to have stuff. More stuff, new stuff, the latest stuff—and it all piles up to be discarded as fast as it was purchased. We have been labeled the disposable society.

No More Gratuitous Shopping

The key to green shopping is to only purchase what is really needed and to buy things that last. Don't purchase ten pairs of shoes when one black pair will coordinate nicely with the majority of your outfits. Don't buy a new iPod just because a newer model came out when the one you have works perfectly fine. By all means, do not buy something just because it has been labeled green.

FACT

According to Seventh Generation, if every household in the United States replaced just one box of facial tissues with 100 percent recycled ones, 87,700 trees and 31 million gallons of water would be saved. Seventh Generation (*www.seventhgeneration.com*) offers a variety of environmentally friendly cleaning and household products.

There is no reason to rip up your perfectly good hardwood flooring and replace it with all new bamboo or cork or get rid of your comfy couch just to buy an expensive and trendy hemp sofa. You don't have to throw all your old clothes out and buy new organic cotton, hemp, or bamboo versions, either. Throwing perfectly good stuff away is not very green. It's a big waste of resources, not to mention money, which also seems to be a dwindling resource for many people.

Don't let commercial consumerism and all the green hype push you into buying things you don't need. If you do need new stuff, then that's okay, and definitely go for the green choices when you do need to purchase new things. All-natural organic cotton blankets, bamboo sheets, and hemp shower curtains are all better choices than the regular synthetic, chemical-laden ones that wouldn't last as long anyway.

Always remember to try to buy items that are recycled, recyclable, organic, fair trade, and made from sustainable material. Take your reusable bags shopping with you and support local businesses that are doing good, green things.

Buying Used

The old saying about one person's trash being another person's treasure is absolutely true. If you've never been one to hit yard sales or resale shops, now might be the time to try it. Look at things from multiple angles. Envision an object as something else with totally different potential uses. For instance, don't look at an old metal bucket as just a bucket; look at it as a tote for your gardening tools or as a chic ice bucket to chill a bottle of wine in.

That old wooden box or crate would make a great storage cubby for your books or old records. That boring old laundry tub or chipped bathtub in the corner of the thrift shop could be turned into an amazing flower bed for your garden. That pile of mismatched silverware could be turned into jewelry, wind chimes, plant stakes, garden tools, or a unique sculpture.

The one thing you shouldn't buy used is an old appliance. New models are often worth the investment because they are made to be energy efficient. Old ones will suck up energy and might break down with no warranty to insure them. Look for Energy Star appliances to know you are getting true energy savings.

Wood furniture (real wood, not pressed junk) is always a great find. It should never end up in the dump, but, sadly, it often does. If it is structurally sound, it is quite easy to give wood a facelift by simply refinishing it and adding some updated hardware. The good news is that there are now environmentally friendly solvents, paint strippers, stains, paints, and finishes that make refinishing and reusing old wood furniture doubly green. If you find a piece that is not in good condition, that's still no reason to consign it to the junkyard. If you or someone you know is pretty good with wood, most repairs can be quite easy and sometimes as simple as replacing a screw, nail, or hinge or re-gluing something.

One of the big benefits of buying used is that it is a way to make sure you have something the majority of the population does not. If you go into an antique store and buy an old table, you will wind up with a unique piece of furniture. On the other hand, if you choose to buy your table from a regular furniture store, many people in your area might have the same mass produced object.

Take a day and hit the resale trail. Go antiquing and shop at all the resale, thrift, and consignment shops in your area. Stop by any yard or garage sales you come across along the way. Think of it as a treasure hunt. Go as a couple, with your best friend, or even your mom. Have fun, pack a picnic, and enjoy yourself. You might get lucky, hit the jackpot, and find a true treasure. At the very least, you'll get out of the house and spend some quality time with someone you care about.

Green Activities

The best way to participate in a green activity is to step outside. Enjoy the fresh air and the natural beauty of the world. Visit your local park, go for a hike, ride your bike along a bike trail, and take part in new experiences. The world is out there waiting to be explored and you can start in your own backyard.

It doesn't matter if you live in a city or out in the country, chances are there is a lot of territory close by that you have not explored. When was the last time you had a picnic in the park? Took a walk on the beach? Visited the local museum, art gallery, or zoo?

FACT

One study found that 84 percent of participants feel that "it is a moral obligation" to care for the environment. Seventy-eight percent said they "would be willing to make a lifestyle change for the good of the environment." The difficulty in separating facts from hype makes it hard for some people to get to the root of the problem and make a solid commitment.

Make it a point to do something new or unusual every day or every weekend. Make a list of all the local places you and your honey should check out. Visit the farmer's market and stock up on locally grown organic produce. Check out all the little art galleries and boutiques along Main Street and support the local artisans and shop owners. Try the new organic deli where you keep meaning to stop for lunch but haven't had the time. Take the time to unwind, unplug, and just simply be. Simplify your life for at least one day a week. Today's world is so full of hustle and bustle that many people never get around to doing the things they really want to do.

Eco-Activism

By choosing to green your lifestyle, you are already participating in activism. You are going against the grain and making choices that have an impact on the world. In addition to choosing eco-friendly products and reducing, reusing, and recycling, you can help make a difference in many other ways as well.

Eco-activism is a great way to really get involved with what matters. You can make your voice heard and really make a difference in the world. When you think of activism, you may have visions of hippies with peace symbols, or picket signs and sit-down strikes. While those are all powerful ways of making a point, no one is asking you to chain yourself to a tree or set up a picket line. No tie-dyed clothes or peace symbols need be involved, either.

When you decide to become actively involved in a cause, the first thing you want to do is some homework. Research everything you can on the topic, from all points of view, and get the facts. The biggest downfall in activism is not knowing the facts. That can knock the wind right out of a petition or campaign in no time.

Next, you need to decide how active you want to become. Are there already organizations working hard and making a difference that you can join, or should you start your own organization? Do you want to work alone or get others involved?

If you choose to work alone or with your significant other, you can start by letter writing. Send letters to your elected representatives and write to any companies or businesses that are part of the problem. If there is a business selling unsafe children's products, write to them and request that they change their products and adopt stricter safety standards. You can also start boycotts of products and companies and create petitions.

The web can be a powerful tool in activism. You can create websites and public personas on sites such as MySpace and Facebook. You can even start your own online petition at *www.thepetitionsite.com*.

If you would like to learn more about activism, check out *www.gender watchers.org/Activist.htm*. The site is geared toward feminist activism, but all the information and links can be modified for any cause you feel strongly about.

If you simply want to contribute as much as you can without going too far out of your way, try e-mail activism, also known as armchair activism. There are sites that offer prewritten letters and already have all the information you need to send the letters to local political figures; all you have to do is personalize it with your name, address, and e-mail address. This is the easiest way to make your voice heard, although it is not necessarily the most effective. Many legislators receive so much e-mail correspondence that they do not read it themselves. Some do not accept e-mail correspondence from their constituents or employ spam filters that may make it difficult for your e-mail to get through.

Many sites offer armchair activism: *www.greenpeace.org, http://action .sierraclub.org, www.nwf.org* (National Wildlife Federation), *www .worldwildlife.org, www.centerforfoodsafety.org, www.foe.org* (Friends of the Earth), *www.wilderness.org, www.forests.org, www.thecampaign.org*, and *www.aspca.org* offer ways to get involved online. You can sign petitions, send e-mails, and even get help writing letters to your local newspaper editor and political figures. However little or much you get involved, just one voice or one signature can make a difference.

Thinking About a Baby?

If you are thinking about having a baby any time in the future, going green is that much more important. Even if you don't plan to have children for a few years, you can start greening your world now to make it a better, more eco-friendly environment for when your little bundle of joy does arrive.

Keeping Everyone Safe and Healthy

Environmental pollutants can be very hazardous to your baby's health, long before it is ever born. A study conducted by the Environmental Working Group in 2004 found 287 different chemicals in randomly tested umbilical cord blood. The parents of these children did not work with chemicals or in any career that involved exposure to various chemicals. Out of the 287 chemicals found, 180 are known carcinogens, 217 are toxic to the brain and nervous system, and 208 cause birth defects or abnormal development.

ALERT!

You may want to have your tap water tested for lead, pesticide residues, and other chemicals that may be lurking in your drinking water. Contact the EPA's Safe Drinking Water Hotline at 1-800-426-4791 or online at *www.epa.gov/safewater* or order a do-it-yourself kit at *www.discovertesting.com*.

Chemical exposures that occur while a baby is in the womb or during infancy can be much more harmful than exposures that occur later in life. Therefore, it is best to minimize exposure to environmental pollution as much as possible and as early as possible. This means cutting down on your own exposure to all toxins and chemicals while you are trying to get pregnant and especially during pregnancy. Eating organic foods minimizes your risk of coming into contact with pesticides. Other things you should avoid include toxic pesticides, harsh cleaning chemicals, paint fumes, tobacco smoke, kerosene heaters or other heating stoves that give off a lot of fumes or smoke, paint fumes, and solvents such as paint thinners. If you must paint, use low- to no-VOC paints. You should also avoid exposure to mercury, lead acetate, parabens, and phthalates (all of which can be found in many things including beauty products). For a helpful web guide for green pregnancies, visit *www.fitpregnancy.com/goinggreen*.

Phthalates

Right now there is also a large controversy surrounding the use of plastics because of phthalates. Phthalates have been linked to cancer, endocrine disruption, birth defects, reproductive problems in men, and thyroid malfunction. Baby boys and pregnant women have been identified as the two groups that are most vulnerable to the effects of phthalates.

FACT

According to the Environmental Working Group, 84 percent of the U.S. population is contaminated with at least six different phthalates. Phthalates have been found in baby bottles, plastic food containers, toys, and bath and body products. People can be exposed through inhalation, ingestion, skin absorption, and even intravenously from medical devices.

To reduce your exposure to phthalates, reduce the amount of plastics that you use. Avoid PVC (polyvinylchloride) products. Make sure the toys and furniture you purchase are PVC free. Do not microwave plastic food containers or baby bottles. Instead, use microwave-safe glass containers to heat food, milk, and formula. Look for baby bottles that are made with polyethylene (#2 or #4) or polypropylene (#5) or opt for old-fashioned glass bottles.

Getting the Nursery Ready

If you want to redo the nursery, consider natural flooring such as real hardwood or cork. If you want carpeting, look for low-VOC carpets such as those that carry the Green Label Plus logo, or look for natural carpeting made from wool, jute, or sisal. Regular carpeting contains a lot of chemicals.

While you plan the nursery, look for natural bedding such as organic cotton and wool blankets, organic cotton, bamboo or hemp comforters, and sheets and mattresses made from organic cotton or organic all-natural rubber stuffing. Also consider using natural cloth diapers or at least unbleached disposable diapers and wipes. Look into organic clothing for the baby, too.

Bringing Baby Home

Once the baby is born, be careful what you rub on his bottom. Popular baby care products by big brands have been found to contain all kinds of chemicals including parabens, phthalates, petroleum by-products, dyes, and fragrances. It all sounds pretty scary, as if you don't have enough to worry about living in this world, but by being informed ahead of time you can prepare yourself and your personal environment to create the best and safest possible nest for a happy, healthy family. If green living has been a part of your life for a long time, making sure you have a happy, healthy, green pregnancy will be a natural and easy thing for you to do. If the green life is new to you, it may be a little more difficult at first, but you don't have to stress about it or do everything all at once.

You can slowly incorporate green ways and products into your life and make choices that are best for you. Every little bit counts. If you can't afford an all-natural mattress but you went for the organic cotton crib set, that is fabulous. It doesn't have to be all or nothing.

Your baby will be quite happy and satisfied with having parents who love and care for her, and won't complain that everything isn't organic or all natural—at least, not until she's a teenager.

CHAPTER 20

Your Green Home: Make Your Nest Eco-Friendly

Your home is your hideaway, your safe haven, a place to relax and recuperate from the stress of daily life. It is where you should be the most comfortable—and the most green. You want it to be the safest, most eco-friendly environment that it can be. Whether you are planning to design a green home from the ground up or make an existing home a green haven, this chapter will help you learn how to feather your nest in the most eco-friendly ways.

Green Homes

The average person spends up to 80 percent of his time indoors, and a big part of that is in his own home. The problem with that is that indoor air can be more than ten times more polluted than outdoor air. Paint, glue, and all the other chemicals used to build a home can result in toxic fumes filling your indoor air, especially in newly built or newly remodeled homes.

Green homes and green building materials are becoming quite popular and easier than ever to come by. In some areas entire green subdivisions have been created. Houses are being remodeled and put on the green market. Real estate agents are becoming eco-agents specializing in the sale of green homes.

ALERT!

Insulating concrete foam is said to lower energy costs and consumption by as much as 40 percent. A geothermal system also promises to lower heating costs by as much as 50 percent and cooling costs by as much as 60 percent depending on your energy source.

Build It Green

It takes a lot to build any home, but building a green home takes a lot of planning and research. You need to search particularly hard to find the best materials and the best person to do the job. If you are interested in having a green home built, hire experts in the field, not someone who says "Yeah, I think I can do it." Work closely with the people you do hire to make sure that you all agree on what's green and what isn't.

Many people think that building green is more expensive than building a regular home, but the truth is that if you hire the right people it can actually be cheaper. If you use recycled, reclaimed, or salvaged materials that are located or made locally, you'll cut down on the costly shipping charges and expensive additions that usually come with new products.

If you are in the market to build a green home, *Building Green: A Complete How-To Guide to Alternative Building Methods* by Clarke Snell and Tim Callahan is a very in-depth book that can help you envision and build your green dream home. Some great websites to consult are *www .greenhomeguide.org*, *www.buildinggreen.com*, and *www.greenhomebuild ing.com*. All three are full of information about building green homes.

Basic Principles of a Green Home

According to *www.greenhomeguide.com*, in addition to being environmentally friendly, a green home is cost-efficient and healthier than a regular home. Green homes use up to 40 percent less energy and 50 percent less water than regular homes, and the construction generates 50 to 90 percent less construction waste. Most green homes are constructed using salvaged and recycled materials or rapidly renewable materials such as bamboo, hemp, and soybean products. Green homes are healthier because they are made with nontoxic materials and use natural ventilation.

Make It Green

If you just want to make your existing environment a little more eco-friendly, check out Danny Seo's *Conscious Style Home: Eco-Friendly Living for the 21st Century*. This is a great book that will help you get simply green. Another very detailed green home book is *Eco-Renovation: The Ecological Home Improvement Guide* by Edward Harland.

Green guru Danny Seo also has several other books that can be useful in other areas of your life; *Simply Green Giving* and *Simply Green Parties* may be helpful to you during your green wedding planning. Some of his simple, sustainable ideas can be modified and used for many different wedding elements.

If you are looking to do a green renovation of your kitchen, check out *Good Green Kitchens: The Ultimate Resource for Creating a Beautiful, Healthy, Eco-Friendly Kitchen* by Jennifer Roberts. This book has everything—flooring, countertops, cabinets, paint, and energy-efficient lighting and appliances. This book addresses some of the main elements that can turn your kitchen green: tankless water heaters, low- and no-VOC paint, energy efficient appliances, fluorescent lighting, high performance windows, skylights, good insulation, and reclaimed or FSC-certified wood products.

Ways to make an existing home green are:

- Insulate, install radiant heat barriers in your attic or under your roof, and caulk all leaks. This will keep heat and air from escaping, making your home energy efficient. Energy efficiency is the number-one attribute of a green home.
- Get a programmable thermostat. Try to keep it at 78°F or higher in the summer and 62°F or lower in the winter for maximum energy savings.
- Switch to CFLs. On average, if you switch twenty bulbs in your home to CFLs you can save around $270 a year. In addition, the bulbs last a long time and can save you hundreds more dollars over their lifetimes. That may not sound like much, but when you figure in all your other green home improvements like a programmable thermostat and sealing up energy leaks and cracks, you can end up saving a lot.
- Install new energy-efficient windows. At the very least, caulk and seal around your existing windows, install screens, and make sure you have no broken windows or cracks. Use good window coverings that offer extra insulation.
- Keep heating and cooling systems tuned up and change filters regularly; use HEPA filters for the best air quality.
- When it's time to replace appliances, choose Energy Star models for maximum energy conservation.
- Reduce your water use by installing aerators on all your sink faucets and switch to low-flow showerheads. Get dual-flush toilets to conserve water.
- Switch to green power. Check with your local energy provider about green energy sources.
- Go solar. Either passively or actively take advantage of the energy the sun provides.
- Plant trees and native plants around your home to provide natural insulation from the outside.

- When you do any remodeling projects, opt for low- to no-VOC products: paint, stains, wood finishes, and even carpeting. Switch to healthy, natural cleaning products.

There are many ways to make your home greener, from simple green elements that add a bit of eco-charm to extensive remodeling that takes you to all-out greendom.

Decorate It Green

Whether you are building a new green home or making an existing home more eco-friendly, you'll want to decorate in green ways as well. You wouldn't want to go to all the trouble to make it thoroughly green only to cover it in paint that's filled with harmful VOCs and synthetic carpet filled with formaldehyde, chloroform, and other harmful petrochemicals.

ALERT!

The American Council for an Energy-Efficient Economy estimates that every year in the United States about $13 billion worth of energy escapes through holes and cracks in residential buildings and homes. By properly sealing up energy leaks, a homeowner can save up to 20 percent on heating and cooling costs. Start by sealing up windows, doors, and cracks and installing proper insulation.

Some great green flooring options are:

- **Reclaimed wood.** It can come from a variety of places: old barns, railroads, or salvaged wood floors. This is a great option because it puts the wood to good use without much reprocessing. Reclaimed wood can offer beautiful coloring, aged patinas, and sometimes an antique finish.
- **FSC-certified wood.** The FSC certifies that this wood has been harvested in ecologically sound ways and that old growth forests are left intact.

- **Cork.** Cork is rising in popularity as flooring material because of its natural and renewable qualities. Cork floors are soft yet durable and provide antimicrobial, fire-resistant, and pest-resistant flooring.
- **Bamboo.** Bamboo flooring has become very popular because it is a rapidly renewable resource and naturally beautiful.
- **Sisal rugs and carpeting.** Sisal is a large leafy plant that's grown all over the world. The pulp is turned into fibers that are woven into coarse-textured rugs and carpeting. Sisal is very strong and durable and resistant to natural elements.
- **Hemp.** Industrial hemp can be woven into strong fabric for beautiful and durable rugs.
- **Jute.** Jute has always been a strong and durable product used in the industrial world for burlap bags, cords, ropes, and mats, yet it also is a nice choice for area rugs.
- **Concrete.** Highly renewable and extremely durable, concrete floors have come a long way. Today they can be polished smooth, painted, or acid-treated to give them unique looks. Concrete is energy efficient and long lasting, but it isn't for everyone. Some people find it too cold and much too hard, and it's especially tough for little ones who can and will fall a lot.
- **Terra cotta.** Just like your flower pots, terra cotta can be used to create tile flooring. Terra cotta—baked clay—is commonly used in warmer climates because it naturally stays cool.
- **Recycled carpet.** Today old carpet can be recycled into new carpet, and it can be an economically sound choice. There is also carpeting made from recycled plastic bottles.
- **Natural, organic carpet.** If you live in a colder climate or have children, nothing beats the warmth and softness of carpet, yet you can gladly live without the chemical odors and toxic materials in new carpeting. Choose natural carpeting made from organic cotton and wool and make sure to pair it with eco-friendly carpet padding and a green, no-VOC glue.
- **Recycled tile.** Tile flooring is being made out of many recycled materials, from recycled vinyl to recycled glass. If you are looking for something unusual and eco-friendly, a glass tiled floor may be the thing.

- **Linoleum.** Real linoleum, not vinyl, is considered to be a renewable resource.

The same materials that are used for eco-responsible flooring can be used in other areas of your home as well. Reclaimed and responsible wood can be used for cabinets and furniture; recycled glass, concrete, or terra cotta tiles for countertops; hemp fabrics for curtains, furniture coverings, sheets, and blankets; and bamboo for everything from sheets to kitchen utensils. Visit local stores and check out the many online retailers that offer sustainable furnishings and great green kitchen items such as Real Goods (*www.realgoods.com*), Greenfeet (*www.greenfeet.com*), Rawganique (*www.rawganique.com*), Green Nest (*www.greennest.com*), and Natural Spaces (*www.naturalspaces.com*).

Sustainable Furnishings

More than 50 percent of the world's forests are gone. When you shop for furniture for your eco-friendly nest, look for furnishings that are made from sustainable resources. You can still buy wood, but look for reclaimed or recycled wood products or at least wood that is FSC-certified. The greenest wood furniture is that which is reclaimed and locally made. Other sustainable furniture options include bamboo, metal, recycled materials, and old furniture that you can renew with a fresh coat of paint or stain.

Improve your indoor air by using natural, healthier choices such as houseplants. Try rock salt lamps, which are negative ion generators that leave you feeling refreshed and energized. Use HEPA filters in your heating and cooling systems and in your vacuum cleaner to remove dust, allergens, mold spores, and other particles from your air. Use a diffuser with all-natural essential oils.

There are many online retailers that offer sustainable furnishing and home products such as daiseye (*www.daiseye.com*), A Natural Home (*www.anaturalhome.com*), Green Logic (*www.greenlogic.com*), GreenSage (*www.greensage.com*), and Green Living (*www.green-living.com*).

Eco-Energy

When you hear the term *green energy* or *eco-energy*, that means the power is supplied in whole or in part from renewable energy resources such as solar, wind, geothermal, or hydropower or sometimes by a combination of them. By using green energy sources you can reduce the need for fossil fuel resources such as coal and natural gas.

Across the United States many energy companies are adding green energy options, so you can purchase green energy straight from your utility supplier. You may also have the option of purchasing Renewable Energy Certificates, also known as green tags, tradable renewable certificates, and green energy certificates. These are certificates that represent the environmental attributes of power produced by renewable energy sources. Green-e is a program that certifies and verifies renewable energy and greenhouse gas reductions in the retail market. Visit *www.green-e.org* to learn about green energy and its sources and to see if you have any local providers of eco-energy.

FACT

By installing a programmable thermostat to turn your heat or air conditioning down when you are sleeping and when you are away from home, you can save at least $100 on annual heating and cooling costs; usually it can save you much more.

You have other options when it comes to green energy, even if you do not have access through a local supplier. You can live off the grid by creating and using your own electricity. The two best sources for individual home use are solar and wind, solar being the most popular and readily accessible. Sometimes you may even produce more power than what your household uses and you will be able to sell it to the electrical company. This is called net metering or sometimes dual metering.

You can create your own energy by setting up a solar energy system for your home. There are two types of solar energy: passive and active.

Passive solar power incorporates energy-efficient design with the use of windows, skylights, roof lights, and proper insulation to make use of the natural energy the sun provides. Simple ways anyone can use passive solar energy are by opening your curtains and blinds during the day to let in heat and light and by closing the curtains at night to keep all the heat in. Combined with good insulation and radiant barriers in your roof, you can effectively conserve energy and keep your home cool in the summer and warm in the winter. There are many design elements and materials that can make the use of passive solar energy even more effective, including using thermal mass, solar slabs, and high tech windows.

Active solar power involves actively collecting solar energy and converting it into usable energy. Solar power can be collected through two main methods: fluid collectors and photovoltaic cells. Fluid collectors use solar power to heat and circulate fluid for energy. The most commonly used form is through photovoltaic cells. Photovoltaic cells can be as small and simple as those on a solar garden light or as complicated as a whole system set up on your home. You can install solar systems that control only one thing in your home (such as your water pump or water heating system), multiple items, or the entire home.

You can even incorporate the use of solar power for simpler elements such as battery chargers, outdoor lighting, even cooking. Gaiam (*www.gaiam.com*) has solar cooking stoves available at its web store. For detailed information about solar power, check out *Solar Living Sourcebook: Your Complete Guide to Renewable Energy Technologies and Sustainable Living* by John Schaeffer. It has information about all aspects of green buildings, including green techniques and building supplies, though it really focuses on the technical side of renewable energy. It is full of highly detailed sections about solar, wind, and hydro power and how it should be installed in your home.

Green Cleaning

Commercial cleaning products often contain many chemicals that are very harmful. Prolonged exposure can cause many health problems. You can be exposed to harmful chemicals every day from the moment you wake up until the time you go to sleep and, depending on indoor air quality, sometimes even while you sleep. Studies show that our bodies and our bloodstreams are filled with hundreds and thousands of chemical residues. Numerous studies have pointed out that chemical exposures do contribute to rising rates of chronic diseases and infertility.

ALERT!

Green cleaning products protect everyone in your household from coming into contact with dangerous substances. They are one step to ensure that your family remains healthy and safe. They also accomplish everything conventional cleaning products do—they sanitize your living space and make it more aesthetically pleasing.

You can lessen the amount of toxic chemicals you are exposed to every day just by changing how you clean your home and what you use to clean it. There are many harmful chemicals in conventional cleaning products. Some ingredients may be mildly irritating, while others are known carcinogens. Some of the most harmful ingredients to watch out for are the following:

- **Chlorine bleach** can be fatal when inhaled or swallowed and can cause severe damage to skin, eyes, and other membranes. It is a respiratory irritant that can cause severe coughing, shortness of breath, and pulmonary edema. In other countries it has been banned and outlawed from use.
- **Ammonia** is listed as a toxic chemical on the EPA's community right-to-know list. Ammonia is in many window cleaners and metal polishes.
- **Chloroform** is sometimes found in fabric softeners. It is a neurotoxin that can damage the central nervous system.

- **Dioxin** may be in any products labeled *antibacterial* or *antimicrobial*. Dioxin has been linked to cancer, birth defects, birth deformities, and damage to immune systems, reproductive systems, and respiratory systems. The antibacterial Triclosan, which is found in many antibacterial soaps, can turn into dioxin.
- **Formaldehyde** has been a known human carcinogen for a long time, but it is still used in many products such as air fresheners, disinfectants, industrial glues, and spray starches. Exposure to formaldehyde can cause skin allergies, asthma attacks, and other breathing difficulties.
- **Hydrochloric acid** can cause burning of the skin and other tissues that can result in permanent scarring. This hazardous material can be found in toilet bowl cleaners, metal cleaners, oven cleaners, and rust removers.
- **Naphthalene** is a suspected carcinogen that can cause eye and skin irritation, kidney damage, and central nervous system damage. It can be found in some mothballs, air fresheners, deodorizers, toilet cleaners, and carpet cleaners.

Skip the toxic chemicals that you can't pronounce and go for natural cleaners that you can make from common ingredients in your kitchen. Basic ingredients for green cleaning include baking soda, distilled white vinegar, lemon juice, hydrogen peroxide, table salt, and essential oils. You don't need toxic cleaners to get your home clean or disinfected. Many essential oils have natural disinfectant properties; some are even antibacterial and antimicrobial. Some of the best are tea tree oil, eucalyptus oil, basil, cloves, thyme, sage, oregano, and rosewood. Oregano, thyme, and rosewood have been proven to destroy strep pneumonia cells, and essential oils have been used effectively to kill the MRSA virus.

Simple, Natural Cleaning Solutions
- Add 2 tablespoons of baking soda to dishwashing soap to cut through grease.
- Clean and disinfect cutting boards with a paste made from 1 tablespoon each of baking soda, salt, and water.
- Add ½ cup of baking soda to laundry to whiten whites and brighten colors.

- Polish silver jewelry with a paste made from ¼ cup baking soda and 2 tablespoons of water.
- Remove blood from fabric by gently dabbing with a cotton ball or cotton swab of hydrogen peroxide on the spot.
- Remove coffee or chocolate from fabric by mixing 1 teaspoon of white vinegar and one quart of cold water. Sponge on, then wash as usual.
- Remove ink from fabric by mixing cream of tartar and lemon juice to form a paste and applying it to the stain. Let it sit for an hour, then rinse and wash as usual.
- Remove grease by mixing baking soda and water or cornstarch and water to form a paste. Cover the spot, let it dry, and brush off.
- Ketchup can be used to clean brass and copper.
- Table salt can remove rust. Combine it with lemon juice to clean copper. Mix salt with vinegar to clean brass. Salt also makes great scouring powders.
- Lemon juice can be used for cleaning many things. It is a natural odor eliminator and can be combined with many other ingredients.

If you don't want to make your own cleaning supplies but still would like natural solutions, there are several companies that make wonderful, safe, and effective cleaning supplies. Seventh Generation (*www.seventh generation.com*), Bi-O-Kleen (*www.biokleen.com*), and Earth Friendly Products (*www.ecos.com*) are a few recommended brands. They can be purchased at many natural and health food stores and even in some supermarkets. They can also be purchased at many online retailers such as Drugstore.com (*www.drugstore.com*) and Kokopelli's Green Market (*www .kokogm.com*). If you would like to learn more about natural cleaning check out *Green This! Greening Your Cleaning* by Deirdre Imus.

Natural Pest Control

Toxic chemicals in pesticides are causing a great deal of harm to the environment and to everyone exposed to them. In addition to purchasing organic foods and other organic materials, you should avoid the use of toxic pesticides in and around your home. The best way to deal with bugs is to avoid having them to begin with. IPM (integrated pest management) is a way to try to stop pest problems before they occur. You can avoid many pest infestations by maintaining a clean and well-kept home. This is why you should always seal cracks, install screens on windows and doors, repair ripped screens, and install door sweeps on your outside doors.

Many natural substances in your kitchen can be used to deter bugs both indoors and out. There are also many other natural and nontoxic solutions that can help repel bugs. Many pests hate strong citrus odors and garlic. Using natural essential oils in citrus scents such as orange or lemon is a good way to repel some critters. Soak cotton balls in the oil and place them in your cabinets or anywhere you seem to have a problem. If you can stand the smell of garlic, it can be used in the same way.

FACT

The EPA defines *IPM* as an effective and environmentally sensitive approach that relies on a combination of common sense practices. IPM is used to manage pest damage through the most economical means with the least possible hazard to people, property, and the environment. IPM chemical pesticide applications should be a last resort after cleaning, prevention, trapping, and repelling.

Crushed garlic, garlic powder, chili powder, and dried hot peppers can also be used to keep bugs at bay, especially ants. Just sprinkle the powders anywhere you see ants crawling around. Other natural ingredients that help repel many types of creepy, crawly critters are biodegradable soaps such as Dr. Bronner's Peppermint Soap, Tabasco sauce and other hot sauces, tea tree oil, and castor oil. *Natural Pest Control: Alternatives to Chemicals for the Home and Garden* by Andrew Lopez is an excellent resource that gives you detailed instructions on how to get rid of several types of pests both indoors and out. Pheromones and natural traps can also be used without the dangers of harmful pesticides.

Diatomaceous earth is another common ingredient used for natural pest control. If you purchase this, make sure to get garden grade (not pool grade) and use goggles and a mask while using it. It contains very small, sharp particles that are not dangerous to touch but can cause severe irritation to your eyes and lungs.

The web store Planet Natural (*www.planetnatural.com*) has a wide variety of all-natural pest control solutions for home and garden. If you have pets, check out the Only Natural Pet Store (*www.onlynaturalpet.com*). In addition to organic food and supplements, natural toys, and bedding the Only Natural Pet Store sells natural flea sprays, baths, collars, pills, and more to keep your pets flea-free. The essential oils pennyroyal, eucalyptus, citrus, citronella, rosemary, and tea tree all work wonders at repelling fleas when used around your home, on pet bedding, and even on the pets.

Organic Gardening

The basic principle of organic gardening is growing things without the use of any synthetic fertilizers or pesticides. When you garden organically, you want to make sure that you manage your whole garden and lawn that way. That means you don't use lawn chemicals on your grass and then say your vegetable garden is organic.

Getting Started

The best way to start an organic garden is with organic seeds or starter plants. Pass up any genetically modified seeds or plants. Try going for organic heritage seeds and plants to preserve natural plant species. To keep care to a minimum, also choose plants that are native to your area.

Even in the garden, you should adopt the principles of reduce and reuse. Collect rainwater and gray water to water your garden. Don't burn yard trash; turn leaves, yard clippings, and organic waste into mulch and compost.

Keeping Pests Away

Having bug problems in your garden? The old-fashioned way to deal with bugs without pesticides is by using an all-natural, biodegradable soap spray. Dr. Bronner's soaps are a good choice. You mix about 3 tablespoons of the soap per gallon of water and spray it directly onto the plants to get rid of pesky bugs. This will kill most soft-bodied insects such as aphids, mealy bugs, spider mites, stinkbugs, crickets, and grasshoppers. Be careful, though, because some plants can be damaged by spraying too much. Cabbage, cucumbers, and melons should not be sprayed with soap mixtures.

Diatomaceous earth can be safely used throughout your garden, as can a natural pesticide derived from chrysanthemums called pyrethrum.

Having problems with mosquitoes while you're working in your garden? Combine a base oil with a strong-smelling essential oil such as mint, eucalyptus, citronella, or tea tree oil and rub the mixture on your body. Vinegar is another natural deterrent if you can stand the smell yourself. Is something nibbling on your growing goodies? Hot sauce sprays and hot pepper powders sprayed or sprinkled on your plants can get keep a variety of critters away from your plants, including many insects, snails, deer, rabbits, and even snakes.

Making your garden and yard a refuge for birds, frogs, toads, and bats will greatly reduce the amount of flies, mosquitoes, and other insects in your vicinity. Ladybugs and praying mantises are beneficial bugs that help keep the bad bugs away. Encourage beneficial insects to frequent your garden by growing plants they like.

Cultivating beneficial plants, insects, and animals are great ways to keep unwanted bugs out of your garden and your home. The growth of pennyroyal and peppermint around your yard will help keep fleas away. Asters repel many insects, basil repels flies and mosquitoes, borage helps deter tomato worm, and calendula and chrysanthemums repel most insects. Garlic will help keep Japanese beetles at bay, while marigolds make sure there are no Mexican bean beetles or nematodes in their area. Peppermint planted next to cabbage can keep away the cabbage butterfly.

Strips of aluminum foil mixed in with the mulch can keep bugs off your plants as well as reflecting light onto them. Ground-up banana peels should be buried into the soil about two inches deep around roses and other plants that are prone to aphid infestations. Bananas are also a great natural fertilizer because they are rich in potassium.

IPM can also be practiced outside. Water plants correctly, physically pick unwanted insects off plants, mulch well, and cover delicate plants with lightweight row covers to keep away pests naturally.

Making your yard wildlife friendly is a very green thing. With their natural habitats dwindling, animals will be drawn to and benefit from the safe areas you create for them. Plant dense shrubs and provide a few dead logs, a rock garden, and a little cave or burrow area. Include a water feature and you've just created a wildlife-friendly habitat for a variety of critters. Add some bird feeders, birdbaths, squirrel feeders, and a couple of bat houses and you'll practically have a nature preserve right in your own yard.

Further Resources

Many organic gardeners also actively compost. If you compost all your food scraps and yard clippings, you should have an unlimited supply of healthy garden fertilizer readily available. Andrew Lopez's *Natural Pest Control: Alternatives to Chemicals for the Home and Garden* has a chapter devoted to composting and gives very helpful advice for the organic gardener. If you really want to learn a lot about organic gardening, Rodale Publishing has put out many books on the topic, including *Rodale's Illustrated Encyclopedia of Organic Gardening*, an all-inclusive one-stop resource for everything about organic gardening.

Gardening is a greatly beneficial way to be a part of nature and live in a green way. The benefits of gardening are many. It will improve your health, help you relax and get in shape, put you out in nature, and give you a sense of accomplishment. Plus, you are growing your own healthy food and beautiful flowers.

Incorporating eco-responsible choices into your world for every aspect of your life does not have to be overly time-consuming or expensive. Green living can and will become a natural part of your life with just a little effort. It really is all worth it to make life a natural and safer experience for you and your family, and it is a wonderful way to reduce your footprint on the planet and make sure that the beauty of nature will be preserved for generations to come.

Driving Green

What if you can't afford to trade in your non-eco-cool wheels for a cleaner greener version? How can you make your own transportation as green as possible? There are several things you can do to make your regular vehicle a little more eco-friendly. The best one is to drive it as little as possible, but you can also purchase carbon credits to offset the time you do drive. You should also consider the maintenance of the vehicle and how you drive it.

- Keep tires properly inflated. This ensures that you get good fuel economy. If tires are below recommended pressure, fuel economy is reduced. Improperly inflated tires can also affect the handling of the vehicle and the life of the tires.

- Get tuneups regularly. This will make sure your fuel efficiency is where it is supposed to be and keeps your vehicle running smooth. Try to find a location that recycles all the vehicle fluids or at least disposes of them properly.

- Get your oil changed on schedule and make sure the oil gets recycled. You can even ask for recycled oil for your vehicle.

- Unless your owner's manual tells you otherwise, use regular gasoline. High-octane fuels do not improve fuel efficiency or performance; they just waste your money.

- Park in the shade or use window shades to help keep your vehicle cooler. This will reduce the need to run the air conditioner. Keeping the vehicle in the shade will also help reduce fuel evaporation that can happen in the heat.

- Avoid driving aggressively. This includes rapid starts and stops.

- Follow the speed limit. The faster you go, the more fuel economy you lose and the more emissions your vehicle creates.

- Combine trips by doing everything you need to in one day or in one location instead of spacing everything throughout the week.

- Carpool as often as possible.

- Clean out your vehicle and don't carry excess stuff you don't need. The more excess weight you carry around, the less fuel economy you have.

Currently there are no miracles on the horizon and no perfect solutions for everyone and everything. Bicycles are not suitable for many, especially those with families and small children or for the elderly and disabled. In addition, many locations in the United States are not bicycle friendly.

Electric-powered vehicles seem to be the optimal solution for many, especially if they are charged with renewable energy such as wind and solar. Yet so far, they do not provide enough range and power for some drivers.

ALERT!

Some cities in California and Arizona have added electric vehicle chargers to places such as shopping malls, grocery stores, hotels, and banks so customers can charge while they are out and about. That is the kind of earth-friendly thinking that needs to be implemented in locations everywhere. Convenience is a big factor when considering change.

Hybrids bridge the gap between the two worlds by increasing fuel efficiency and combining it with electric power to go farther and faster, but the problem is that hybrids still rely on petroleum fuel. Alternative fuels don't get as much mileage and can't be used in every vehicle currently on the road. There is no one-size-fits-all solution, but the important thing is that we all do what is necessary to reduce our dependence on oil and utilize greener methods of traveling from point A to point B and back again. The near future holds promise as many companies scramble to find solutions to reduce our dependence on dwindling supplies of petroleum.

APPENDIX A

Wedding Planning Timeline and Checklist

9–12 MONTHS BEFORE THE WEDDING

❑ **Announce your engagement.** Send out e-mails or electronic announcements to save on trees.

❑ **Have an eco-friendly engagement party.** Allow for organic, locally grown food and sustainable accessories.

❑ **Arrange for your parents to get together.** Schedule a sit-down so you can all discuss your engagement and upcoming wedding.

❑ **Envision your wedding.** Sit down with your fiancé and discuss your idea of the perfect wedding, complete with green trimmings.

❑ **Create a budget.** You'll need to know how much everyone (both families) and the two of you plan on spending on your big day.

❑ **Set up a planning team.** Who's going to help you plan? Are you hiring a wedding planner? If you plan to hire one, start looking early and interview several before deciding on one.

❑ **Select a date.** You might want to pick a couple of optimal dates in case you have trouble booking a location. Flexibility is a great asset when planning a wedding.

❑ **Start looking for great green locations.** Search for green venues for your ceremony and reception (or both in one location) and book the best ones.

❑ **Start planning your guest list.** Start compiling names and addresses of everyone you plan to invite. Put stars by the most important people in case you have to cut some people from the list later.

❑ **Meet with your officiant.** If you don't have a minister or priest, start searching for someone to officiate your wedding.

❑ **Shop for the gown.** Start your quest for the perfect gown. Flip through magazines, hit the online vendors, and shop for your beautiful organic, sustainable, used, or vintage gown.

❑ **Hit the resale trail.** Take a day and visit all the resale stores in your area to get a feel for what each store carries.

6–9 MONTHS BEFORE THE WEDDING

❑ **Interview caterers.** Look for caterers who offer locally grown and organic menus, possibly even vegetarian, vegan, and raw choices.

❑ **Select your wedding party.** Ask everyone whom you would like to be a part of your big day.

❑ **Choose a color scheme and/or theme.** If you plan to have a specific color scheme or theme, decide on it early so your wedding attire and décor can all match up.

❑ **Order your wedding gown.** Make sure you order early so you have plenty of time to get special ordered gowns and alterations.

❑ **Shop for bridesmaids' dresses.** Let your bridesmaids be involved. Look for fabulous green options such as hemp, bamboo, or organic cotton fabrics, or let them choose something they will wear again.

❑ **Pick photographers.** Look for digitally green photographers and videographers and pick the ones whose style suits you best. Remember: This is not an area in which you should go for the cheapest choice.

❑ **Hire a florist.** Decide on your floral options. Go for the greenest and most convenient possibilities.

❑ **Book the musicians or deejay.** Schedule musicians for the ceremony (if necessary) and reception or choose a great deejay.

❑ **Create a gift registry.** It is best to start one early. You can always add to it or modify it as you go along. Online registries make this very easy to do.

❑ **Start shopping for unique décor.** If you are planning on having décor such as vintage accessories, start shopping early to ensure plenty of time to find what you need. Visit all your local stores and scout out online retailers.

❑ **Send out save-the-date announcements.** E-mail these reminders, especially if you have a lot of out-of-town guests coming in, if you are having a destination wedding, or if your wedding is on a holiday weekend.

❏ **Consider honeymoon destinations.** Start researching the places you may like to go for your honeymoon.

❏ **Think about wedding insurance.** Wedding insurance is a relatively new thing that you can purchase in case anything goes wrong on your wedding day, or even if your wedding gets cancelled. You might have to purchase liquor liability insurance if you are going to be serving alcohol at your reception. Make sure you find out from the venue.

❏ **Reserve rentals.** Book tents, chairs, tables, fountains, arbors, or any other rentals early so you know you'll have them. If you are borrowing them from family and friends, make sure everything you want is available and in good shape. Pull anything out of storage so you can check it out and see if it needs any minor repairs or a good cleaning.

4–6 MONTHS BEFORE THE WEDDING

❏ **Order your wedding stationery.** Order all your invitations (on recycled, handmade, or tree-free paper) or the supplies you need to make your own invitations. If you are getting really creative, such as making your own paper, make sure you get this done long before the invitations need to be mailed out. (Invitations should be sent out six to eight weeks before the wedding.)

❏ **Calligraphy.** Practice your hand at fancy writing or find someone else who is good at it. Hire someone if necessary. With the fancy fonts available on home computers, you could also try printing out each envelope.

❏ **Eat cake—and order one while you're at it.** Taste test cake flavors and frostings before you make your decision. It may take a while to make a choice and order your wedding cake (made from organic ingredients if possible).

❏ **Complete your guest list.**

❏ **Order bridesmaids' dresses.** Place your orders for everything; also order flower girl dresses and any accessories for your female attendants.

❑ **Plan your honeymoon.** Make your reservations for transportation and accommodations.

❑ **Arrange the rehearsal dinner.** Book a location for the rehearsal dinner in a green location.

❑ **Book your wedding day transportation.** Look for unique green transportation, hybrids, biofuels, or something fun.

❑ **Look for wedding rings.** If you have not picked out your wedding rings, get them ordered now so they can be sized and ready for the big day. Hit vintage jewelers and antique stores for something really unique or meet with local artisans to have something specially made.

❑ **Make sure your passports are up to date.** If you are leaving the country, you'll need a passport. Get one or renew yours.

❑ **Look for guest accommodations.** Scout out great green lodging choices for your guests. Talk to the hotels; many times you can get group discount rates if you have a large number of guests coming in from out of town.

❑ **Book beauty treatments.** Schedule prewedding pampering and book your stylists for the big day.

❑ **Have a DIY party.** Are you making a lot of crafts for your wedding? Have a get-together and let your friends and family help.

2–4 MONTHS BEFORE THE WEDDING

❑ **Finalize tuxedo rentals.** Order tuxedos for the guys or decide on their attire options.

❑ **Get the information on the marriage license.** Call your county clerk's office to get all the details on what you need to bring and when you need to apply.

❑ **Meet with your vendors.** Sit down with all your vendors, especially caterers, to pick menus, select wine, and cover all the little details.

❑ **Choose your music.** Pick out the music selections for your ceremony and your special songs for the reception.

❏ **Customize your ceremony.** If you are planning anything special, such as handfasting ceremonies, rose ceremonies, or lighting the unity candle, decide on exactly what you want to do and when in the ceremony it will happen.

❏ **Start working on your vows.** Think about what makes you love your fiancé, and choose unique but not overly personal wording.

❏ **Purchase gifts.** Pick out thank-you gifts for all your attendants. Consider choosing sustainable and green items they are sure to use. Get gifts for your parents and any other special people as well. Don't forget something special for your fiancé while you're at it.

❏ **Pick out favors and other wedding accessories.** Try to choose greenly.

❏ **Get a room.** Book a nice hotel room for the actual wedding night.

❏ **Get showered.** Bridal showers and other prewedding parties are usually held a month to three months before the wedding. Bachelor and bachelorette parties are within the same time frame. Do not ever have them the night before. You'll have enough to do, and no one wants a hangover on their wedding day.

❏ **Accessorize.** If you haven't already done so, make sure you have all your bridal accessories for the big day: veil or tiara or other headpiece, stockings, garter, shoes, undergarments for the wedding, lingerie for the honeymoon, a purse or little handbag, and anything you need for the wedding such as a flower girl basket, ring bearer pillow, toasting goblets, or cake knife.

4–8 WEEKS BEFORE THE WEDDING

❏ **Mail your invitations.** Invitations should be sent out six to eight weeks before the wedding.

❏ **Try it out.** Spend a day trying out hair styles (with your headpiece) and makeup colors.

❏ **Complete any alterations you need done to your gown.**

❑ **Call your wedding party.** Get in touch with all your attendants. Make sure that all of the guys have been fitted for their suits or tuxes and that all of the ladies have their dresses and shoes. Make sure the flower girl and everyone else has everything they need.

❑ **Touch base with your vendors.** Connect with and confirm all details with your vendors to make sure everything is running smoothly.

❑ **Make your DIY purchases.** Are you planting flowers or making any food for your big day? Get your list together for everything you need and start gathering your ingredients.

2–4 WEEKS BEFORE THE WEDDING

❑ **Finalize your RSVP list.** Go over your guest list, and call anyone you haven't heard from.

❑ **Make seating charts.** If you are planning to create a seating chart, now's the time to do it. Or you can go the green route and skip the hassle and the place cards.

❑ **Write your toast now so you'll be ready.**

❑ **Do your final fitting.** Get your final gown fitting and make sure the gown gets cleaned and pressed before you bring it home.

❑ **Print your place cards, favor tags, or seating chart.**

❑ **Confirm, confirm, confirm.** Get last-minute confirmations, finalize times with vendors, and give the musician or deejay a copy of your song list. Be sure to include must-have songs and songs to definitely avoid.

❑ **Get your hair cut.** This goes for both the bride and groom.

❑ **Plant it.** Now is the time to transfer any potted flowers or plants into the containers they will be in for the wedding. This should give them time to establish roots and fill out a little before the big day.

❑ **Assembly line.** Any favors, tags, table tent cards, or other crafts that are nonperishable and that have not been assembled yet should be done now. Get friends and family involved so it all gets done.

1 WEEK BEFORE THE WEDDING

❑ **Do a final head count.** You'll probably need to turn in a final guest count to the caterer. Don't forget to include photographers, deejays, bartenders, waitstaff, and any other vendors and staff you will be feeding.

❑ **Round up reliable people.** Get your reliable people together to collect all your stuff from the reception if you plan to leave without doing it yourself. Make sure you appoint people to do cleanup if your location or catering service does not do all that.

❑ **Call your transportation.** If you have scheduled rental transportation, make sure the vendor has the right times and locations.

❑ **Arrange carpools and shuttles.** Make sure all your eco-friendly carpooling and shuttle buses are ready to roll on the right date and time.

❑ **Beautify yourself.** Get all your final beauty treatments done.

❑ **Pack.** Get everything together and pack for your honeymoon.

❑ **Take care of money.** Place all your final vendor payments in envelopes ready to be delivered on the wedding day.

❑ **Double check.** Are all your crafts done? Do you have everything you need? Is everything ready to go to the location?

1–2 DAYS BEFORE THE WEDDING

❑ **Rehearse the ceremony and have the rehearsal dinner.** Make sure everyone is clear on where they are supposed to be and what they are supposed to be doing during the ceremony.

❑ **Set up.** Some locations may allow you in the night before to decorate and set up. Take advantage of it and get everything done ahead of time.

❑ **Flower power.** If you are doing your own (real) flowers, get them now and put them all together to be ready for your wedding.

❑ **Relax.** Take a deep breath and enjoy everything. Find a little quiet time for yourself.

APPENDIX B

Green Resources

Green Wedding Planning Resources

Portovert
A magazine and website devoted to green weddings and wedding planning
www.portovert.com

Green Elegance Weddings
Full of advice and resources and links to help you plan your green wedding
www.greeneleganceweddings.com

Everything Green Weddings and More
Advice, links, resources, articles, and more to help you plan your green wedding and live in an eco-friendly way
www.everythinggreenweddings.blogspot.com

Ethical Weddings
A U.K.-based resource that has advice and vendor listings for all over the world
www.ethicalweddings.com

Eco-Chic Weddings
Companion site to the book *Eco-Chic Weddings* by Emily Anderson
www.ecochicweddings.com

EcoArt Weddings
A helpful resource for green wedding planning
www.ecoartweddings.com and http://blog.ecoartweddings.com

Green Weddings
A good resource for green wedding planning
www.greenweddings.net

Great Green Weddings
Another great resource to help you plan your green wedding
www.greatgreenwedding.com

Wedding Attire

Organic and Sustainable Wedding Attire

Rawganique
Organic cotton, linen, and hemp wedding gowns, bridesmaid dresses, men's suits, and shoes; Rawganique also carries a variety of home goods and linens
www.rawganique.com

Thread Head Creations
Offers beautiful gowns made from bamboo and other sustainable fabrics
www.threadheadcreations.com

Earth Speaks
Organic fashions; several beautiful dresses are suitable for bridesmaid attire
www.earthspeaks.com

Conscious Clothing
A variety of wedding gowns, bridesmaid and flower girl dresses, and men's suits made from hemp and hemp blends; semi-pricey
www.getconscious.com

Olivia Luca
Offers several organic fabric options for custom-made bridal gowns
www.olivialuca.com

Boll Organic
Sells only organic cotton men's dress shirts
www.bollorganic.com

Faernyn's Grove
High-fashion wedding gowns and corsets at designer prices
www.mycorset.com

Vintage Wedding Gowns and Accessories

Vintage Vixen
A large selection of vintage fashions, including many wedding gowns
www.vintagevixen.com

Vintageous
Vintage formalwear; mainly cocktail dresses
www.vintageous.com

The Frock
Vintage formalwear and wedding gowns
www.thefrock.com

Posh Girl Vintage
Authentic gowns from the '20s to the '80s; more formal gowns than bridal
www.poshgirlvintage.com

Vintage Wedding
Lots of vintage gowns and information about vintage wedding attire
www.vintagewedding.com

Cherished Bride
Vintage wedding gowns
www.cherishedbride.com

Antique Dress
Vintage wedding dresses
www.antiquedress.com

Used and Charity Wedding Gowns

Used Wedding Dresses
All gently used gowns; nothing over $250
www.usedweddingdresses.com

Bridal Garden
A charity organization that sells gowns for charity; boutique located in New York City
www.bridalgarden.org

Making Memories—Brides Against Breast Cancer
Buy or donate clothing to help patients with breast cancer
www.makingmemories.org

Blue Sky Bridal
Gently used and organic gowns; 10 percent of proceeds from each sale are donated to charity
www.blueskybridal.com

Encore Bridal
Offers gently used wedding gowns with some new off-the-rack and sample gowns mixed in
www.encorebridal.com

Preowned Wedding Dresses
A selection of preowned gowns available for purchase
www.preownedweddingdresses.com

Eco-Undies

Green Knickers
Great green underwear from a U.K. company
www.greenknickers.org

Gaiam
Organic cotton underwear
www.gaiam.com

Enamore
Organic, sustainable and sexy lingerie, based in the U.K.
www.enamore.co.uk

g=9.8
French designer of organic, eco-friendly and very sexy lingerie made from pine; available at the USA Pivot Boutique in Chicago or online through Noblivity (*www.noblivity.com*)
www.g98.fr

Eco Body Wear
Organic underwear; comfortable but not sexy
www.ecobodywear.com

Good Humans
Organic cotton underwear
www.goodhumans.com

Other Organic and Sustainable Clothing

The Green Loop
High end eco-fashions and accessories
www.thegreenloop.com

Cool Not Cruel
Urban chic clothing with a conscience
www.coolnotcruel.com

EcoLution
Hemp clothing
www.ecolution.com

Alternative Outfitters
Vegan boutique
www.alternativeoutfitters.com

Anna Cohen
Bamboo dresses and other sustainable clothing
www.annacohen.com

Downbound
Vegan, organic, and sweatshop-free hemp clothing and accessories
www.downbound.com

Tara Lynn Designs
Tara Lynn designs natural fiber gowns custom made for brides
www.taralynnstudio.com

Eco-Friendly Jewelry

Brilliant Earth
Sells only conflict-free diamonds
www.brilliantearth.com

Green Karat
Uses recycled gold for their jewelry
www.greenkarat.com

Leber Jewelry
Sells nonconflict, nondirty gold and free trade jewelry
www.leberjeweler.com

Sumiche
Handcrafted jewelry made from sustainable materials
www.sumiche.com

Signet group, Kay and Sterling Jewelers
Has pledged to sell only nondirty gold
www.kay.com and *www.sterlingjewelers.com*

Seraglia Couture Gems and Jewelry
Uses antique, reclaimed, and unusual materials to create one-of-a-kind jewelry
www.seraglia.com

Smart Glass Jewelry
Uses sterling silver and recycled glass to create earrings, necklaces, bracelets, and more
www.smartglassjewelry.com

Junk to Jewels
Turns junk into eco-fashion
www.junktojewels.net

Global Hand Crafters
Sells jewelry from all over the world
www.globalhandcrafters.com

Repurposed 4 You
Has creative rings and bracelets made out of soda can tabs
www.repurposed4you.com

Topazery
Offers a tremendous selection of heirloom, antique, vintage, and estate jewelry from the 1800s to the present
www.topazery.com

The Marlene Harris Collection
Carries one-of-a-kind antique and estate jewelry
www.marleneharriscol.com

Fay Cullen
Offers a very large assortment of jewelry styles from Victorian to modern
www.faycullen.com

Sylvia's Antiques
Carries a wide variety of antiques, including beautiful engagement rings spanning the eras from Victorian to Contemporary
www.sylviasantiques.com

Columbia Gem House
Fair trade gemstones
www.columbiagemhouse.com

Chicago Joinery
Unique selection of wood wedding rings
www.chicagojoinery.com

Touch Wood Rings
Beautiful, handcrafted wooden wedding bands
www.touchwoodrings.com

Simply Wood
Handcrafted wood wedding rings
www.simplywoodrings.com

Natural Health and Beauty Websites

Cosmetic Database
Learn what is really in your cosmetics and find safer alternatives
www.cosmeticdatabase.com

Safe Cosmetics
Join the fight for safe cosmetics at the Campaign for Safe Cosmetics site
www.safecosmetics.org

Drugstore.com
Sells many items, including several brands of natural beauty products such as JASON, Desert Essence Organics, and Kiss My Face and cleaning and personal care products such as Tom's of Maine, Seventh Generation, and Earth Friendly Products
www.drugstore.com

Beauty.com
This site can be accessed on its own or through its partner site, Drugstore. com; it sells various brands of organic and natural cosmetics
www.beauty.com

Alima Cosmetics
Offers 100 percent natural mineral cosmetics
www.alimacosmetics.com

Saffron Rouge
Sells organic face and skin care products
www.saffronrouge.com

Terressentials
Make handcrafted certified organic skin, hair, and baby care products using USDA-certified organic food grade ingredients
www.terressentials.com

Avalon Natural Products
Organic body care products and cosmetics by Avalon Organics and Un-Petroleum products by Alba
www.avalonnaturalproducts.com

Tom's of Maine
All-natural personal care products
www.tomsofmaine.com

Origins
Organic beauty brand, a division of Estée Lauder; sells cosmetics and bath and body products
www.origins.com

Trillium Organics
Nice selection of natural, organic products
www.trilliumorganics.com

JASON
Organic skin care products
www.jason-natural.com

Garden of Eve
Natural and organic products
www.garden-of-eve.com

Purely Shea
Organic shea butter skin care
www.purelyshea.com

Mother Nature
Wide variety of personal care products from all the big companies
www.mothernature.com

Modern Wife
All-natural health and beauty advice and recipes
www.modernwife.com

CranberryLane.com
DIY cosmetic, bath, and beauty advice, recipes and supplies
www.cranberrylane.com

Mountain Rose Herbs
DIY products and supplies, essential oils, teas, herbs, and more
www.mountainroseherbs.com

Eco-Invitations

Of the Earth
Offers a wide variety of recycled, handmade, and tree-free invitations; also sells seeded paper, handmade invitations, eco-ribbons, and wedding accessories
www.custompaper.com

Greenfield Paper

Offers tree-free and recycled paper products; a decent selection of wedding invitations

www.greenfieldpaper.com

Twisted Limb Paper

More than twenty wedding invitation designs, all handcrafted and 100 percent recycled; also sells accessories, thank-you notes, place cards and favors, guest books, menus, programs, and more

www.twistedlimbpaper.com

Acorn Designs

Uses only eco-friendly papers and inks; has a small selection of wedding invitations

www.acorndesigns.org

Earthly Affair.com

Invitations printed on 100 percent postconsumer waste recycled paper and cotton paper

www.earthlyaffair.com

Invite Site

Green, eco-friendly wedding invitations made from tree-free and 100 percent recycled fibers and do-it-yourself kits

www.invitesite.com

Oblation Papers

Tree-free wedding invitations in a European style made from recycled cotton fiber

www.oblationpapers.com

Botanical Paperworks.com

Plantable papers, invitations, and favors

www.botanicalpaperworks.com

Plant A Memory.com

Plantable papers, invitations, and favors

www.plantamemory.com

Ecoparti

Plantable papers, invitations, and favors

www.ecoparti.com

Evite
Paperless announcements, save-the-date cards, and invitations all delivered online
www.evite.com

Sendomatic
Paperless announcements, save-the-date cards, and invitations all delivered online
www.sendomatic.com

Seal-N-Send.com
All-in-one unique wedding invitations with removable response cards
www.seal-n-send.com

Organic, Vegetarian, Vegan, and Raw Food Information

The Organic Report
Information on organic foods
www.theorganicreport.com

Food News
Information on organic foods
www.foodnews.org

Organic Consumers
Information on organic foods
www.organicconsumers.org

Center for Food Safety
Information on the safety of the foods you purchase
www.centerforfoodsafety.org

Blue Sky
Natural and organic soda
www.drinkbluesky.com

Eat Locally
Locate organic farms, restaurants, and stores that sell organic products
www.eatwellguide.org, www.localharvest.org and *www.sustainabletable.org*

Lydia's Organics
Organic and raw foods
www.lydiasorganics.com

Gold Mine Natural Food
Big selection of organic, raw, vegan, and other specialty foods
www.goldminenaturalfood.com

Eden Foods
Organic and natural products
www.edenfoods.com

Walnut Acres
Products are sold both in stores and at online retailers
www.walnutacres.com

Raw Guru
Information on the raw foods diet
www.rawguru.com

The Organic Wine Company
Earth-friendly wines made with certified organically grown grapes
www.theorganicwinecompany.com

Bonterra
Organic wines
www.bonterra.com

Flower Power Essentials

AFloral
Clips, holders, and other flower supplies for DIY wedding flowers
www.afloral.com

Organic Bouquet
Organic growers and providers of all organic flowers; will ship directly to you or to a florist in your area
www.organicbouquet.com

California Organic Flowers
Will ship large amounts of organic flowers directly to you; special wedding packages
www.californiaorganicflowers.com

VeriFlora
Flowers or potted plants that were produced in socially and environmentally responsible ways
www.scscertified.com/csrpurchasing/veriflora/

Recycling Information

Recycling Markets
A list of where to recycle anything
www.recyclingmarkets.net

The National Recycling Coalition
Gives a lot of useful information about recycling
www.nrc-recycle.org

Earth 911
Information on recycling and finding local recycling facilities in your area
www.earth911.org

Green Wedding Décor and Accessories

Earthware Biodegradables
Carries compostable/biodegradable cups, plates, bowls, and eating utensils
www.earthwarebiodegradables.com

Kokopelli's Green Market
Offers napkins made from 100 percent recycled paper along with other household items and personal care products
www.kokogm.com

Blue Corn Naturals
All-natural beeswax and soy candles
www.beeswaxcandles.com

Green Space Candles
Carries a variety of soy and other eco-wax choices
www.greenspacecandles.com

Way Out Wax
Offers a variety of soy and other enviro-friendly candle choices
www.wayoutwax.com

Smart Candle
Big variety of LED flameless candles, some of which are even rechargeable
www.smartcandle.com

Wedding Rice
Environmentally and bird-friendly wedding rice
www.weddingrice.com

Victoriana
Victorian weddings and Victorian décor
www.victoriana.com

Fabulously Green Favors

Tree in a Box
Choose from many styles of tree favors
www.treeinabox.com

Arbor Day Foundation
A wedding favor package that consists of your choice of redwoods, pines, or spruces
www.arborday.org

Favors With Seeds
All kinds of beautiful seed favors, kits, and seed packets
www.favorswithseeds.com

Green World Project
Wide variety of reasonably priced live tree seedlings, wildflowers, tree seeds, and wedding birdseed; also offers custom-printed wedding seed packets and other earth-friendly favors
www.greenworldproject.net

Beauty Without Cruelty
Sells mini bottles of organic bath and body products, perfect size for favors
www.beautywithoutcruelty.com

June Taylor Jams
Organic jams and other tasty organic goods
www.junetaylorjams.com

Green Mountain Coffee
Organic and fair trade coffee
www.greenmountaincoffee.com

Gifts That Matter
Edible organic treats and gift baskets
www.giftsthatmatter.com

Endangered Species Chocolate

Individually wrapped bite-size chocolates and large chocolate bars suitable as favors; 10 percent of the company's net profits are donated to support wildlife species and their habitats
www.chocolatebar.com

I Do Foundation

Choose the charity to donate to, and favor cards are printed and sent to you for your guests
www.idofoundation.org

The World Wildlife Fund

Donate in lieu of favors and download table tent signs for the reception that can be printed from home
www.justgive.org/worldwildlifefund/weddings/index.jsp

The Nature Conservancy

Dedicated to environmental conservation
www.nature.org

The National Wildlife Federation

Wildlife preservation
www.nwf.org

CocoaVino

Brooklyn company that makes handcrafted bonbon favors
www.cocoavino.com

Green Home Goods

BambuHome

Sells a variety of household goods made from bamboo
www.bambuhome.com

Hemp Traders

Hemp fabrics, textiles, clothing, and many more household goods
www.hemptraders.com

Hemp Fabric Shop

Sells hemp fabrics for clothing and furniture
www.hempfabricshop.com

Bamboo Fabric Store
Sells bamboo and bamboo fabric blends
www.bamboofabricstore.com

Bamboosa
Bamboo fabrics, clothing, and other bamboo products
www.bamboosa.com

Green Culture
Eco-friendly furniture
www.eco-furniture.com

Ecowork
Sustainable office furnishings
www.ecowork.com

Metaform Studio
Modern furniture made from recycled waste materials
www.metaformstudio.com

Ecologic, Inc
Furniture made from recycled materials
www.ecoloft.com

Natural Tree Furniture
Furniture made from branches and tree trunks
www.naturaltreefurniture.com

Airedale Woodworks
Furniture and wood flooring made from the reclaimed wood from old tobacco barns
www.airedale-woodworks.com

Jay Sanders Furniture
Beautiful home furnishings made from reclaimed wood
www.jaysanders.com

Organic Food, Farms, Vineyards, and Other Organic Information

Local Harvest
Search for organic farms, orchards, farmers markets, and more
www.localharvest.org

Local Food Works
Learn about local and organic food in your area
www.localfoodworks.org

Zenith Vineyard
Vineyard in Salem, Oregon, that offers wedding packages
www.zenithvineyard.com

5 Oaks Organic Farm
A beautiful organic farm in Washington
www.5oaksorganicfarm.com

Green Acres Lavender Farm
Farm in California that offers wedding location packages
www.greenacreslavenderfarm.com

Rock Basin Vineyards
A vineyard in Santa Margarita, California, open for wedding rentals
www.rockbasinvineyards.com

Summerhill Pyramid Winery
Vineyard in Kelowna, British Columbia
www.summerhill.bc.ca

BoaVentura De Caires Winery
Five-acre winery located on a 100-year-old ranch; available to accommodate up to 150 guests in Livermore, California
www.boaventuravineyard.com

Deer Ridge Vineyards
Ridgetop winery in California; a popular destination for weddings
www.deerridgevineyards.com

Wolffer Estate Vineyards and Stables
Popular wedding location in New York
www.wolffer.com

Research Green Companies, Services, and Products, Green Certifications

Co-op America
Publishes the Green Pages and sustainable shopping guide for green products and businesses
www.coopamerica.org

Sweat Free
Shop for items that were not made in sweatshops
www.sweatfree.org

Fair Trade Federation
Get information on fair trade and see what products are available
www.fairtradefederation.org

Green Hotels Association
Research green hotels
www.greenhotels.com

Green Seal
Research the products that have been stamped with the Green Seal of approval
www.greenseal.org

EcoLogo
Information on proven green products
www.ecologo.org

New Dream
Helpful green guides, alternative gift registry, shopping recommendations, and the responsible shopping guide
www.newdream.org

Greenwashing Index
Evaluate companies and their commercials
www.greenwashingindex.com

Scientific Certification Systems
Complete listing of certified green products
www.scscertified.com

Energy Star
Energy Star–certified appliances
www.energystar.gov

Green Registries

I Do Foundation
Large retailers have partnered with the I Do Foundation and will donate up to 10 percent of purchases from your registry to the charity of your choice
www.idofoundation.org

Green Feet
Online green retailer with a variety of home goods
www.greenfeet.com

Rawganique
Hemp and organic cotton clothing, household goods, raw foods, and more
www.rawganique.com

3rLiving
Green retailer with a variety of home goods
www.3rliving.com

Re-Modern
Green retailer with a variety of home goods
www.re-modern.com

Green Nest
Great store full of everything for a green home
www.greennest.com

Gaiam
One of the original green stores and still one of the best
www.gaiam.com

Natural Spaces
Green home goods
www.naturalspaces.com

Green Sage
All-natural green products for your home
www.greensage.com

Green-Living
Home goods
www.green-living.com

GX Online Store
Green home goods
www.gxonlinestore.org

The Alternative Gift Registry
Combine with your other registries and add heartfelt desires and wishes,
things that have no monetary value
www.alternativegiftregistry.org

Charity Organizations

Charity Guide
www.charityguide.org

Network for Good
www.networkforgood.org

Charity
www.charity.com

Just Give
www.justgive.org

Give
www.give.org

Habitat for Humanity
A worldwide organization that helps build homes for low-income families
www.habitat.org.

Terra Pass
Carbon credit company with a wedding package
www.terrapass.com

Carbon Fund
ZeroCarbon wedding package
www.carbonfund.org

Wedding Webcasters

Webcast My Wedding
www.webcastmywedding.net

Vowcast
www.vowcast.com

Live Wedding Broadcast
www.liveweddingbroadcast.tv

Green Transportation

Eco-Limo
Eco-friendly limo service in Los Angeles, San Francisco, and Washington, D.C.
www.eco-limo.com

Elite Green Car
Green rental service in Atlanta
www.elitegreencar.com

Green Limousine
Biodiesel rentals in Colorado
www.greenlimousinecolorado.com

Green Car Limo
Hybrid rental service in California
www.greencarlimo.com

LimoGreen
Rental service with a fleet of natural gas Lincoln Towncars in New York City
www.limogreen.net

Bauer's Limousine
A service in Northern California that rents electric buses
www.bauerslimousine.com/content/green.html

EvoLimo
Limo service in California with low emissions vehicles; it hopes to have zero emissions vehicles available soon
www.evolimo.com

EV Rental
California Company that rents hybrids
www.evrental.com

Enterprise Rent-A-Car
Enterprise, National Car Rental, and Alamo offer FlexFuel and hybrid rentals
www.enterprise.com

Fox Rent A Car
Fox Rent A Car offers hybrid rentals in many of its locations
www.foxrentacar.com

Hybrid Technologies
Learn more about hybrid vehicles
www.hybridtechnologies.com

Green Travel

Green Spa Network
Lists mostly day spas but has a few eco-friendly spa resorts in the network
www.greenspanetwork.com

The Sierra Club
Many types of outings: kayaking, canoe trips, bicycle trips, backpack trips, service/volunteer trips, and even international getaways
www.sierraclub.org/outings/

Green Hotels Association
Lists green lodging
www.greenhotels.com

The Blue Flag Program
An eco-label awarded to beaches and marinas all over Europe, South Africa, Morocco, New Zealand, Canada, and the Caribbean
www.blueflag.com

Green Globe
Environmental information about international destinations; the Green Globe label is used by resorts, vacation tours, and rental car companies
www.greenglobe.org

Green Key
An eco-label for tourism products used throughout Europe
www.green-key.org

The International Ecotourism Society
The world's oldest and largest ecotourism organization; information on eco-tourism and a searchable database of tours and trips
www.ecotourism.org

National Park Service
A listing of national parks
www.nps.gov

Planeta
Information on planning an ecotour vacation or honeymoon
www.planeta.com

Green Living Resources

Be Green Now
Information on green living
www.begreennow.com

Campaign Earth
Resources and advice for living green
www.campaignearth.org

The Green Guide
Online and print green living magazine by *National Geographic*
www.thegreenguide.com

Green Living Tips
Great tips and resources for green living
www.greenlivingtips.com

National Resources Defense Council
Tips for green living
www.nrdc.org/greenliving

Care2
Tips and advice for green and natural living
www.care2.com/greenliving

Green Living Journal
Information on green living
www.greenlivingjournal.com

Green Living Online
A green living magazine
www.greenlivingonline.com

***Amaze* Magazine**
Print and online publication devoted to "organic, natural beauty, holistic, green living, and eco-friendly content"
www.amazemag.com

E/The Environmental Magazine
Bimonthly print publication with online articles and resources
www.emagazine.com

Sierra (Sierra Club's Magazine)
Bimonthly magazine put out by the Sierra Club
www.sierra.org/sierra

Plenty Magazine
Magazine devoted to eco-friendly living
www.plentymag.com

Ideal Bite
Daily dose of green living tips sent right to your inbox
www.idealbite.com

On Earth
Green Living magazine
www.onearth.org

Green Matters
Green advice from Crissy Trask, author of *It's Easy Being Green*
www.greenmatters.com

Grist Magazine
Online magazine devoted to environmental issues
www.grist.org

Natural Home
Green living on the home front focusing on green designs and decorating
www.naturalhomemagazine.com

Earth 911
Devoted to all aspects on environmental issues but focuses on recycling
www.earth911.org

Thinking about a Baby?

Fit Pregnancy Magazine's Green Guide
A guide to going green during pregnancy
www.fitpregnancy.com/goinggreen

Alternative Baby
Organic cotton diapers, clothing, toys, and more
www.alternativebaby.com

Classy Kid
Biodegradable diaper sacks and disposable placemats
www.classy-kid.com

Earthy Birthy Mama
Natural bath, body, and skin-care products for mom and baby; cloth diapers and clothing
www.earthybirthymama.com

EcoBaby Organics
Organic crib bedding, mattresses, clothing, toys, and more
www.ecobaby.com

The Real Milk Paint Company
Natural paint made from milk protein
www.realmilkpaint.com

EPA
Information on water quality in your area and where to get your drinking water tested
www.epa.gov/safewater

Water Safe Test Kits
DIY testing kits you can order online
www.discovertesting.com

Earth Mama Angel Baby
Natural products for pregnancy, postnatal care, breast feeding, and infant care
www.earthmamaangelbaby.com

Giggle
Organic baby clothing, furniture, and skin-care products
www.giggle.com

Hanna Anderson
Organic cotton children's clothing
www.hannaanderson.com

Kiddopotamus
Organic cotton swaddlers and sleep sacks
www.kiddopotamus.com

Green Homes

Green Nest
Online retailer that offers everything for your green home
www.greennest.com

Green Home Guide
A complete resource for green home building and remodeling
www.greenhomeguide.com

Energy Star
Research Energy Star ratings and products
www.energystar.gov

Globus Cork
Big selection of natural cork flooring in a variety of styles and colors
www.corkfloor.com

Natural Cork
Natural cork and bamboo flooring
www.naturalcork.com

Trestle Wood
Flooring and wood products made from salvaged wood
www.trestlewood.com

Plyboo
Bamboo products for flooring, cabinets, and building materials
www.plyboo.com

Building Green
Loads of information about building green homes
www.buildinggreen.com

Green Home Building
Information on green building
www.greenhomebuilding.com

Salvage Web
Find architectural salvage
www.salvageweb.com

Green Homes for Sale
Find online listings for green homes that are for sale
www.greenhomesforsale.com

Green Cleaning, Pest Control, and Pets

Seventh Generation
All-natural cleaning and home products
www.seventhgeneration.com

Bi-O-Kleen
All-natural cleaning products
www.biokleen.com

Earth Friendly Products
Highly recommended brand of natural products for your home needs.
www.ecos.com

Kokopelli's Green Market
Retailer that sells Seventh Generation, Earth Friendly Products, Bi-O-Kleen
and several other brands all in one place
www.kokogm.com

Planet Natural
A great store for all-natural gardening supplies
www.planetnatural.com

Only Natural Pet Store
Natural food, vitamins and supplements, food and treats, herbal remedies,
and natural flea products
www.onlynaturalpet.com

Natural Pet Market
Natural food, flea products, and more for your pets
www.naturalpetmarket.com

Nature's Pet
All-natural pet products
www.naturespet.com

Plant Native
Information on plants that are native to your region and where to purchase
them
www.plantnative.org

Green Energy

The Green Power Network
Information on green power, renewable energy, and more
www.eere.energy.gov/greenpower/

Green-e
Find a local provider of green energy
www.green-e.org

Buy Energy Efficient
Tips on being green and saving energy
www.buyenergyefficient.org

Energy Guide
Your guide to energy efficient products
www.energyguide.com

Index

THE EVERYTHING SERIES!

BUSINESS & PERSONAL FINANCE

Everything® Accounting Book
Everything® Budgeting Book, 2nd Ed.
Everything® Business Planning Book
Everything® Coaching and Mentoring Book, 2nd Ed.
Everything® Fundraising Book
Everything® Get Out of Debt Book
Everything® Grant Writing Book, 2nd Ed.
Everything® Guide to Buying Foreclosures
Everything® Guide to Fundraising, $15.95
Everything® Guide to Mortgages
Everything® Guide to Personal Finance for Single Mothers
Everything® Home-Based Business Book, 2nd Ed.
Everything® Homebuying Book, 3rd Ed., $15.95
Everything® Homeselling Book, 2nd Ed.
Everything® Human Resource Management Book
Everything® Improve Your Credit Book
Everything® Investing Book, 2nd Ed.
Everything® Landlording Book
Everything® Leadership Book, 2nd Ed.
Everything® Managing People Book, 2nd Ed.
Everything® Negotiating Book
Everything® Online Auctions Book
Everything® Online Business Book
Everything® Personal Finance Book
Everything® Personal Finance in Your 20s & 30s Book, 2nd Ed.
Everything® Personal Finance in Your 40s & 50s Book, $15.95
Everything® Project Management Book, 2nd Ed.
Everything® Real Estate Investing Book
Everything® Retirement Planning Book
Everything® Robert's Rules Book, $7.95
Everything® Selling Book
Everything® Start Your Own Business Book, 2nd Ed.
Everything® Wills & Estate Planning Book

COOKING

Everything® Barbecue Cookbook
Everything® Bartender's Book, 2nd Ed., $9.95
Everything® Calorie Counting Cookbook
Everything® Cheese Book
Everything® Chinese Cookbook
Everything® Classic Recipes Book
Everything® Cocktail Parties & Drinks Book
Everything® College Cookbook
Everything® Cooking for Baby and Toddler Book
Everything® Diabetes Cookbook
Everything® Easy Gourmet Cookbook
Everything® Fondue Cookbook
Everything® Food Allergy Cookbook, $15.95
Everything® Fondue Party Book
Everything® Gluten-Free Cookbook
Everything® Glycemic Index Cookbook
Everything® Grilling Cookbook
Everything® Healthy Cooking for Parties Book, $15.95
Everything® Holiday Cookbook
Everything® Indian Cookbook
Everything® Lactose-Free Cookbook
Everything® Low-Cholesterol Cookbook

Everything® Low-Fat High-Flavor Cookbook, 2nd Ed., $15.95
Everything® Low-Salt Cookbook
Everything® Meals for a Month Cookbook
Everything® Meals on a Budget Cookbook
Everything® Mediterranean Cookbook
Everything® Mexican Cookbook
Everything® No Trans Fat Cookbook
Everything® One-Pot Cookbook, 2nd Ed., $15.95
Everything® Organic Cooking for Baby & Toddler Book, $15.95
Everything® Pizza Cookbook
Everything® Quick Meals Cookbook, 2nd Ed., $15.95
Everything® Slow Cooker Cookbook
Everything® Slow Cooking for a Crowd Cookbook
Everything® Soup Cookbook
Everything® Stir-Fry Cookbook
Everything® Sugar-Free Cookbook
Everything® Tapas and Small Plates Cookbook
Everything® Tex-Mex Cookbook
Everything® Thai Cookbook
Everything® Vegetarian Cookbook
Everything® Whole-Grain, High-Fiber Cookbook
Everything® Wild Game Cookbook
Everything® Wine Book, 2nd Ed.

GAMES

Everything® 15-Minute Sudoku Book, $9.95
Everything® 30-Minute Sudoku Book, $9.95
Everything® Bible Crosswords Book, $9.95
Everything® Blackjack Strategy Book
Everything® Brain Strain Book, $9.95
Everything® Bridge Book
Everything® Card Games Book
Everything® Card Tricks Book, $9.95
Everything® Casino Gambling Book, 2nd Ed.
Everything® Chess Basics Book
Everything® Christmas Crosswords Book, $9.95
Everything® Craps Strategy Book
Everything® Crossword and Puzzle Book
Everything® Crosswords and Puzzles for Quote Lovers Book, $9.95
Everything® Crossword Challenge Book
Everything® Crosswords for the Beach Book, $9.95
Everything® Cryptic Crosswords Book, $9.95
Everything® Cryptograms Book, $9.95
Everything® Easy Crosswords Book
Everything® Easy Kakuro Book, $9.95
Everything® Easy Large-Print Crosswords Book
Everything® Games Book, 2nd Ed.
Everything® Giant Book of Crosswords
Everything® Giant Sudoku Book, $9.95
Everything® Giant Word Search Book
Everything® Kakuro Challenge Book, $9.95
Everything® Large-Print Crossword Challenge Book
Everything® Large-Print Crosswords Book
Everything® Large-Print Travel Crosswords Book
Everything® Lateral Thinking Puzzles Book, $9.95
Everything® Literary Crosswords Book, $9.95
Everything® Mazes Book
Everything® Memory Booster Puzzles Book, $9.95

Everything® Movie Crosswords Book, $9.95
Everything® Music Crosswords Book, $9.95
Everything® Online Poker Book
Everything® Pencil Puzzles Book, $9.95
Everything® Poker Strategy Book
Everything® Pool & Billiards Book
Everything® Puzzles for Commuters Book, $9.95
Everything® Puzzles for Dog Lovers Book, $9.95
Everything® Sports Crosswords Book, $9.95
Everything® Test Your IQ Book, $9.95
Everything® Texas Hold 'Em Book, $9.95
Everything® Travel Crosswords Book, $9.95
Everything® Travel Mazes Book, $9.95
Everything® Travel Word Search Book, $9.95
Everything® TV Crosswords Book, $9.95
Everything® Word Games Challenge Book
Everything® Word Scramble Book
Everything® Word Search Book

HEALTH

Everything® Alzheimer's Book
Everything® Diabetes Book
Everything® First Aid Book, $9.95
Everything® Green Living Book
Everything® Health Guide to Addiction and Recovery
Everything® Health Guide to Adult Bipolar Disorder
Everything® Health Guide to Arthritis
Everything® Health Guide to Controlling Anxiety
Everything® Health Guide to Depression
Everything® Health Guide to Diabetes, 2nd Ed.
Everything® Health Guide to Fibromyalgia
Everything® Health Guide to Menopause, 2nd Ed.
Everything® Health Guide to Migraines
Everything® Health Guide to Multiple Sclerosis
Everything® Health Guide to OCD
Everything® Health Guide to PMS
Everything® Health Guide to Postpartum Care
Everything® Health Guide to Thyroid Disease
Everything® Hypnosis Book
Everything® Low Cholesterol Book
Everything® Menopause Book
Everything® Nutrition Book
Everything® Reflexology Book
Everything® Stress Management Book
Everything® Superfoods Book, $15.95

HISTORY

Everything® American Government Book
Everything® American History Book, 2nd Ed.
Everything® American Revolution Book, $15.95
Everything® Civil War Book
Everything® Freemasons Book
Everything® Irish History & Heritage Book
Everything® World War II Book, 2nd Ed.

HOBBIES

Everything® Candlemaking Book
Everything® Cartooning Book
Everything® Coin Collecting Book
Everything® Digital Photography Book, 2nd Ed.

Everything® Drawing Book
Everything® Family Tree Book, 2nd Ed.
Everything® Guide to Online Genealogy, $15.95
Everything® Knitting Book
Everything® Knots Book
Everything® Photography Book
Everything® Quilting Book
Everything® Sewing Book
Everything® Soapmaking Book, 2nd Ed.
Everything® Woodworking Book

HOME IMPROVEMENT

Everything® Feng Shui Book
Everything® Feng Shui Decluttering Book, $9.95
Everything® Fix-It Book
Everything® Green Living Book
Everything® Home Decorating Book
Everything® Home Storage Solutions Book
Everything® Homebuilding Book
Everything® Organize Your Home Book, 2nd Ed.

KIDS' BOOKS

All titles are $7.95
Everything® Fairy Tales Book, $14.95
Everything® Kids' Animal Puzzle & Activity Book
Everything® Kids' Astronomy Book
Everything® Kids' Baseball Book, 5th Ed.
Everything® Kids' Bible Trivia Book
Everything® Kids' Bugs Book
Everything® Kids' Cars and Trucks Puzzle and Activity Book
Everything® Kids' Christmas Puzzle & Activity Book
Everything® Kids' Connect the Dots
   Puzzle and Activity Book
Everything® Kids' Cookbook, 2nd Ed.
Everything® Kids' Crazy Puzzles Book
Everything® Kids' Dinosaurs Book
Everything® Kids' Dragons Puzzle and Activity Book
Everything® Kids' Environment Book $7.95
Everything® Kids' Fairies Puzzle and Activity Book
Everything® Kids' First Spanish Puzzle and Activity Book
Everything® Kids' Football Book
Everything® Kids' Geography Book
Everything® Kids' Gross Cookbook
Everything® Kids' Gross Hidden Pictures Book
Everything® Kids' Gross Jokes Book
Everything® Kids' Gross Mazes Book
Everything® Kids' Gross Puzzle & Activity Book
Everything® Kids' Halloween Puzzle & Activity Book
Everything® Kids' Hanukkah Puzzle and Activity Book
Everything® Kids' Hidden Pictures Book
Everything® Kids' Horses Book
Everything® Kids' Joke Book
Everything® Kids' Knock Knock Book
Everything® Kids' Learning French Book
Everything® Kids' Learning Spanish Book
Everything® Kids' Magical Science Experiments Book
Everything® Kids' Math Puzzles Book
Everything® Kids' Mazes Book
Everything® Kids' Money Book, 2nd Ed.
Everything® Kids' Mummies, Pharaoh's, and Pyramids
   Puzzle and Activity Book
Everything® Kids' Nature Book
Everything® Kids' Pirates Puzzle and Activity Book
Everything® Kids' Presidents Book
Everything® Kids' Princess Puzzle and Activity Book
Everything® Kids' Puzzle Book

Everything® Kids' Racecars Puzzle and Activity Book
Everything® Kids' Riddles & Brain Teasers Book
Everything® Kids' Science Experiments Book
Everything® Kids' Sharks Book
Everything® Kids' Soccer Book
Everything® Kids' Spelling Book
Everything® Kids' Spies Puzzle and Activity Book
Everything® Kids' States Book
Everything® Kids' Travel Activity Book
Everything® Kids' Word Search Puzzle and Activity Book

LANGUAGE

Everything® Conversational Japanese Book with CD, $19.95
Everything® French Grammar Book
Everything® French Phrase Book, $9.95
Everything® French Verb Book, $9.95
Everything® German Phrase Book, $9.95
Everything® German Practice Book with CD, $19.95
Everything® Inglés Book
Everything® Intermediate Spanish Book with CD, $19.95
Everything® Italian Phrase Book, $9.95
Everything® Italian Practice Book with CD, $19.95
Everything® Learning Brazilian Portuguese Book with CD, $19.95
Everything® Learning French Book with CD, 2nd Ed., $19.95
Everything® Learning German Book
Everything® Learning Italian Book
Everything® Learning Latin Book
Everything® Learning Russian Book with CD, $19.95
Everything® Learning Spanish Book
Everything® Learning Spanish Book with CD, 2nd Ed., $19.95
Everything® Russian Practice Book with CD, $19.95
Everything® Sign Language Book, $15.95
Everything® Spanish Grammar Book
Everything® Spanish Phrase Book, $9.95
Everything® Spanish Practice Book with CD, $19.95
Everything® Spanish Verb Book, $9.95
Everything® Speaking Mandarin Chinese Book with CD, $19.95

MUSIC

Everything® Bass Guitar Book with CD, $19.95
Everything® Drums Book with CD, $19.95
Everything® Guitar Book with CD, 2nd Ed., $19.95
Everything® Guitar Chords Book with CD, $19.95
Everything® Guitar Scales Book with CD, $19.95
Everything® Harmonica Book with CD, $15.95
Everything® Home Recording Book
Everything® Music Theory Book with CD, $19.95
Everything® Reading Music Book with CD, $19.95
Everything® Rock & Blues Guitar Book with CD, $19.95
Everything® Rock & Blues Piano Book with CD, $19.95
Everything® Rock Drums Book with CD, $19.95
Everything® Singing Book with CD, $19.95
Everything® Songwriting Book

NEW AGE

Everything® Astrology Book, 2nd Ed.
Everything® Birthday Personology Book
Everything® Celtic Wisdom Book, $15.95
Everything® Dreams Book, 2nd Ed.
Everything® Law of Attraction Book, $15.95
Everything® Love Signs Book, $9.95
Everything® Love Spells Book, $9.95
Everything® Palmistry Book
Everything® Psychic Book
Everything® Reiki Book

Everything® Sex Signs Book, $9.95
Everything® Spells & Charms Book, 2nd Ed.
Everything® Tarot Book, 2nd Ed.
Everything® Toltec Wisdom Book
Everything® Wicca & Witchcraft Book, 2nd Ed.

PARENTING

Everything® Baby Names Book, 2nd Ed.
Everything® Baby Shower Book, 2nd Ed.
Everything® Baby Sign Language Book with DVD
Everything® Baby's First Year Book
Everything® Birthing Book
Everything® Breastfeeding Book
Everything® Father-to-Be Book
Everything® Father's First Year Book
Everything® Get Ready for Baby Book, 2nd Ed.
Everything® Get Your Baby to Sleep Book, $9.95
Everything® Getting Pregnant Book
Everything® Guide to Pregnancy Over 35
Everything® Guide to Raising a One-Year-Old
Everything® Guide to Raising a Two-Year-Old
Everything® Guide to Raising Adolescent Boys
Everything® Guide to Raising Adolescent Girls
Everything® Mother's First Year Book
Everything® Parent's Guide to Childhood Illnesses
Everything® Parent's Guide to Children and Divorce
Everything® Parent's Guide to Children with ADD/ADHD
Everything® Parent's Guide to Children with Asperger's
   Syndrome
Everything® Parent's Guide to Children with Anxiety
Everything® Parent's Guide to Children with Asthma
Everything® Parent's Guide to Children with Autism
Everything® Parent's Guide to Children with Bipolar Disorder
Everything® Parent's Guide to Children with Depression
Everything® Parent's Guide to Children with Dyslexia
Everything® Parent's Guide to Children with Juvenile Diabetes
Everything® Parent's Guide to Children with OCD
Everything® Parent's Guide to Positive Discipline
Everything® Parent's Guide to Raising Boys
Everything® Parent's Guide to Raising Girls
Everything® Parent's Guide to Raising Siblings
Everything® Parent's Guide to Raising Your
   Adopted Child
Everything® Parent's Guide to Sensory Integration Disorder
Everything® Parent's Guide to Tantrums
Everything® Parent's Guide to the Strong-Willed Child
Everything® Parenting a Teenager Book
Everything® Potty Training Book, $9.95
Everything® Pregnancy Book, 3rd Ed.
Everything® Pregnancy Fitness Book
Everything® Pregnancy Nutrition Book
Everything® Pregnancy Organizer, 2nd Ed., $16.95
Everything® Toddler Activities Book
Everything® Toddler Book
Everything® Tween Book
Everything® Twins, Triplets, and More Book

PETS

Everything® Aquarium Book
Everything® Boxer Book
Everything® Cat Book, 2nd Ed.
Everything® Chihuahua Book
Everything® Cooking for Dogs Book
Everything® Dachshund Book
Everything® Dog Book, 2nd Ed.
Everything® Dog Grooming Book

Everything® Dog Obedience Book
Everything® Dog Owner's Organizer, $16.95
Everything® Dog Training and Tricks Book
Everything® German Shepherd Book
Everything® Golden Retriever Book
Everything® Horse Book, 2nd Ed., $15.95
Everything® Horse Care Book
Everything® Horseback Riding Book
Everything® Labrador Retriever Book
Everything® Poodle Book
Everything® Pug Book
Everything® Puppy Book
Everything® Small Dogs Book
Everything® Tropical Fish Book
Everything® Yorkshire Terrier Book

REFERENCE

Everything® American Presidents Book
Everything® Blogging Book
Everything® Build Your Vocabulary Book, $9.95
Everything® Car Care Book
Everything® Classical Mythology Book
Everything® Da Vinci Book
Everything® Einstein Book
Everything® Enneagram Book
Everything® Etiquette Book, 2nd Ed.
Everything® Family Christmas Book, $15.95
Everything® Guide to C. S. Lewis & Narnia
Everything® Guide to Divorce, 2nd Ed., $15.95
Everything® Guide to Edgar Allan Poe
Everything® Guide to Understanding Philosophy
Everything® Inventions and Patents Book
Everything® Jacqueline Kennedy Onassis Book
Everything® John F. Kennedy Book
Everything® Mafia Book
Everything® Martin Luther King Jr. Book
Everything® Pirates Book
Everything® Private Investigation Book
Everything® Psychology Book
Everything® Public Speaking Book, $9.95
Everything® Shakespeare Book, 2nd Ed.

RELIGION

Everything® Angels Book
Everything® Bible Book
Everything® Bible Study Book with CD, $19.95
Everything® Buddhism Book
Everything® Catholicism Book
Everything® Christianity Book
Everything® Gnostic Gospels Book
Everything® Hinduism Book, $15.95
Everything® History of the Bible Book
Everything® Jesus Book
Everything® Jewish History & Heritage Book
Everything® Judaism Book
Everything® Kabbalah Book
Everything® Koran Book
Everything® Mary Book
Everything® Mary Magdalene Book
Everything® Prayer Book

Everything® Saints Book, 2nd Ed.
Everything® Torah Book
Everything® Understanding Islam Book
Everything® Women of the Bible Book
Everything® World's Religions Book

SCHOOL & CAREERS

Everything® Career Tests Book
Everything® College Major Test Book
Everything® College Survival Book, 2nd Ed.
Everything® Cover Letter Book, 2nd Ed.
Everything® Filmmaking Book
Everything® Get-a-Job Book, 2nd Ed.
Everything® Guide to Being a Paralegal
Everything® Guide to Being a Personal Trainer
Everything® Guide to Being a Real Estate Agent
Everything® Guide to Being a Sales Rep
Everything® Guide to Being an Event Planner
Everything® Guide to Careers in Health Care
Everything® Guide to Careers in Law Enforcement
Everything® Guide to Government Jobs
Everything® Guide to Starting and Running a Catering
    Business
Everything® Guide to Starting and Running a Restaurant
**Everything® Guide to Starting and Running
    a Retail Store**
Everything® Job Interview Book, 2nd Ed.
Everything® New Nurse Book
Everything® New Teacher Book
Everything® Paying for College Book
Everything® Practice Interview Book
Everything® Resume Book, 3rd Ed.
Everything® Study Book

SELF-HELP

Everything® Body Language Book
Everything® Dating Book, 2nd Ed.
Everything® Great Sex Book
**Everything® Guide to Caring for Aging Parents,
    $15.95**
Everything® Self-Esteem Book
Everything® Self-Hypnosis Book, $9.95
Everything® Tantric Sex Book

SPORTS & FITNESS

Everything® Easy Fitness Book
Everything® Fishing Book
Everything® Guide to Weight Training, $15.95
Everything® Krav Maga for Fitness Book
Everything® Running Book, 2nd Ed.
Everything® Triathlon Training Book, $15.95

TRAVEL

Everything® Family Guide to Coastal Florida
Everything® Family Guide to Cruise Vacations
Everything® Family Guide to Hawaii
Everything® Family Guide to Las Vegas, 2nd Ed.
Everything® Family Guide to Mexico
Everything® Family Guide to New England, 2nd Ed.

Everything® Family Guide to New York City, 3rd Ed.
**Everything® Family Guide to Northern California
    and Lake Tahoe**
Everything® Family Guide to RV Travel & Campgrounds
Everything® Family Guide to the Caribbean
Everything® Family Guide to the Disneyland® Resort, California
    Adventure®, Universal Studios®, and the Anaheim
    Area, 2nd Ed.
Everything® Family Guide to the Walt Disney World Resort®,
    Universal Studios®, and Greater Orlando, 5th Ed.
Everything® Family Guide to Timeshares
Everything® Family Guide to Washington D.C., 2nd Ed.

WEDDINGS

Everything® Bachelorette Party Book, $9.95
Everything® Bridesmaid Book, $9.95
Everything® Destination Wedding Book
Everything® Father of the Bride Book, $9.95
Everything® Green Wedding Book, $15.95
Everything® Groom Book, $9.95
Everything® Jewish Wedding Book, 2nd Ed., $15.95
Everything® Mother of the Bride Book, $9.95
Everything® Outdoor Wedding Book
Everything® Wedding Book, 3rd Ed.
Everything® Wedding Checklist, $9.95
Everything® Wedding Etiquette Book, $9.95
Everything® Wedding Organizer, 2nd Ed., $16.95
Everything® Wedding Shower Book, $9.95
Everything® Wedding Vows Book, 3rd Ed., $9.95
Everything® Wedding Workout Book
Everything® Weddings on a Budget Book, 2nd Ed., $9.95

WRITING

Everything® Creative Writing Book
Everything® Get Published Book, 2nd Ed.
Everything® Grammar and Style Book, 2nd Ed.
Everything® Guide to Magazine Writing
Everything® Guide to Writing a Book Proposal
Everything® Guide to Writing a Novel
Everything® Guide to Writing Children's Books
Everything® Guide to Writing Copy
Everything® Guide to Writing Graphic Novels
Everything® Guide to Writing Research Papers
Everything® Guide to Writing a Romance Novel, $15.95
Everything® Improve Your Writing Book, 2nd Ed.
Everything® Writing Poetry Book